BEYOND *JERUSALEM*: MUSIC IN THE WOMEN'S INSTITUTE, 1919–1969

This book is dedicated to the women of Britain.

Beyond *Jerusalem*: Music in the Women's Institute, 1919–1969

LORNA GIBSON
University College London, UK

ASHGATE

© Lorna Gibson 2008

All rights reserved. No part of this publication may be reproduced, stored in a retrieval system or transmitted in any form or by any means, electronic, mechanical, photocopying, recording or otherwise without the prior permission of the publisher.

Lorna Gibson has asserted her moral right under the Copyright, Designs and Patents Act, 1988, to be identified as the author of this work.

Published by
Ashgate Publishing Limited
Gower House
Croft Road
Aldershot
Hampshire GU11 3HR
England

Ashgate Publishing Company
Suite 420
101 Cherry Street
Burlington, VT 05401-4405
USA

Ashgate website: http://www.ashgate.com

British Library Cataloguing in Publication Data

Gibson, Lorna
  Beyond Jerusalem : music in the Women's Institute, 1919–1969
  1. National Federation of Women's Institutes – History
  2. Feminism and music – Great Britain – History – 20th century 3. Women musicians – Great Britain – History – 20th century 4. Music patronage – Great Britain – History – 20th century
  I. Title
  780.8'2'0941

Library of Congress Cataloging-in-Publication Data

Gibson, Lorna
  Beyond Jerusalem : music in the Women's Institute, 1919–1969 / by Lorna Gibson.
     p. cm.
  Includes bibliographical references (p.   ) and index.
  ISBN 978-0-7546-6349-2 (alk. paper)
  1. National Federation of Women's Institutes–History. 2. Feminism and music–England–History–20th century. 3. Women musicians–England–History–20th century. I. Title.

ML27.E5N384 2007
780.82'0941–dc22

2007023669

ISBN: 978-0-7546-6349-2

Printed and bound in Great Britain by MPG Books Ltd, Bodmin, Cornwall.

Contents

List of Figures   *vii*
Foreword   *ix*
Acknowledgements   *xi*
List of Abbreviations   *xiii*

Introduction   1

1   Music Policy and its Implementation in the Women's Institute   7

2   Education, Empowerment and *The Acceptable Face of Feminism*   31

3   The Changing Roles of Folk Song and Part Song in the Women's Institute   49

4   *Folk Songs of the Four Seasons* and the First National Singing Festival   71

5   *The Brilliant and The Dark* and the Second Music Festival   89

6   Afterburn: The National Society Choir, 1969–1975   113

Conclusion   133

Bibliography   *137*
Personalia   *153*
Appendices
1   'Jerusalem' – Words by William Blake (1757–1827)   175
2   'The story of Jerusalem' (NFWI, 1934)   176
3   'Jerusalem' (NFWI, 1950)   177
4   'An Institute Song' from 'Letters to the Editor' in Home and Country   178
5   Music courses held at Denman College, 1948–1969   186
6   Society of Women Musicians concerts and events conducted by women   189
7   Contents of The Women's Institute Song Book *(London: NFWI, 1925)*   192
8   Contents of The Women's Institute Second Song Book *(London: NFWI, 1926)*   193
9   National Federation National Events, 1928–1980   194

Index   *195*

List of Figures

1.1	Cavendish and Pentlow (West Suffolk) choir winners, from *Home and Country* vol. 12 (1930) p. 20	10
1.2	Original manuscript of *Jerusalem* by Parry	24
3.1	Angle WI (Pembrokeshire) Ladies' Choir, from *Home and Country* vol. 3 (1921) p. 9	52
5.1 and cover	The premiere of Malcolm Williamson's *The Brilliant and The Dark*	107
6.1	Antony Hopkins and Janet Cannetty-Clarke with the Avalon Singers	117

Foreword

The Women's Institute is an organization dear to my heart. As many members know, the first WI in England and Wales was founded at Llanfairpwll in Anglesey on 11 September 1915, under the auspices of the British Agricultural Organization Society. Those involved in the establishment of the first Women's Institute included my father-in-law's cousin, Colonel Stapleton-Cotton. He and his wife spent much of their life in the West Indies and had a special interest in rural and agricultural life. After an accident, Colonel Stapleton-Cotton became a paraplegic and Lord Anglesey invited him and his wife to make a new life at Plas Llwynnon at Llanfairpwll. Others who were working with him during the Women's Institute's early years were Sir Harry Reichel (Principal of Bangor University College), Mrs Madge Watt and Mr Nugent Harris. Indeed, Colonel Stapleton-Cotton is said to have remarked that if a non-party, sectarian organization for country women could be established and thrive in rural Wales, it could survive anywhere. This is certainly the case – the Women's Institute has been a remarkably successful and powerful organization which has influenced the lives of women in Britain and throughout the world. It currently has over 211,000 members in 70 counties in Britain alone.

I joined the Women's Institute soon after my marriage in 1948 when I moved to Anglesey. I served on Committees both locally and at county and national level, and was National Federation Chairman from 1966 to 1969. I was very involved during the preparations and the premiere of Malcolm Williamson's *The Brilliant and The Dark*, and got to know Ursula Vaughan Williams well.

As a member, and later Chairman, of the Women's Institute, I was acutely aware of the importance of the 'artistic' and cultural side of the organization. The singing of *Jerusalem* which still opens many monthly WI meetings throughout Britain, has provided an important means of uniting the organization and given it a sense of identity. However, as this book demonstrates, music-making within the organization is more than just the singing of *Jerusalem* and includes many other aspects, such as choral singing, conducting, instrumental music and music appreciation, and much more.

This book offers an interesting insight into the 'artistic' aspect of the organization's role and to music in particular. It draws on evidence from a selection of sources, ranging from the archives of the National Federation, to those outside of the organization, such as the BBC and personal collections, and offers a broad, historical perspective, of music-making within the Women's Institute. It reminds us of the contribution the organization has made to the education of women and rural life and its important role within British cultural life. I very much hope that in future, particularly at Denman College and in the county federations, that these aspects of Institute life continue, and that this book will be available to members for discussion and action within the WI itself.

Shirley Anglesey

Signed Lady Anglesey, April 2007

Acknowledgements

Special thanks must go to Susan Stockley and Anne Ballard, without whose support this study would not have been possible. I am immensely grateful for their co-operation, kindness and encouragement over the past four years. I would also like to thank the National Federation's General Secretary, Jana Osbourne, who has been very supportive of my research. I am also grateful to Anne Stamper for her assistance in obtaining the photographs for this book, and the administrative staff at Denman College who treated me with great kindness during every visit.

Outside the National Federation, I am particularly grateful to Malcolm Taylor at the Vaughan Williams Memorial Library for his practical advice and input, and Jeff Walden at BBC Written Archives Centre in assisting me to follow up leads and check references. Other individuals I would like to thank include the Women's Library, who gave me access to the National Federation's material whilst the archives were being recatalogued. I am also grateful to staff at the following libraries: the Royal College of Music, the Royal Academy of Music, the Britten-Pears foundation, the Victoria and Albert Archives, and the British Library.

My research has also involved liaising with individuals who were involved in the National Federation's national events examined in the book. I am grateful to Simon Campion, Elizabeth Lamb, and Janet Cannetty-Clarke for allowing me to speak to them about their involvement in *The Brilliant and The Dark*. I would also like to thank Ursula Vaughan Williams and Antony Hopkins for allowing me to visit them in their homes and for answering my many questions. I am also grateful to staff in the Music Department at Royal Holloway who have given me practical advice over the past four years, in particular, my supervisor, Prof. Katharine Ellis who was a source of great encouragement throughout my research, Erik Levi, Prof. Lionel Pike, Prof. David Charlton and Prof. John Rink.

Whilst it is beyond the scope of this section to acknowledge all the individuals who have been influential in the bringing together of this book, I would like finally to give a special mention Heidi May at Ashgate, my colleagues at University College London, Sarah Smith, William Knottenbelt, and my parents.

Copyright information

I acknowledge the copyright of the material referred to and cited in this book from the following sources: Ms Alyson Laverick, Prof. Lionel Pike, Mr Humphrey Stone, the BBC Written Archives Centre, the Arts Council of England, the English Folk Dance and Song Society archives, Royal College of Music library, the archives of the National Federation of Women's Institutes, and the Britten-Pears Foundation. The quotations from the letters of Benjamin Britten are © copyright of the Trustees of the Britten-Pears Foundation and may not be further reproduced without the written permission of the Trustees.

List of Abbreviations

AOS	Agricultural Organization Society
BFMCF	British Federation of Music Competition Festivals
CUKT	Carnegie UK Trust
EFDS	English Folk Dance Society
EFDSS	English Folk Dance and Song Society
ELPS-C	Education, Literature and Publicity Sub-Committee
FPA	Family Planning Association
FSS	Folk Song Society
GJS-C	Golden Jubilee Festival Ad Hoc Sub-Committee
LEA	Local Education Authorities
MDDcS-C	Music Drama and Dancing Sub-Committee
MDS-C	Music and Drama Sub-Committee
MFS-C	Music Festival Ad Hoc Sub-Committee
MS-C	Music Sub-Committee
MSCh	Music Society Choir Sub-Committee
NCSS	National Council for Social Service
NFMS	National Federation of Music Societies
NFWI	National Federation of the Women's Institute
NUSEC	National Union of Societies for Equal Citizenship
NUTG	National Union of Townswomen's Guilds
NUWSS	National Union of Women's Suffrage Societies
OFS-C	Office and Finance Sub-Committee
RMSA	Rural Music School's Association
SESS-C	South Eastern Section Sub-Committee
SFS-C	Singing Festival Ad Hoc Sub-Committee
SWM	Society of Women Musicians
TAS	The Avalon Singers Sub-Committee
VCO	Voluntary County Organizers
WN-WSC	Wales and North West Choir Sub-Committee
YMSO	Young Musicians' Symphony Orchestra

Introduction

Until the early 1990s, traditional histories of Western music included few references to women.[1] This is partly due to a lack of evidence regarding female composition, as women often used their single and married names, or worked under pseudonyms. The composer Shena Fraser, for example, who was involved in her local Women's Institute's music activities, also composed under her married name of Shena Neame and the pseudonym Sebastian Scott. Their absence is also due to women often composing in genres considered to be of secondary importance in traditional music histories (for example, small-scale works such as songs) and because compositions by women have not gained the same recognition as those of their male counterparts. As a result, women have been excluded from the musical canon upon which traditional music histories are based.

The second wave of feminism during the 1970s brought with it awareness about women and their lack of presence in music history, and what followed was an unearthing of information about women's involvement in music history. It became clear that women's involvement in music history was not confined to the sphere of composition, but also included performance, pedagogy and patronage, and that traditional music history (which is both elitist and document-based) was unsuitable and ill-equipped for dealing with the topic of women.[2] Although scholars in feminist studies and women's history revealed the inadequacy of such 'traditional' histories, discussions in musicology have continued to centre on one aspect of women's achievements – composition.[3] Topics such as performance, amateur music-making and patronage (which have been shown to be important areas of women's involvement) have remained at the edges of the discipline. It seems that musicology is unwilling to address what 'new' music history should be about, and how the topic should be tackled.

More generally, musicological discussions of music in the twentieth century have returned to the 'traditional' model, and have thus been dominated by men, composing, and modernism.[4] Compositions that do not adhere to the modernist ideology have been given little (if any) attention within musicology, and topics such as folk songs go unmentioned. However, social histories of music in Britain during the twentieth

---

1 Traditional music histories include, for example, Donald J. Grout and Claude V. Palisca (eds), *A History of Western Music*, 4th ed. London: Norton, 1988.

2 Examples include Karin Pendle (ed.), *Women in Music: A History*, Bloomington: Indiana University Press, 1991, and Jane Bowers and Judith Tick (eds), *Women Making Music: The Western Art Tradition, 1150–1980*, Chicago: University of Illinois Press, 1987.

3 Publications include Susan McClary, *Feminine Endings: Music, Gender and Sexuality*, London: University of Minnesota Press, 1991, and Marcia Citron, *Gender and the Musical Canon*, Cambridge: Cambridge University Press, 1993.

4 For example, Arnold Whittall, *Musical Composition in the Twentieth Century*, Oxford: Oxford University Press, 1999, which focuses on the works of composers such as Stravinsky, Bartók, Messiaen, Tippett and Ligeti.

century offer a solution to the limitation of seeing music history from the viewpoint of avant-garde composition alone, by providing an opportunity to recognize the existence of other forms of music-making.[5] That said, there is a gap in social histories of British music which, broadly speaking, falls between 1920 and the early 1960s; publications either have a time-span that covers music in the late Victorian era to the first decade of the twentieth century, or are concerned with popular musical culture and the early decades of the 1960s. Andrew Blake's *The Land Without Music*, for example, reflects this trend: it has a chapter that examines music during the 'English Musical Renaissance' and the early decades of the twentieth century, followed by a chapter on British pop music from the 1960s. The interim period (which in this study broadly falls from the mid 1920s to the 1950s), when 'great' British figures such as Elgar, Gustav Holst, and Ralph Vaughan Williams were actively composing, is mentioned only fleetingly.[6] Indeed, this appears to be the trend: rather than being valued for the contribution it makes to knowledge about musical culture, the social history of music is used as a means to fill the gap in musicology when there is an absence of significant British musical works to be discussed.

The National Federation's archive provides a valuable source of information about women in twentieth-century Britain as performers and patrons of music, as well as reveals the organization's wider contribution to British musical culture (namely its promotion of folk music, amateur music-making and music in British rural communities). In addition, it not only fills a gap in social histories of music during the period from 1919 to 1969, but also reveals the ways in which compositions by two 'great' British figures during this period worked within the culture for which they were commissioned.

The research for this book has drawn heavily on the archives, which, when I embarked on this study in 2000, were uncatalogued and kept in a garage at the National Federation's residential establishment, Denman College, in Oxfordshire. The collection was in the process of being arranged into files by two members who had held influential positions within the organization; an ex-Chairman of the National Federation, Susan Stockley, and an ex-General Secretary, Anne Ballard. Their roles were to arrange archival documents into thematic files, and to destroy duplicate documents (the majority of which appear to have been carbon copies of correspondence sent by the National Federation, and ephemera).

The files on music and drama were compiled in the late 1980s. The archival documents for music consisted of a series of files arranged by topic and usually labelled with references beginning 'J', each dealing with a topic of music making: for example 'JCBB23 Singing Festival *Folk Songs of the Four Seasons* (5 June 1950)'. Within these folders, the material was usually arranged chronologically. Files on music included the National Federation's official papers (such as correspondence,

---

5 Examples include Dorothy de Val, 'The Transformed Village: Lucy Broadwood and Folk Song', in Christina Bashford and Leanne Langley (eds), *Music and British Culture, 1785–1914: Essays in Honor of Cyril Ehrlich*, Oxford: Oxford University Press, 2001, pp. 341–67. Folk song is a genre that has typically been overlooked in musicological discussions.

6 Andrew Blake, *The Land Without Music: Music, Culture and Society in Twentieth-Century Britain*, Music and Society Series, Manchester: Manchester University Press, 1997.

outlines of budgets, excerpts of Committee meeting minutes, etc), memoranda, personal papers of members, newspaper reviews, photographs, programmes, scores, etc. Other material consulted at these archives for this research included files on policy and procedure, national events, membership, and collections of newspaper cuttings.

In addition to examining archival material at Denman College, I spent many months based at the National Federation's Head Office in London. Here I was able to consult not only editions of *Home and Country* and the NFWI Annual Reports, but also a complete set of the minutes of Executive Committee meetings from 1917 to the present (they supplemented those at Denman College which were often incomplete and illegible due to their poor condition). This provided a valuable source of information about the role of music within the organization, and how music policy was decided and implemented.

In an attempt to safeguard their long-term preservation and make them accessible to the public, the National Federation's archives were moved to The Women's Library on 20 March 2002, and those held at the London Headquarters followed a day later. In total, the collection consisted of over 300 archive boxes. Two curators of the Women's Library, Liza Giffen and Claire Ashcroft, spent the next two years recataloguing the material into seven sections: policy, administration, organizations, public affairs, education, agriculture and publications. Within this system, music (and drama) is catalogued under 'policy' (along with other Sub-Committees) and is referred to under its 'Box' number (for example 'NFWI Box 71').

In view of the relocation of the National Federation's archives and the change in cataloguing, the system of referencing used throughout this book for this material is based on an abbreviation that refers to the title of the document (and not to the file where it can now be found at The Women's Library). With regard to references from the National Federation's minute books, the volume of the Executive minute book from where the minutes are taken is listed first (if known), followed by Sub-Committee (if it is not the Executive Committee), the date of the meeting in brackets, and page number (if known). For example, 'Executive Minutes, vol. 6 MS-C (10 July 1923), p. 198' refers to a meeting of the Music Sub-Committee held on 10 July 1923, listed in the Executive Committee minutes in volume 6, page 198. If minutes do not appear in the Executive Committee volumes, only the title of the Sub-Committee is listed. The List of Abbrieviations provides a full list of abbreviations used.

In order to minimize the risk of the book being 'top heavy' in its reliance on the National Federation's minute books and archival documents, attempts have been made to include personal recollections found in the archival sources of Institute members whenever possible. Interviews were conducted with members and non-members who had been involved in music activities during this period (namely Simon Campion, Elizabeth Lamb, Janet Canetty-Clarke, Ursula Vaughan Williams and Antony Hopkins), and provided a valuable means to corroborate information found in the archives. Transcripts have not been included in the appendices so as to maintain a consistent methodology (i.e. being primarily archive-based rather than including elements of oral history). I also refer to the 'Correspondence' and 'News from the Institutes' sections in *Home and Country*, as well as references to 'local' activities in the National Federation's minutes, in order to gauge, to the extent that it is possible, the relationship between the National Federation and village Institutes. Whilst it might be useful to examine the records of individual Institutes, it would be difficult to gauge from them how representative they are of activities within the organization unless an extensive study were conducted.

It has also proved useful to look 'outside' the Women's Institute and examine its relationship with other institutions in order to understand the organization's role within both the amateur music scene and rural music making. Although I have been unable to gain access to the archives of the Rural Music Schools Association or the National Union of Townswomens' Guilds, their official publications (namely histories of the organizations and journal articles) have proved to be valuable sources of information.[7] Other archives consulted during the research for this book include the BBC Script Archives, V&A Archives, Britten-Pears library, Ralph Vaughan Williams library (for the English Folk Dance and Song Society archives), The Women's Library, and the Newspaper Library. By examining the Women's Institute's music making activities through archival documents, and relating them to their wider historical and cultural context, I hope to more than justify the importance of recognizing the Women's Institute's contribution to British musical culture.

The book begins with an examination of the role of music in the Women's Institute. It examines the role of the National Federation's Music Sub-Committee and the organization's relationship with other organizations that promoted amateur music-making, and shows how music policy was implemented. In the second section, the role of *Jerusalem* and the National Federation's changing interpretations of the hymn are discussed. This in turn provides a background to assess the organization's relationship with suffrage, as well as other issues discussed throughout the book, namely the importance of rurality and empowerment, and the context for the two national music events discussed in Chapters 4 and 5.

The organization's promotion of conducting since the 1930s, an activity which is considered (even nowadays) to be a male dominated sphere, is discussed in Chapter 2 in the context of its being a potentially feminist activity within the organization. The National Federation's policy on conducting is discussed in detail, focusing on its involvement with the Schools for Conductors during the 1930s, and the conducting courses held at Denman College from the late 1940s until the late 1960s. For comparison, women's conducting activities outside the organization are examined, which includes conducting classes held at London's music conservatoires and concerts held by the Society of Women Musicians, to assess whether the National Federation sought to challenge societal constructs of gender in its conducting

---

[7] Official histories of the NUTG include Mary Stott, *Organization Women: The Story of the National Union of Townswomen's Guilds* (London: Heinemann, 1978), and Caroline Merz, *After the Vote: The Story of the National Union of Townswomen's Guilds in the Year of its Diamond Jubilee* (Norwich: NUTG, 1988). The NUTG's monthly journal (which has been published since 1933) is called *The Townswoman*. The most detailed information about the RMSA to date is Mary Ibberson, *For the Joy That We Are Here: Rural Music Schools, 1929–1950* (London: NCSS, 1977), and its monthly journal (first published in 1937 as *Rural Music* and renamed in 1946) is called *Making Music*.

activities. The term 'feminism' and its applicability to the Women's Institute are discussed in the final section.

The third chapter is an investigation into the National Federation's promotion of folk song and its contribution to the Folk Revival of the twentieth century. Examination of the National Federation's song books, song lists, and articles on music in *Home and Country* published during the 50-year period reveals that folk song was at its most popular during the 1920s–1930s, and that its decline after the *Folk Songs of the Four Seasons* commission was part of a general trajectory away from the genre and its associations in the post-war era. In addition the extent of the Institutes' interaction with other organizations that promoted amateur music-making is revealed and highlights the National Federation's wider contribution to music-making within Britain's rural communities.

Detailed archival studies of the National Federation's music commissions follow in the next two chapters. In Chapter 5, the commissioning of Ralph Vaughan Williams' *Folk Songs of the Four Seasons* is located within the organization's tradition of singing folk songs and shown to be somewhat old-fashioned for its time. In Chapter 6, the complex genesis of Malcolm Williamson's *The Brilliant and The Dark* is traced and linked to attempts at embracing modernism to a recruitment campaign to attract younger members to the organization. The study of both of these works not only provides an insight into the National Federation's music policy, but also reveals composers' interactions with amateurs – a topic that has been overlooked in both music histories and biographies of composers. In addition to Vaughan Williams and Williamson, the involvement of Britten, Imogen Holst and Elizabeth Poston in the National Federation's music activities is also discussed and reveals the organization's involvement with composers active in Britain's music scene during the 1950s and 1960s.

The final chapter examines the National Society Choir, which was formed as a direct result of *The Brilliant and The Dark* and performed at prestigious venues (such as the Purcell Room in London). Chapter 6 briefly discusses the three works that that the Choir premiered: Antony Hopkins' *Riding to Canobie*, Joan Littlejohns's *The Bonny Earl of Murray* and Ralph Nicholson's *Herrick's Carol*, and examines the organization's commitment to amateur music-making.

Chapter 1

Music Policy and its Implementation in the Women's Institute

Despite being Britain's largest women's organization, the Women's Institute has attracted the attention of only a few scholars.[1] The popular perception of the Women's Institute is of a church-related organization, with a membership of predominantly middle-aged women, whose activities centre on singing *Jerusalem*, jam making, handicrafts and organizing village fetes. To date, the most significant work written by outsiders includes Maggie Andrews' *The Acceptable Face of Feminism*, Alyson Laverick's 'The Women's Institute: Just Jam and Jerusalem?', Caitriona Beaumont's article on concepts of citizenship and feminism in mainstream women's organizations between 1928–1939, and Lynne Thompson's work on the Lancashire Federation.[2] In each case, the authors have sought to dispel the image of the Women's Institute being old-fashioned and conservative, and raise questions about the significance of the organization within the lives of its members. Broadly speaking, Beaumont, Andrews and Laverick reveal the organization to be a site of 'feminist' activity (discussed further in Chapter 2), whereas Thompson argues that the Women's Institute has provided a means for individuals' self-advancement (in both local politics and in education). However, Andrews has been the only scholar so far to examine the artistic side of the Women's Institute.[3] Thus, the image of music-making in the Women's Institute comprising women standing to patriotically sing

---

1 There are currently 215,000 Women's Institute members in England, Wales, and the Islands. National Federation of Women's Institute website (Accessed 12 February 2005), <http.www.womensinstitute.org.uk>.

2 Maggie Andrews, *The Acceptable Face of Feminism: The Women's Institute as a Social Movement*. London: Lawrence and Wishart, 1997, Alyson Laverick, 'The Women's Institute: Just Jam and Jerusalem?', MA. Dissertation in Women's Studies, University of Wales, 1990, Caitriona Beaumont, 'Citizens not Feminists: the boundary negotiated between citizenship and feminism by mainstream women's organizations in England, 1928–1939', *Women's History Review* vol. 9 no. 2 (2000): pp. 411–29, Lynne Thompson, 'The Promotion of Agricultural Education for Adults: The Lancashire Federation of Women's Institutes', *Rural History* vol. 10 no. 2 (1999): pp. 217–34, and '"Conservative" Women and Feminist History: The Case of The Women's Institute Movement in England and Wales 1915–1945', unpublished paper given at the 'Conservative Women' Conference at University College Northampton in November 2001.

3 Andrews argues that the organization's promotion of arts and crafts provided members with a female cultural space to explore new skills, gain confidence and engage in leisure time. *The Acceptable Face of Feminism*, pp. 59–78.

Jerusalem for the opening of their monthly meetings, often accompanied by an old and out-of-tune village hall piano, has not been addressed, until now.

Apart from these recent publications, all that has been available about the Women's Institute are instructional publications issued by the National Federation (such as the *WI Handbook*, *Procedure at Meetings* and *Keeping Ourselves Informed*)[4] and histories of the organization written either by members themselves (which include Ignez Jenkins' *A History of the Women's Institute Movement of England and Wales* and Anne Stamper's *Rooms Off the Corridor*), or commissioned by the National Federation (such as Piers Dudgeon's *Village Voices*).[5] These publications only briefly discuss 'internal' issues of policy and procedure, and are either concerned with depicting the structure of the Committees, or showing how local Institutes have been able to take part in directing national policy through resolutions discussed and voted on at the Annual General Meeting (AGM).[6]

Andrews discusses the Women's Institute's policies and how they changed in Chapter 2 of her *The Acceptable Face of Feminism*; but her examination is confined to the period from 1915 to the mid-1920s. In addition, the ways in which policies were implemented are dismissed on the grounds that, like the three-tiered arrangement of the organization, they have remained unchanged since the organization's beginnings.[7] The structure may not have altered greatly since the time of its gaining independence from the Board of Agriculture in 1919, but overlooking the internal mechanisms of the organization has meant that discussions have over-simplified the decision-making process and have not accounted for changes in policy.

Background to the Organization

The Women's Institute was founded in Britain in the autumn of 1915, although the roots of the organization can be traced to Canada. Following an address by a certain Mrs Hoodless of Hamilton on the need for special domestic science teaching for girls in Ontario's schools in 1896 (at a meeting held at the Ontario Agricultural College), the first Women's Institute was formed on 19 February 1897. It began as the Women's Department of Domestic Economy in affiliation with the Farmers' Institute of South Wentworth, and as the organization expanded, later became known as the Stoney Creek Women's Institute.[8] The organization was brought to Britain

---

4 The *WI Handbook* has been published annually since 1946, *Procedure at Meetings* (which is about how to hold and record a WI meeting) was first published in 1949, and *Keeping Ourselves Informed* (which details the correct procedure for the resolutions discussed at the AGM) was published in 1964.

5 Ignez Jenkins, *The History of the Women's Institute of England and Wales*, Oxford: Oxford University Press, 1953, Anne Stamper, *Rooms Off the Corridor; Education in the WI and 50 years of Denman College, 1948–1998*, London: WI Books, 1998, and Piers Dudgeon, *Village Voices*, London: Pilot Productions Ltd., 1989.

6 Examples include Dudgeon, *Village Voices*, p. 47, and Laverick, 'The Women's Institute: Just Jam and Jerusalem?', pp. 31–2.

7 Andrews, *The Acceptable Face of Feminism*, p. xii.

8 Jenkins, *The History of the Women's Institute of England and Wales*, pp. 5–11.

by a Canadian woman, Madge Watt, who had been a founder member of the first Women's Institute formed in British Columbia.[9] However, it was not until she was invited to speak at an annual meeting of the Agricultural Organization Society (AOS) in 1915 by its secretary, Mr Nugent Harris, that the idea of Women's Institutes attracted attention in Britain. The first British Women's Institute, founded in a small village called Llanfair in Anglesey, had its first monthly meeting of members on the 25 September 1915.

The original aim of the British Women's Institute was to provide a female counterpart to the male-dominated Agricultural Organization Society, an organization founded in 1901 to promote co-operation amongst farmers, small-holders and growers, to increase agricultural production.[10] If British countrywomen could be educated, it would, the founders believed, improve rural life and the conditions of Britain's villages. Indeed, it is significant that the resolution to set up a Women's Institute Committee under the auspices of the AOS was passed and carried at a time when women's involvement in the organization was seen as a way of maximizing food production as part of the war effort.[11]

As with its Canadian predecessors, the education of rural women remained high on the agenda from the organization's beginnings in Britain. In addition to providing members with information (by means of lectures, presentations and displays), the monthly Institute meeting also provided women with opportunities to socialize with fellow members.[12] Although many village communities had the local pub and organizations such as the British Legion, ex-servicemen's clubs, working men's clubs, and farmers' clubs, they tended not to cater for women (apart from the Women's Section of the British Legion, which usually met only twice a year).[13] The Women's Institute provided an opportunity for women to socialize beyond church-based activities (such as the Mothers' Union and serving on church councils)[14] and also, what was for many, the first time to have an existence outside the rural home.

---

9 Further information about Madge Watt's involvement can be found in Stamper, *Rooms Off the Corridor*, p. 24.

10 References to the British Agricultural Organization Society can be found in Jenkins, *The History of the Women's Institute of England and Wales*, pp. 3–4.

11 The Women's Institute continued to aid food production as part of the war effort when it transferred affiliation to the Women's Branch of the Board of Agriculture in 1917 and, in 1919, became an independent organization.

12 The minutes of the first British Women's Institute meeting (in Llanfair, Wales) on 18 June 1915 reported that the President, Mrs Stapleton Cotton, had been chosen, a Committee formed, and meetings of 'an educational and social character' arranged to take place on the first Tuesday of each month starting at 2pm, cited from Stamper, *Rooms Off the Corridor*, pp. 26–7.

13 H.E. Bracey, *English Rural Life – Village Activities, Organizations and Institutions*, London: The Humanities Press, 1959, p. 158.

14 According to Dr Cordelia Moyse, archivist of the Mothers' Union, there was no widespread culture of music-making in the organization beyond taking part in church worship.

Figure 1.1: Cavendish and Pentlow (West Suffolk) choir winners

Music and the Social Half Hour

Music featured in the Social Half Hour, a section at the end of the Institute meeting allocated to the promotion of the educational value of leisure activities. For many members, the Social Half Hour provided the first opportunity for leisure-time and relaxation outside of the home.

The music activities of the Social Half Hour were in keeping with the organization's ideological concern of promoting communality and community spirit by allowing all members to take part, irrespective of ability or resources, and tended to focus on choral singing or, where Institutes were unable to train choirs, community singing of simple and well-known songs sung in unison (discussed in Chapter 3). It is within this context that music for pipes and percussion bands was recommended in the National Federation's monthly magazine, *Home and Country* (which was first published in February 1919) – as a means to accompany folk songs and folk dancing rather than to enable individuals to perform concerts, thus adhering to the Women's Institute ideology of communal music-making.[15] Other activities recommended by the National Federation for this part of the meeting were handicrafts, games, acting and listening to visiting speakers. However, it was music (and drama) that enabled Institutes to infiltrate village life, by extending communal action to include men from the local villages in Institute activities (discussed further in Chapter 2).

Although there is little archival material on the topic of music for the years before the National Federation's Music Sub-Committee was established in 1923, references to music in *Home and Country* indicate that music was a feature of many early Institute meetings (discussed further in Chapter 3). A letter printed in the October

---

15 Music recommended includes publications by The Year Book Press for pipe music and Joseph Williams' repertoire for percussion bands in Gertrude Lampson, 'Music Reviews', *Home and Country* vol. 15 no. 2 (February 1933): p. 86.

edition of 1920 requesting information about the necessary instruments for Haydn's or Romberg's *Toy Symphony*, and a review of a performance by the Wadsworth String Quartette a month later, indicate that instrumental music had been a feature of some Institute meetings since their early years.[16]

The NFWI Music Sub-Committee

The establishment of the National Federation Music Sub-Committee formalized the organization's music activities. The first meeting of the National Federation Music Sub-Committee was held on 9 July 1923.[17] It consisted of the three Officers of the National Federation (who presided on every National Federation Sub-Committee): the Chairman, Vice-Chairman and Treasurer.[18] The Music Sub-Committee consisted of both elected and co-opted members, as well as advisers from outside the organization (discussed later). There appears to have been no pre-requisite qualification to join a National Federation Sub-Committee apart from being interested in the organization and being able to seek expert advice from outside the National Federation when required. Janet Cannetty-Clarke (discussed in Chapter 6) appears to have been among only a handful of Sub-Committee members who had a music qualification: she had obtained a BMus from the Royal Academy at the age of 21.

Some members of the Music Sub-Committee served at the same time on other National Federation Sub-Committees.[19] The first Music Sub-Committee, for example, included Viscountess Boyne (who was also on the Executive Committee and the Agriculture and Horticulture Sub-Committee), Lady Margaret Boscawen (who also served on the Education, Literature and Publicity Sub-Committee and the *Home and Country* Sub-Committee) and Mrs H.G. Stobart (who was also on the Executive, Education, Literature and Publicity Sub-Committee as well as the *Home and Country* Sub-Committee). Although some members had a lengthy membership (Gertrude Lampson, for example, served from 1923 to 1936), the Music Sub-Committee was elected annually and fluctuated in size with a membership (excluding the Officers) ranging from 13 in 1928 to 6 in 1932.

The Sub-Committee's official name changed throughout the 50-year period: in 1926 the 'Music Sub-Committee' changed to the 'Music, Drama and Dancing Sub-Committee', then in 1936 split into 'Music and Dancing' with a separate 'Drama' section. In 1941 the Sub-Committees amalgamated into 'Music and Drama' and 'Dancing' was deleted from the title. In 1949 it changed again to 'Music and Dancing', and in 1957 to 'Music and Drama'. In 1970, it reverted to its original name, the 'Music Sub-Committee'. But despite these changes in its official title, examination of the Terms of Reference (which featured annually in the minute books) reveals that the Sub-Committee's role did not alter greatly.

---

16 'Correspondence' by Mrs S.D. Boys, Vice-President of North Cadbury WI *Home and Country* vol. 2 no. 8 (October 1920): p. 17, and 'A Musical Experiment' by a WI member in vol. 2 no. 9 (November 1920): p. 17.
 17 Executive Minutes vol. 6 (10 July 1923), p. 198.
 18 In 1927, a second Vice-Chairman was added to the Sub-Committee.
 19 Executive Minutes vol. 8 (8 June 1926), p. 46.

Broadly speaking, the Music Sub-Committee's responsibility was twofold: to encourage music-making within the organization and to strive to maintain 'high standards'. Although it was not stated which types of music were to be encouraged or the level of musicianship that was to be reached – words such as 'amateur' or 'professional' were not used – the National Federation was committed to amateur music-making.

The Sub-Committee's goals varied slightly year by year and can be traced through an examination of the 'Plan of Work' section which was created each time a new Sub-Committee was elected. It usually included organizing music conferences and Schools for Conductors, arranging visits to the counties from either Sub-Committee members or those on the 'Music Panel' (who were people recommended by the County Federation Music Committees as being suitable to undertake work in the Institutes), assisting and advising on the publication of National Federation literature on music, and planning national music events for which new works were commissioned (Ralph Vaughan Williams's *Folk Songs of the Four Seasons* for the 1950 Singing Festival and Malcolm Williamson's *The Brilliant and The Dark* for the 1969 Music Festival) which aimed to include Institutes nationwide.[20] It is unclear from the wording of the minute books what was the procedure for the proposal and discussion of topics at meetings, but it appears that decisions were made as the result of a democratic process (which might entail another member of the Committee seconding a proposal or a vote being taken).[21]

Although the Sub-Committee was responsible for setting and ensuring the implementation of music policy within the organization, the Executive Committee made most of the important decisions regarding the national music events. These include the recommendation in 1962 and 1964 to approach Britten for the organization's second musical commission (discussed in Chapter 5). Furthermore, it was the Executive Committee's decision not to repeat a performance of *Folk Songs of the Four Seasons* in 1951, and their backing that ensured a second national music event would take place.[22]

That said, an incident recorded in the minute books indicates that the Executive Committee did not always have the last word. At a meeting of the Executive Committee on the 8 January 1929 it was decided to invite the contralto Dame Clara Butt to sing solos at the two-day AGM. On the first day she would sing *England*, and a solo (unspecified) on the second.[23] Butt had become a well-known figure following

---

20 The Music Sub-Committee's role also included suggestions for agendas and courses on music at Denman College (discussed in Chapter 2). However, it appears that the General Education Committee took over this role around 1955 and the Music Sub-Committee merely vetted their suggestions.

21 There appears to be only one reference in the minute books to a private session of the Music Sub-Committee being held on 9 March 1951.

22 The decision not to repeat *Folksongs* is recorded in the Executive Minutes, vol. 22 (27 July 1950), p. 1039, and the request for a second national music event is recorded in the Executive Minutes vol. 28 (6 February 1961), p. 1025.

23 Executive Minutes vol. 9 (8 January 1929), p. 280. 'England' is most likely to refer to a song composed by Parry, the words of which were paraphrased from Shakespeare by Sir Esme Howard (published by The Yearbook Press Series of Unison Songs and Part Songs, 1919).

her performance in the Royal College of Music's production of Gluck's opera *Orpheus* at the Lyceum Theatre in 1892. By the late 1920s, she was a much sought-after concert soloist and had made numerous recordings.[24] However, the National Federation later withdrew the invitation to Butt. The minutes for the next meeting of the Music, Drama and Dancing Sub-Committee (which was held on the 7 February 1929) reported that a Miss [C.J.] Gaskell protested at the precedent of the Executive Committee deciding matters that affected the work of the Sub-Committee without its consent, following which the topic appears to have been dropped.[25]

Outside the Music Sub-Committee

The Music Sub-Committee often sought advice from outside the organization, whether from individuals or organizations. There are a few references to individuals being approached. In 1926, the English writer, educationist and composer, William Henry Hadow (who was also the older brother of Grace Hadow, the National Federation's first Vice-Chairman) was asked for his opinion about the suitability of *The Community Songbook* for use in the Institutes: he criticized it for containing 'a good deal of second-rate material'.[26] He had given an address at the National Federation's AGM in 1924 on 'Music for Country People' which encouraged music-making within the Institutes as a way of introducing members to the enjoyment of music. W.H. Hadow's recommendations included Institutes holding lectures at meetings on musical subjects followed by sessions of practical music-making, training Institute members as conductors (discussed in Chapter 2), singing 'simple' music (such as rounds and national songs) and promoting musical appreciation (by listening to records and performances by local organists).[27] Other individuals include a Major J.T. Bavin who was also asked whether there was a song book already published that could be adapted for the organization, or whether the National Federation should produce its own (discussed in Chapter 2).[28]

The National Federation also approached the British Federation of Music Competition Festivals (BFMCF) for advice about music suitable for festivals and music activities in the Institutes. The minutes for a meeting of the Executive Committee on 12 July 1927, for example, refers to a letter from a member, Mrs Lampson, requesting advice from the National Federation about music suitable for

---

24 Anonymous: 'Dame Clara (Ellen) Butt', *The New Grove Dictionary of Music Online* ed. L. Macy (Accessed 4 May 2004), <http.www.grovemusic.com>.

25 Executive Minutes vol. 9 (12 February 1929), p. 313, and Executive Minutes vol. 9 (12 March 1929), p. 341 respectively.

26 I have been unable to locate this song book. Executive Minutes vol. 8 (14 December 1926), p. 163. Further information about W.H. Hadow can be found in Nigel Fortune's article, *The New Grove Dictionary Online* ed. L. Macy (Accessed 4 May 2004) <http.www.grovemusic.com>.

27 W.H. Hadow's speech was published in *Home and Country* vol. 6 no. 5 (July 1924): pp. 614–16.

28 Major [J.T] Bavin's articles include 'The Care of the Piano', *Home and Country* vol. 10 no. 1 (January 1928): pp. 32–3.

festivals held in the counties. It was recommended that she contact the BFMCF directly.[29] It seems likely that the National Federation's early contact with the BFMCF (which was previously known as the Association of Musical Competition Festivals) was the result of William Henry Leslie's involvement in both: around the same time he was advising the National Federation's music policy, Leslie was Treasurer of the AMCF.[30] Indeed, Leslie soon became an important figure in creating and leading the Women's Institute's policy on music until he died in 1926 (discussed in Chapter 3).

The Music Sub-Committee also liaised with the Rural Music Schools Association (RMSA), an organization founded in 1929 by Mary Ibberson to promote the teaching of mainly instrumental music (although choral music may have also featured as part of training in musicianship) to amateurs in rural Britain.[31] However, information about the organization's relationship with the National Federation is scarce. The minutes reveal that a member of the Music Sub-Committee, Lady Listowel, attended the Founder's Day gathering of Hertfordshire Rural Music School in 1934 and the weekend Rural Music School in Roehampton in 1947.[32] From being represented on the RMSA Committee, it seems that the National Federation severed its link at least on a national level, following the change in the RMSA's Constitution in 1939 which would have made the National Federation a guarantor and therefore financially liable.[33]

There are also signs of links with the Women's Institute's urban counterpart, the National Union of Townswomen's Guilds (NUTG), which was founded in 1928 following the disbanding of the National Union of Women's Suffrage Societies.[34] The minutes for a meeting of the Music and Dancing Sub-Committee on 6 May 1936 refers to ten members of the NUTG being invited to attend the National Federation's demonstration of music in the Social Half Hour which was held at Cecil Sharp House on 19 May 1936. In addition, the minutes for a meeting of the Music and Dancing Sub-Committee on 7 December 1951 refer to Tennant's (who was serving on the Executive Committee at the time) attendance of the NUTG Music Conference. However, it seems unlikely to have been anything more than a reciprocal arrangement of inviting representatives from other organizations to attend music conferences.

---

29 This may be the same Mrs [Gertrude] Lampson who served on the Music Sub-Committee (1923–1936). Executive Minutes vol. 8 (12 July 1927), p. 310.

30 Little is known about the BFMCF apart from its originating from a movement pioneered by Mary Wakefield at the end of the nineteenth century as a means to stimulate amateur music-making.

31 Mary Ibberson, *For the Joy That We Are Here: Rural Music Schools, 1929–1950* provides a valuable insight into the early history of the organization.

32 MDDcS-C (3 January 1934), n.p, and MDS-C (14 April 1947), n.p.

33 Executive Minutes vol. 17, OFS-C (7 February 1939), p. 527.

34 The NUWSS disbanded into the National Union for Equal Citizenship, the Fawcett Society, and the NUTG. The most detailed information about the organization can be found in Mary Stott, *Organization Women: The Story of the National Union of Townswomen's Guilds* and Caroline Merz, *After the Vote: The Story of the National Union of Townswomen's Guilds in the Year of its Diamond Jubilee.*

Nevertheless, the organization's relationship with the NUTG provides an insight into the importance of the rurality in the identity of the Women's Institute (which can also be seen in its repertoire, discussed in detail in Chapter 3).[35] Writing 50 years after the formation of the first Townswomen's Guild, Mary Stott states that the organizations' distinct identities have prevented any merger into a single body:

> It has been suggested several times that the time has come when the Townswomen and the Women's Institutes might merge into a single organisation. The general boundaries have not made much sense for years, with the villages receiving more 'incomers' from towns and the reorganisation of the local government system destroying the 'county federation' basis of the Women's Institutes. But the Townswomen would not like to be 'swallowed up' by the larger organisation, and the Women's Institutes would not like their essentially rural interests to be dominated by the 'townies'.[36]

The NUTG had a clear sense of its identity from its inception; during the 1920s, when the Women's Institute was concerned with the promotion of agricultural and food production, the NUTG based its 'urban' identity on an active training of its members in citizenship and an ideology of comradeship.[37]

However, it appears that the NUTG adopted features of the Women's Institute. Stott refers to the use of training schools (which were also a feature of the Women's Co-operative Guild), the recruitment and training of Voluntary County Organizers, and the use of advisory committees for specialist activities.[38] Indeed, comparisons can be made between the NUTG and the Women's Institute in their music activities: in addition to focusing on choral (rather than instrumental) music-making, both organizations had music advisers, held music schools, schools for conductors, and commissioned works for national events.[39]

The only occasion when the National Federation rejected an allegiance was with a musical organization called the Empire Musical Fellowship in 1934.[40] The minutes state: 'The [Music] Sub-Committee decided to recommend that the Federation should not co-operate in this scheme, as it was felt that it was outside the scope of the Federation's work.'[41] In view of the National Federation's allegiances with the

---

35 The title of the Women's Institute's magazine, *Home and Country*, also symbolises the organization's promotion of the countryside, as well as incorporating patriotic overtones.

36 Stott, p. 228.

37 Stott states that the aims of the NUTG were 'To enable women as citizens to make their best contribution towards the common good and to obtain all such reforms as are necessary to secure a real equality of liberties, status and opportunities for men and women', pp. 23–4. These topics never appear to have been specifically addressed in WI policy.

38 Ibid., p. 22.

39 The NUTG commissioned Armstrong Gibbs' *The Gift* which was premiered by the London Federations in 1959 and Imogen Holst who wrote *The Sun's Journey* for the National Festival in 1965. Further information about the NUTG's music activities can be found in Stott's *Organization Women*, pp. 90–99.

40 Despite conducting detailed searches on the British Library catalogue and at the EFDSS archives, I have been unable to find any further references or information about this organization.

41 MDS-C (12 September 1934), n.p.

English Folk Dance and Song Society (EFDSS) (discussed in Chapter 3) and the RMSA, the most likely explanations for this decision are either that the Empire Musical Fellowship was an organization that promoted professional rather than amateur music-making, or that the National Federation considered anything beyond the national as being outside their remit.

The National Federation also had contacts with the leading grant-awarding bodies – the Carnegie UK Trust (CUKT) and the Arts Council (preceded during the Second World War as the Council for the Encouragement of Music and the Arts). The main difference between the two organizations was that whereas the CUKT gave financial aid to promote amateur work in the Arts (and in particular amongst adults), the Arts Council concentrated on promoting the Arts in the professional sphere.[42] Information about their relationship with the Women's Institute is reliant on the National Federation's minute books, as references to the organization in the archives of the Arts Council (which incorporate the archives for the CUKT) are limited to Imogen Holst's correspondence.[43]

The National Federation's commitment to promoting amateur music-making rather than music in the professional sphere may explain why the organization was more closely involved with the CUKT than with the Arts Council. Furthermore, an entry in the minute books indicates that tension existed between the Arts Council and the National Federation, at least on a national level. The minutes of a meeting with a member of the Executive Committee, Mrs Gowring, and a representative from the Arts Council, Mona Tatham, reported: 'Means of closer co-operation with the [Arts] Council had been discussed. It was noted that the NFWI had the reputation for wanting "something for nothing"'.[44] The Executive Committee dismissed the derogatory comment as the Arts Council having an 'urban' rather than rural outlook, but seized the opportunity five months later to remind the Arts Council of the importance of the Women's Institute in spreading the Arts Council's news in rural areas.[45] Although it is difficult to gauge what was behind the jibe, a letter to Miss Glasgow (then Secretary of the Arts Council) in Imogen Holst's correspondence (dated 7 August 1941) about a request from Worcester Federation for her to conduct the singing at their AGM, suggests that the Institutes may have approached the Arts Council too often, requesting potentially free help with their music activities.[46]

By contrast, the relationship with the CUKT was highly beneficial for the National Federation. The organization had been set up during the 1930s to help with the development of music, and channelled its activities through the National Federation

---

42 In 1950, the Arts Council took over the responsibility of the Carnegie UK Trust and began its promotion of bringing amateur and professional musicians together.

43 This includes a letter from E.M. Stokes (dated 1 May 1941), a letter from Miss Glasgow (dated 29 June 1941) that refers to Joan Brocklebank, and another (dated 9 August 1941) regarding performing at Worcester WI's annual meeting, from a file labelled EL2/51 at the V&A archives.

44 Executive Minutes vol. 21, MDS-C (9 September 1946), p. 352 and Executive Minutes vol. 21, MDS-C (14 April 1947), p. 650.

45 Executive Minutes vol. 21 (25 September 1947), p. 796.

46 A letter from Imogen Holst to Miss Glasgow (dated 7 August 1941) from a file labelled EL2/51 at the V&A archives.

of Music Societies (NFMS).[47] In addition to bringing together organizations involved in amateur music-making and providing a centre for the exchange of advice, the CUKT provided financial assistance, which was administered by a Joint Committee of representatives from the Trust and the NFMS. The CUKT provided the Women's Institute with two major grants for the training of conductors and producers of drama within the organization (discussed in Chapter 2).

The National Federation's involvement with outside organizations through music not only refutes its popular image as an insular organization, but also reveals that the Women's Institute recognized music as having a wider role within community life. In addition to providing elementary musical instruction for members, the National Federation saw itself as having a role in fostering a network in the community that could enable members to develop their musicianship (as individuals) beyond the organization. In comparison with allegiances to drama organizations outside the Women's Institute (essentially limited to the British Drama League), the National Federation had a far wider interaction with the community through music.

Music Policy and Tools for Implementation

As mentioned earlier, historians' accounts of the policy-making process within the organization have focused on the AGM and how individual Institutes have affected the resolutions passed. However, music never formed a significant feature of the AGM despite the topic being discussed at meetings of the Consultative Council (which met biannually as an advisory body to the Executive Committee).[48] Music policy, it seems, was mainly created in response to feedback from music events (to which county representatives were invited) organized by the National Federation. An early example is the Summer School of Music arranged and held at the home of W.H. Leslie in September 1922 which included sessions led by Walford Davies (who at the time was Professor of Music at Aberystwyth University and adviser on the Welsh National Council of Music).[49] A report by a Sub-Committee member, Miss Nightingale, stated that the aim of the summer school had been to examine the possibility of Women's Institutes taking over the organization of music-making within villages, and to provide instruction for leaders of music (in villages) in sight-singing, conducting and descant singing (the latter is referred to as 'melody

---

47 The NFMS was founded in 1933 to provide a central body that supported the promotion of amateur choral and orchestral societies. H.E. Bracey's *English Rural Life* provides a useful insight into the history of the Carnegie UK Trust (pp. 176–8).

48 The Consultative Council comprised members of the National Executive Committee and one representative elected by each Federation. In 1946, Tennant gave a statement at a meeting of the Consultative Council on the Carnegie policy on music and drama which is recorded in the Executive Minutes vol. 21, MDS-C (9 September 1946), p. 351.

49 Executive Minutes vol. 5 (10 October 1922), p. 15. Further information about Walford Davies can be found in the article by Hugh Ottaway and Lewis Foreman, 'Sir (Henry) Walford Davies', *The New Grove Dictionary of Music Online* ed. L. Macy (Accessed 4 May 2004), <http.www.grovemusic.com>.

making').[50] It can be seen that, as a result, summer schools proliferated (such as the one held annually in Oxford) and Schools for Conductors began to be regularly held in the counties. These events were frequently promoted in *Home and Country*.

In 1924 and 1934 questionnaires were sent to the counties as a means to gather up-to-date information about music activities (in order for the Music Sub-Committee to plan its work accordingly). It seems that in 1924 little action was taken due to a poor response to the questionnaire.[51] The minutes reveal that another questionnaire was sent to the Institutes a decade later, following which an interview was arranged with Mr Farquharson (who was secretary of the CUKT's Joint Committee) to discuss how the requests could be best carried out.[52] However, the nature of the responses or even the questions posed is unknown, as none of the questionnaires have been kept.

The Music Sub-Committee implemented music policy through the official literature published by the National Federation and distributed to the Institutes. This comprised leaflets on music topics (such as the two on *Jerusalem* discussed later), song books and song lists recommending items suitable for Institute music-making (discussed in Chapter 3), and newsletters sent via the county federations (usually during preparations for a national event). In addition, articles on music and advertisements for local and national music events were published in *Home and Country*.[53]

The format of *Home and Country* did not change greatly from 1921.[54] Amidst articles on a range of subjects, the magazine included regular features. Broadly speaking, these comprised 'Editor's Notes' (which ranged from information about WI successes at local competitions to special announcements), a 'Diary of Coming Events' (which included a list of council meetings, conferences, and training schools), 'Office Notes' (written by the General Secretary and usually concerned with the running of the organization such as annual meetings, the current state of funds, membership levels, etc), 'Correspondence to the Editor' (consisting of letters from members predominantly with queries or comments about aspects of the organization), a column advertising items for private sale, a list of recommended publications, and 'County Federation Notes' (which reviewed Institutes' activities in

---

50 Executive Minutes vol. 3, EC (10 October 1922), n.p. For more information on W.H. Leslie (known as Henry Leslie, 1860–1926) see H.C. Colles and E.D. Mackerness: 'Leslie, Henry (David)', *The New Grove Dictionary of Music Online* ed. L. Macy (Accessed 30 January 2001), <http: www.grovemusic.com>.

51 The minutes reported that Lady Denman was asked at the Consultative Council meeting to draw attention 'at some convenient time' to the lack of information supplied by many counties. Executive Minutes vol. 7, MS-C (10 February 1925), p. 262.

52 Executive Minutes vol. 12, MDcS-C (11 July 1934) p. 244. It is unclear whether Mr Farquharson was a relation of Olive Farquharson who wrote articles on opera for *Home and Country*.

53 *Home and Country* appears not to have been sold or distributed outside of the organization.

54 The first editor of *Home and Country* was Alice Williams in 1919, who was succeeded in 1920 by Mrs Nugent Harris. In 1936, Mrs Nugent Harris was replaced by joint editors – Margery Sidgwick and Irene Clephane. Detailed information about the magazine and can be found in the *Home and Country* Sub-Committee minutes.

the counties and later became known as 'News from the Institutes'). 'Music Reviews' (discussed in Chapter 3) became a regular music feature in *Home and Country* from 1929, recommending music suitable for Institute choirs and catering for varying choral abilities. It ranged from simple children's songs to works for mixed choirs. The majority of the articles on music were written by members of the Music Sub-Committee or representatives from other organizations, in particular by prominent figures in the EFDSS and the RMSA.[55] Authors whose writings frequently appeared in *Home and Country* include W.H. Leslie, Lampson, Tennant, Kathleen Talbot and Dorothy Erhart (to name only a few).

The magazine also featured advertisements from outside companies. From the mid-1920s, the publishers Curwen dominated the advertisements for music with repertoire from their catalogue deemed suitable for use in the Women's Institutes (namely folk songs, national songs and song books for communal singing). However, Curwen's monopoly appears to have ended by the mid-1930s as music published by other companies (mostly Boosey and Hawkes) appeared. Indeed, outside influence in *Home and Country* was closely controlled. The minutes for a meeting of the Executive Committee on 9 June 1955 reveal the degree of vetting of the subject, authors and the content of articles. The minutes state:

> The various Sub-Committees shall, as at present, decide the subject of their article, and make recommendations as to the authors, but the invitation to write shall come from the Editor, after consultation with the Chairman of the relevant Sub-Committee. The Editor is empowered to offer a few suggestions and to exercise the usual editorial control.[56]

In addition, the decision to reject an offer from a certain Miles Henslow for a magazine (entitled 'Music') on Institutes' music activities in the counties indicates that rival publications were not welcomed.[57]

The National Federation used the County Federation Committees to ensure that music policy was taken to the grassroots of the organization. The County Federation Committees (to which County Music Organizers were affiliated) had oversight of the 'official' visits from Voluntary County Organizers (VCOs), Music Advisers and occasionally, members of the Music Sub-Committee. Little is known about County Federation Committees apart from their involvement in the preparations for the National Music Festivals, or who the VCOs were or what they actually did (apart from their official role which was to establish new Institutes and to deal with the needs of individual counties).[58]

---

55 However, before 1923 articles had tended to be short and written by a variety of unknown authors: M. Radford, 'On hearing music', *Home and Country* vol. 3 no. 2 (June 1921): p. 17; M.E. Hobbs, 'Singing', *Home and Country* vol. 3 no. 3 (July 1921): p. 6; and Lilian Belletti, 'Women's Institute Choirs', *Home and Country* vol. 4 no. 6 (November 1922): p. 8.

56 Executive Minutes vol. 24 (9 June 1955), p. 1056.

57 Executive Minutes vol. 23, MDS-C (12 October 1951), p. 188.

58 Ignez Jenkins writes: 'A first training-school for Voluntary County Organisers was arranged at Burgess Hill in Sussex. It was a residential school which lasted for three weeks … The syllabus of instruction for this first school was, in its general conception, clear and comprehensive. The teaching and the advice given on propaganda, programme planning,

There is, however, more detailed archival information about the National Federation's Music Adviser, who, it seems, remained at the heart of the Women's Institute's implementation of music policy from the mid-1930s until 1948 when the National Federation's residential establishment opened, Denman College (discussed in Chapter 2). The position was created in 1935 following a suggestion from a Sub-Committee member, Gertrude Lampson, as a means to co-ordinate music-making within the organization. The minutes for a meeting of the Music and Dancing Sub-Committee on 2 October 1935 stated:

> That in view of the lack of liaison between the different parts of the country as regards [to] musical activities, the NFWI should employ the services of a part-time Organiser who should go to counties on planned tours, attend Committee meetings, give lecture-demonstrations, advisory visits, etc., and report to the NFWI Music Sub-Committee.[59]

Iris Lemare appears to have been the first choice, although it was Nancy Tennant who took up the position in December 1935. A year later, Tennant resigned from her position as Music Adviser. The job was advertised in *Home and Country*, *The Times*, *The Daily Telegraph* and *Time and Tide* magazine. There were 87 applications. Ten applicants were interviewed by the Executive Committee, and three were called for second interviews by the Music Sub-Committee.[60] Tennant was succeeded by Joan Brocklebank who served until 1938 and was replaced by Elsie Rigg in 1940 (which was slightly later than anticipated due to lack of funds), who worked intermittently, it seems, until 1948. Brocklebank appears to have been the only one who had studied music at an institution, having attended the Musikheim in Frankfurt (an establishment which, she states, promoted the technical side of music as well as communal music-making).[61]

One of the qualifications for the job appears to have been experience in organizing Women's Institute music events. Prior to her appointment, Tennant had served on the National Federation's Music Sub-Committee since 1930; Brocklebank had been heavily involved in the music activities in the Dorset Federation (organizing festivals and conducting schools); and Rigg had served on the Music Panel since 1931, and was involved in numerous engagements within the organization which included giving lectures on music in the Institutes, leading community singing, choir training, taking sessions at conductors schools, adjudicating, the production of operettas, and

---

instruction of committee members and the rest, were all that is sound and practical.' *A History of the Women's Institute Movement of England and Wales*, p. 23. The only references I have found in the National Federation's minutes to VCOs and music refers to W.H. Leslie giving a lecture at a VCO Conference in 1922 (Executive Minutes vol. 6 (12 December 1922), p. 42), music being included at the 'Social Half Hour' School in 1934 and copies of the first notice of the Singing Festival being sent to the VCOs (MDS-C (10 January 1949), n.p).

59 MDcS-C (2 October 1935), n.p.
60 MDcS-C (9 September 1936), n.p.
61 Joan Brocklebank wrote an article on her experiences at the Musikheim, which was signed 'J.B.' titled 'A Home of Music in Germany', *Home and Country* vol. 19 no. 4 (April 1937): p. 187. I have been unable to find out any other information about this establishment.

leading pipe classes.[62] It is unclear from the minute books why Rigg was chosen over Miss Merritt who, out of a total of eight applicants, was also called for interview. However, the decision to recommend Merritt as a suitable person for Institute work on the 'technical side' suggests that her speciality was in musical performance whereas Rigg was considered to have a wider range of musical abilities.[63]

The role of the Music Adviser appears to have been varied and demanding. Although she was contracted on a part-time basis, Tennant's official responsibilities included organizing music schools and conferences, speaking at council meetings, attending meetings of the Music Sub-Committee, and visiting county federations.[64] Her work in the counties was broadly divided into two categories: advisory visits (when she visited County Federation Committees and Music Sub-Committees and gave advice on music policy, choice of music and the organization of music activities) and instructional visits (which were concerned with elementary tuition either at council or group meetings, or schools organized by county federations).[65] Brocklebank had the additional responsibility of adjudicating elementary festivals (or Area Festivals) and revising the National Federation's song book. In addition, she appears to have been the most prolific writer (as Music Adviser) of articles on music for *Home and Country*.[66] Although it is difficult to gauge the effectiveness of the Music Adviser in implementing music policy, the reviews of Brocklebank's and Rigg's work indicate that there was a real demand in the counties for advice on music. The minutes report that in 1937 Brocklebank spent 50 days visiting 16 county federations; and Rigg is recorded to have worked 90 days (instead of her contracted 80) in 1947.[67]

Only one significant incident was recorded in the minutes of an Institute deliberately violating the National Federation's policy. It occurred in 1956 at the Devon Federation Annual Meeting when the General Secretary of the Federation, Lady Sidmouth, stated that the use of prayer at the monthly meeting was a breach of the non-sectarian ruling of the Constitution.[68] Her statement was reproduced in the press and was broadcast on the West Region of the BBC. However, this opinion appears not to have been held countywide and the matter was resolved following a deputation from members of the Executive Committee to meet those involved.[69]

It seems surprising therefore that *Jerusalem*, which is replete with Christian sentiments in its references to the 'Holy Lamb of God' and 'Countenance Divine', has become adopted, albeit unofficially, as the Women's Institute's anthem (see

---

62 Listed in a document titled 'Music Panel: speakers' WI engagements during the last three years' (dated in hand writing June 1937).

63 It is possible that the 'Miss Merritt' was Kathleen Merritt who is mentioned in Mary Stott's Organization Women (pp. 91–9). In 1937 she became the NUTG's music adviser.

64 MDcS-C (30 October 1935), n.p.

65 'Notes from Headquarters', *Home and Country* vol. 8 no. 2 (February 1936): p. 76.

66 Her responsibilities are listed in the minutes of the MDcS-C (4 November 1936), n.p.

67 MDcS-C (1 February 1938), n.p. and Executive Minutes vol. 21, MDS-C (9 February 1948), p. 1014.

68 Executive Minutes vol. 125 (24 May 1956), p. 489.

69 The matter was resolved following a meeting with Lady Sidmouth and the National Federation Chairman, Lady Dyer, recorded in the Executive Minutes vol. 26 (25 October 1956), p. 1.

Appendix 1).[70] Were it not for the fact that *Jerusalem* has been ritualistically sung at Women's Institute monthly meetings and national events since the 1920s, its significance within the organization might be overlooked. However, examination of the hymn reveals it to be central to various aspects of members' experience of the Women's Institute such as singing, communality and empowerment. In addition, because *Jerusalem* has been sung in the Institutes since the mid-1920s and become the organization's unofficial anthem, it also provides a valuable means to judge music policy. Has it remained static or fluctuated in response to the organization's wider policy? If the latter is the case, then it raises further questions about what *Jerusalem* can tell us about where music fits within the organization and whether the National Federation's two music commissions in 1950 and 1969 (discussed in Chapters 4 and 5 respectively) should be seen as representative of music-making within the organization at their respective times. Examination of the meaning of *Jerusalem* and members' reaction to it therefore provides a useful barometer of political change within the Women's Institute and shows the centrality of music within the organization's identity.

Music and the Constitutional Ruling

The non-sectarian ruling, which prevents the organization from having any affiliation to a particular denomination and so insulates members from being discriminated against on religious grounds, has occupied more discussion than any other aspect of the Constitution.[71] The topic has been frequently addressed in *Home and Country* (the first such mention was in the November edition of 1927) and tends to focus on the relationship of the Women's Institute with churches.[72]

The absence of references to music in these articles might lead one to infer that the non-sectarian rule has not affected the National Federation's music policy.[73] But the two were in fact intimately linked. The topic was addressed at a meeting of the Music and Dancing Sub-Committee on 11 July 1949:

> The Committee noted this [i.e. the non-political and non-sectarian ruling] but wished to point out that a number of mixed choirs are called WI choirs and therefore permission to allow WI members to perform in mixed groups at party political or sectarian functions was not in itself a solution to this problem.[74]

---

70 For the sake of clarity, I refer to Blake's poem as 'Jerusalem' although it is officially titled 'Milton'.

71 For further information see 'Interpretation of the Non-Sectarian Rule. 29.12.50. Ref. 2440/1'. It was not until 1951 that a definition of 'non-sectarian' was included in the WI Handbook.

72 The NFWI archives include the draft of Lady Denman's article called 'Statement published in July, 1929', Grace Hadow's draft 'The NFWI Ruling re: Prayer at Institute Meetings' and an extract from a circular sent to county federations dated 14 December 1941.

73 A list titled 'National Federation of Women's Institutes Non-Sectarian Rule', dated (in handwriting) June 1956, sets out the issues that had been discussed with regard to the non-sectarian ruling.

74 MDcS-C (11 July 1949), n.p.

Questions of whether the performance of choirs (and drama groups) at church and chapel functions contravened the non-sectarian ruling continued to be raised during the 1950s and 1960s. Each time, the Executive Committee reiterated that in order for the Women's Institute to uphold its ruling, members could sing at religious services as individuals but not as an official Women's Institute choir.[75] An exception appears to have been made regarding the participation of Women's Institute choirs at the re-dedication of the Five Sisters Window in York Minster in 1950. After examining the policy of other voluntary, non-sectarian organizations (the Girl Guides and the British Red Cross Society), the Executive Committee decided that the Yorkshire Federation could join in the Service (because it was of national importance) but that any participation would be strictly on a voluntary basis.[76]

Jerusalem's Past

On 17 March 1917, Parry conducted a performance of *Jerusalem* at a suffrage meeting held at the Royal Albert Hall. The words 'bring me my arrows of desire' and 'I will not cease from mental fight, nor shall my sword sleep in my hand' made it a suitable choice because they could be seen as alluding to the campaigners' strife in gaining women's suffrage, as well as having a nationalist wartime message. However, it appears that, ironically, Millicent Fawcett regarded the music as being better suited to the suffrage campaign than the words. In a letter to Parry, she wrote:

> The music said for us what no words could say, and it was an added delight that you were in charge of it all, with memories going back to Rhoda and Agnes in their young days and of Harry with all his chivalries and enthusiasms. The Council passed a special vote of thanks to you, the Bach Choir, and the Orchestra yesterday, but this is a little personal line. Your *Jerusalem* ought to be made the Women Voter's [sic] Hymn.[77]

Parry's response indicates that he was sympathetic to the suffrage cause. He wrote accepting Fawcett's suggestion and replied that the concert was '… a glorious occasion for you and everyone concerned. Quite thrilling. I thought myself very lucky to be allowed to take part in it'.[78]

However, Jeremy Dibble reveals in his biography of Parry that *Jerusalem* was originally composed following a request from Robert Bridges that Parry set the opening verses of Blake's poem 'Milton' for Fight for the Right, an organization that had been founded by General Sir Francis Younghusband as a means to counter

---

75 Executive Minutes vol. 25 (24 May 1956), p. 489.
76 Executive Minutes vol. 22 (25 May 1950), p. 982.
77 Graves notes that the letter refers to Harry Fawcett (who was Millicent's husband), Agnes Garrett and her cousin, Rhoda (who were neighbours of the Fawcetts at their residence in Rushington). Charles L. Graves, *Hubert Parry: His Life and Works*. Vol. 2. London: Macmillan and Co. Ltd., 1926, p. 92.
78 Ibid., p. 92. Graves' biography refers to Parry attending suffrage meetings and being impressed by the speeches of 'old friends' such as Millicent Fawcett, Mrs Creighton and Maude Royden.

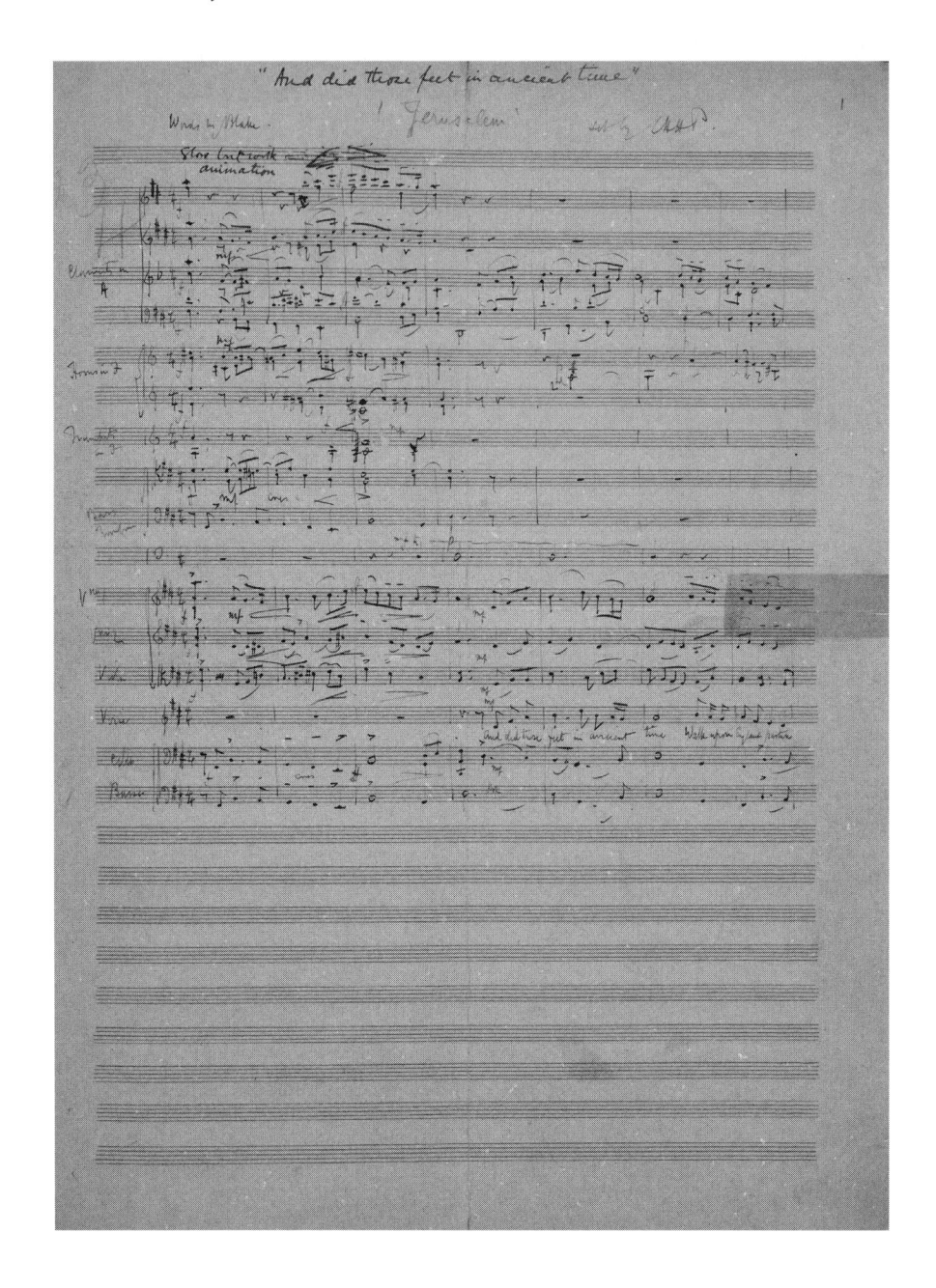

Figure 1.2: Original manuscript of *Jerusalem* by Parry.

German wartime propaganda.[79] It was first performed on 28 March 1914 at the Queen's Hall by a choir of volunteers from London's main choral societies, with organ accompaniment, conducted by Walford Davies. Parry, however, did not have nationalistic illusions about the war, and overt patriotism appears to have unnerved him: he not only rejected a request from another organization for unison songs that could be used for patriotic purposes, but also withdrew his support from the Fight for the Right movement in May 1917.

A letter published in *Home and Country* in December 1923 refers to its being Grace Hadow's suggestion that Parry's *Jerusalem* be adopted as the Institutes' song. She wrote: 'Both words and music are simple and dignified and are easy to learn. Incidentally, the learning would give pleasure to any WI and would afford an excellent opportunity for a short talk either on Blake's poetry, or on poems about England.'[80] A song competition was held in 1924, which, it was hoped, would find an Institute song and suitable lyrics that could be set to music in a later competition or by an 'eminent' composer. The decision to continue singing rather than to choose from entrants of the song competition or to commission its own song raises questions about what meaning the Women's Institute identified with the hymn.[81] The Women's Institute's first singing of the hymn at a national event took place at the organization's eighth AGM in 1924, after which it became a feature of Institute meetings.

The National Federation printed two pieces of official literature on *Jerusalem*. They are leaflets with the words printed on one side and a brief history of Blake's poem on the other. Published in 1934 and 1950, neither makes any reference to *Jerusalem*'s suffrage past.[82] Although a network of membership in women's organizations (discussed in detail in Chapter 2) might suggest that the Women's Institute's early use of the hymn was not totally devoid of associations with the suffrage movement, it is likely that *Jerusalem*'s associations with nationalism replaced the hymn's connections with suffrage. This is likely to have occurred at a concert at the British Empire Exhibition on 23 April 1924, when Elgar conducted *Jerusalem* in a programme that included his *Imperial March*, *Land of Hope and Glory* and the *National Anthem*. The move from suffrage to patriotism may also explain why, in 1926, the British Federation of Music Competition Festivals also took on *Jerusalem* as their hymn.

---

79 Jeremy Dibble, C. *Hubert H. Parry: His Life and Music*, Oxford: Clarendon Press, 1992, p. 483. Although Parry completed a simple orchestral arrangement of the accompaniment soon after (in November 1914) for use in large-scale concerts, it is Elgar's more lavish re-orchestration for large orchestra which is now most commonly heard. Elgar's version was first performed at the Leeds Music Festival in 1922.

80 'Letters to the Editor', *Home and Country* vol. 5 no. 6 (December 1923): pp. 355–6. A reference in Helen Deneke's biography to her attending the speeches of Mrs Fawcett at Queen's Hall on 18 March 1918 indicates that Grace Hadow was supportive of the suffrage cause. *Grace Hadow*, Oxford: Oxford University Press, 1946, p. 86.

81 The requirements of the competition are outlined in the Executive Minutes vol. 5 (13 December 1921), p. 73.

82 The first leaflet is unsigned and stamped '23 November 1934'. The second publication is signed 'Nancy Tennant' and dated 'reprint 1950'.

The Meaning of *Jerusalem* in the Women's Institute

The first leaflet, published in 1934, is a celebration of rurality and reflects the important place of folk songs within the National Federation's music policy (to continue until the late 1940s).[83] It refers to *Jerusalem* as 'the ideal City of God', a heavenly place of love and compassion associated with rurality (see Appendix 2). The commentary for the first eight lines of the poem refers to the legend that Christ visited England accompanied by his uncle Joseph of Arimathea (who was engaged in the tin trade that existed between Phoenicia and Cornwall), and the 'dark Satanic mills' to the mines Blake saw on his visit to the small village of Priddy (contrasting with the idyllic image of green and unspoilt hills of the countryside). The second stanza also links rurality with religious sentiments but remains vague enough to cover all beliefs, as the commentary highlights:

> He [i.e. Blake] prays for the bow and arrow of burning enthusiasm, for the spear for closer battle, and above all, for the spiritual forces of heaven, the 'Chariot of Fire', to carry him onwards, till his vision of peace shall find fulfilment in the fertile and smiling English land.[84]

Examination of the leaflet published 16 years later (which was the same year the National Federation premiered its first music commission from Vaughan Williams) reveals that by 1950 *Jerusalem* had lost all its religious associations, at least officially (see Appendix 3). This appears somewhat curious in view of the publication of critiques about Blake published around this time that celebrated his associations with Christianity: Margaret Bottrall's *The Divine Image* (1948) examines Blake's writings within the context of the Christian tradition based on the claim that he was 'a soldier of Christ'[85] and Bernard Blackstone's publication *English Blake* (1949) describes 'Milton' as 'an expression of Blake's devotion to the cause of Christ'.[86]

By 1950, the National Federation had gained a more general humanist sense of individual empowerment which was reflected in the National Federation's post-war plans to construct the organization's own educational establishment. The only similarity between the two commentaries is the reference to the legend that Christ visited England. The later one describes *Jerusalem* as 'a state of mind which is attained by practising the virtues of love and the healing power of constructive imagination'. Tennant, then Chairman of the Music and Drama Sub-Committee, wrote:

> The first verse has as its theme the legend that Christ came to Britain as a child, but it really throws out a challenge. Blake is asking us what we think about our country, what

---

83 It is likely that the 1934 publication (entitled 'The story of Jerusalem') was written by Mrs Clarke of Somerset, who was the author of a letter sent to Upper Hardies WI on the topic which is cited in the Executive Minutes vol. 12 (11 April 1934), p. 151.

84 Leaflet titled 'The story of Jerusalem'.

85 Margaret Bottrall, *The Divine Image: A Study of Blake's Interpretation of Christianity*, Oxford: Oxford University Press, 1948, p. 7.

86 Bernard Blackstone, *English Blake*, Cambridge: Cambridge University Press, 1949, p. 375.

does it mean to us with all its beauty and traditions? Do the right spiritual and physical conditions prevail in it for its people to develop what is best in themselves? In the second verse he answers the challenge and as we sing it we answer it too, for it is a challenge to the individual. 'Bring me my bow of burning gold,' 'I will not cease from mental fight.'[87]

The self-questioning in the 1950 leaflet has an assertive tone and sense of individual empowerment that seems to be more in keeping with the 'feminist' libretto (written by Ursula Vaughan Williams) for the National Federation's second music commission, rather than Vaughan Williams' *Folk Songs of the Four Seasons* with which it coincides. Although the absence of commentaries published after 1950 makes it more difficult to gauge the second commission, if the 1950 commentary is used, then it appears that *The Brilliant and The Dark* was also on the side of traditionalism.

Members' Interpretations

A series of letters published in *Home and Country* from June to October 1937 reveals that the National Federation's policy on *Jerusalem* was met with a degree of resistance from members to the extent that some even questioned whether the hymn was still relevant to the organization's work (see Appendix 4). In June 1937, M.C. Browning wrote to the Editor requesting a new Institute song on the grounds that village Institutes dragged out the singing of *Jerusalem*, creating a slow and dull rendition, that it had unsuitable words and that it lacked a striking melody.[88] This letter sparked a heated argument. The four-month-long debate that ensued highlighted members' differing interpretations of Blake's poem. E.M. Tovey wrote that the meaning of *Jerusalem* was symbolic of women's work to avert war, strife and bitterness; Margaret Baines stated that it referred to the desecration of England's holy countryside as a result of 'urbanization'; whilst Mary L. Pendered wrote: 'I doubt if one hundred of our members grasp its symbolism and I have never heard it sung at a village meeting with the least enthusiasm.'[89] Although it is unclear whether she associated 'symbolism' with Blake's poem or the hymn's associations with suffrage, this suggests that she associated the poem with urban (rather than rural) concerns.

Although it is difficult to gauge how representative these members' letters were, they show how members effectively appropriated Blake's eighteenth-century poem for the early twentieth century. Examination of members' objections to 'dark Satanic mills' also reveals a parochial view of rurality shared by members who seem to have regarded the working class and urban concerns as 'Other'. In addition, it highlights the importance of members' sense of rural identity. Marjory R. Ruggles-Brise wrote on behalf of the Southern and Eastern members that the hymn lacked any relevance to

---

87 The leaflet titled 'Jerusalem'.
88 'Letters to the Editor', *Home and Country* vol. 9 no. 5 (June 1937): p. 323.
89 'Letters to the Editor', *Home and Country* vol. 9 no. 8 (August 1937): p. 437, vol. 9 no. 10 (October 1937): p. 539, and vol. 19 no. 8 (August 1937): p. 437 respectively.

members' lives: 'We have not got "dark Satanic mills" and have never seen them.'[90] A. Shillabeer from Cornwall wrote that it did not reflect the nature of the Institute meeting: 'We go from a weary round of toil to join in about "dark Satanic mills" and the warlike arrow, spear and fiery chariot, which does not tend to refreshment.'[91] And a member of Wotton-under-Edge Women's Institute, M.S. Walker, criticized the Institutes' singing of Blake's poem as hypocritical. She wrote:

> In this little Cotswold town, where a considerable part of the population depends, regularly and happily, on employment in two prosperous local textile factories, belonging to a resident and popular land owner, it is rank insincerity to wail about 'dark Satanic mills,' nor, I hope, do we women want bows and arrows, spears and swords, however figuratively, to gain our ends.[92]

Although Walker's comment suggests that she thought there to be 'ends' for women to gain, it seems that she associated the Women's Institute with Constitutional changes, rather than the militant activism that has (until recently) dominated writings about feminist history (discussed further in Chapter 2). The official statement by the Chairman of the Music and Dancing Sub-Committee, Lady Listowel, which was published in the November edition, urging members to persevere with the singing of *Jerusalem* (although it was not obligatory), appears to have stifled discussion.[93]

Alternatives to *Jerusalem* were suggested, including an adaptation of the tune *Onward Christian Soldiers*, *Land of Hope and Glory* (words by Arthur C. Benson), *I vow to thee, my country* (words by Sir Cecil Spring-Rice set to the hymn tune by Gustav Holst), 'The Women's Institute's [Canadian] Ode' (set to *Auld Lang Syne*) and *The Song of the Musicmakers* (words by Rodney Bennett set to music by Martin Shaw), although none appears to have been seriously considered at the level of the National Executive.[94] Apart from *Onward Christian Soldiers*, which would have contravened the non-sectarian ruling of the Constitution, the reasons for rejecting the other suggestions are open to speculation.

Examination of the National Federation's music policy and its implementation reveals that the structures and mechanisms of the organization provided a highly efficient framework for action where music was concerned. Music policy was planned and regulated by the National Federation's Music Sub-Committee, promoted through official publications, conferences, and courses (both internally and externally organized) and taken to even the smallest Institutes (through VCOs, visits from the Music Adviser and County Federation Music Committees). In addition, the National Federation promoted and supported music policy throughout the organization – from small-scale events (such as local music festivals) to the major undertakings of the national music events (in 1950 and 1969).

---

90 'Letters to the Editor', *Home and Country* vol. 9 no. 5 (June 1937): p. 383.

91 'Letters to the Editor', *Home and Country* vol. 9 no. 5 (June 1937): p. 383. Original italics.

92 'Letters to the Editor', *Home and Country* vol. 19 no. 10 (October 1937): p. 539.

93 'Letters to the Editor', *Home and Country* vol. 19 no. 11 (November 1937): p. 599.

94 'Letters to the Editor', *Home and Country* vol. 9 no. 7 (July 1937): p. 383, vol. 9 no. 10 (September 1937): p. 485, and vol. 9 no. 10 (October 1937): p. 540 respectively.

Although for many, music has been viewed as a pastime within the Institutes, examination of *Jerusalem* reveals that music has been at the heart of the organization's policy and identity. It also provides a gateway to examine other issues, for example adherence to Constitutional ruling, the organization's relationship with suffrage, and the importance of rurality, which provide a valuable insight into the nature and identity of the Women's Institute. Thus, the idea that like the structure of the organization, music policy has not changed, is deceptive. If we are to understand the importance of the Women's Institute's music activities, we must not only explore its nature and role within the organization, but also what it meant for members who took part.

Chapter 2

Education, Empowerment and *The Acceptable Face of Feminism*

The Women's Institute is likely to have trained more women conductors than any other single organization in twentieth-century Britain. Conducting was first introduced into the Institutes in the 1930s as a means to end the shortage of village conductors, following which it became a regular part of the organization's musical activities. It continued to be promoted at the National Federation's residential establishment, Denman College, which became the National Federation's centre for training conductors until the late 1960s.

It is interesting that conducting continued to be promoted even after the need for more village conductors had been met; it thus took on a purpose beyond its initially pragmatic one. Whilst for some members, conducting was a means of musical training, for others it is likely to have provided the opportunity to explore empowering qualities of leadership and assertion. Since conducting was traditionally regarded as an 'unfeminine' activity, should the National Federation's training of women conductors be seen as means of empowering women? If this is the case, where does the Women's Institute and conducting fit within discussions of 'feminism'?

Educational Policy

Whereas during the First World War the Institutes had been mainly concerned with practical things such as the production of food, after 1919 there was a shift in emphasis towards promoting rural development and the education of members. The 1919 Constitution stated:

> The main purpose of the Women's Institute movement is to improve and develop conditions of rural life. It seeks to give all countrywomen the opportunity of working together through the Women's Institute organisation, and of putting into practice those ideals for which it stands.[1]

The National Federation's educational policy aimed to cater for a wide variety of rural women's needs. These included providing information (by means of lectures, demonstrations, etc.) that was both practical and developed the mind; training women in the principles of democracy (through the structure and procedures of the organization) and in citizenship (for example, by lectures on both local and national issues) in order to participate in rural life; and enabling local women to interact (and

---

1 Cited from Anne Stamper, *Rooms Off the Corridor*, p. 39.

thus promote community spirit) in order to aid the rejuvenation of Britain's rural villages, many of which had been blighted by the effects of war.[2]

A significant element in the National Federation's educational policy was to improve the lives of members on a day-to-day basis, in their roles as housewives, mothers and farmers. Examination of some of the articles in *Home and Country* reveals an array of featured subjects: 'Helpful Hints for the Busy Housewife' (on cleaning, clearing the ashes from the grate, and preparing breakfast) in 1922, 'A Short Article on Washing up' in 1931, 'Ration-al Cookery' in 1940, 'Managing an Earth Closet' in 1944 and 'The Feeding and Management of Your Pig' in 1950.[3]

In addition to practical advice which helped women to do their jobs more efficiently and effectively, the National Federation also promoted cultural subjects such as music, drama, and handicrafts (to name only a few), which not only educated members about their national heritage, but also served as a means towards personal and community development.[4] Conducting was originally introduced by the National Federation as a means to assist in the development of music within village communities (for example, choral societies), but the fact that courses on conducting continued within the organization for more that 30 years suggests that for some members at least, they catered for members' personal development.

The Training of Conductors in the Women's Institute

Examination of the National Federation's promotion of conducting reveals that it became a regular feature of Institute activities in the 1930s. The topic of conducting in the Institutes appears to have been first raised at W.H. Leslie's summer school of music, held at his home in Llansantffraid, Shropshire, in September 1922. His reputation, however, appears to have been based on his ability to raise standards of singing amongst amateurs, rather than conducting *per se*. The minutes for a meeting of the Executive Committee on 14 November 1922 reported:

> Miss Gildea had reported having been at the Hertfordshire Council Meeting, when Mr Leslis [*sic*] had made 400 presumably unmusical people sing melodies with descants – much to their enjoyment ... It was AGREED to recommend that Mr Leslie be invited to

---

   2   For further information on this topic see Pamela Horn, *Rural Life in England in the First World War*, New York: St Martins Press, 1984.

   3   Penny Kitchen, *For Home and Country: War Peace and Rural Life As Seen Through the Pages of the WI Magazine, 1919–1959*, London: NFWI, 1996, p. 12, 22, 83, 36, and 90 respectively.

   4   With regard to music, the National Federation can be seen to have promoted a distinctly English heritage of music in its choice of repertoire (folk songs and part songs). Stamper notes (in *Rooms Off the Corridor*, p. 50) that, during her time as Vice-Chairman, Grace Hadow was heavily involved in the early promotion of such topics in the Institutes; she gave lectures on plays, poetry, and village histories throughout her local Federation of Oxfordshire. However, it is difficult to gauge how influential she might have been in the early formation of the National Federation's policies on cultural topics.

attend the next Conference for VCOs [Voluntary County Organisers] on November 23rd in order to teach the VCOs to sing.[5]

Nevertheless, it appears that Leslie was to some extent also involved in the training of conductors, as the minutes for a meeting on 8 April 1924 refer to him leading a conductors' class at the Forum Club in London.[6]

The first scheme for the training of conductors in the Women's Institute was launched in response to a crisis that threatened to hamper music-making activities within the organization. An entry in *Home and Country* in 1925 reported that Women's Institute choirs were having difficulty in finding competent conductors, and that as a result their musical progress was being held back.[7] It appears that the shortage was not confined to the National Federation: in 1930, the CUKT commissioned a survey of conductors in the villages by the Hickers Committee in order to decide upon the future direction of their music policy, following which courses on conducting (both residential and non-residential) were included in the programmes of Local Education Authorities (LEAs) and County Music Organizers.[8]

As a result of the grant issued by the CUKT, the National Federation started a joint scheme for the training of conductors and producers of drama in 1927. The CUKT hoped that the grant would be used to develop music-making in the Women's Institute into mixed (rather than single-sex), amateur, community-based groups. However, it is difficult to assess whether this was ever achieved. The project involved Institutes applying to attend master-class type demonstrations (rather than workshops), which were then followed by regular weekly or fortnightly classes that were aimed at helping 'backward' counties (i.e. those lacking in music or drama activities) and instigating activities in areas that had been overlooked by LEAs. The minutes reported that only a small number of counties were making use of this opportunity, and it is therefore unlikely to have been regarded as a successful project.

The National Federation's other 'national' scheme for training conductors was launched at the Music Conference on 16 March 1967 in an attempt to create uniformity during the preparations for the second National Music Festival (held in 1969). It involved members attending two-hour sessions over a ten-week period, with classes led by professional tutors on sight reading, aural training, baton technique, singing, repertoire, voice production, choir training, accompaniment and music appreciation. During the years that separate these two schemes, the National Federation promoted conducting by organizing advisory visits to Institute choirs, and encouraged contact

---

5 Original capitals. Executive Minutes vol. 6 (14 November 1922), p. 18.

6 Executive Minutes vol. 7 (8 April 1924), p. 85. It is likely that this class refers to one held at another organization called the 'Women's Institute' (formed in 1897) which had its meetings at the Forum Club. There appears to have been no links with the National Federation.

7 'Notes from the Music Sub-Committee', *Home and Country*, vol. 7 no. 7 (July 1925): p. 254.

8 This survey is referred to in H.E. Bracey, *English Rural Life* (p. 176), although I have been unable to locate a copy of the report in the V&A archives or the British Library.

with LEAs and County Federation Music Committees by advertising events (such as summer schools) in *Home and Country*.

The National Federation was also involved in the Schools for Conductors that were held annually (in London) in collaboration with the BFMCF and the National Council of Social Services. Little is known about these early Schools apart from the fact that attendance was not restricted to women.[9] The minutes refer to Mr Bower, conductor of the Sandhurst WI choir, being granted a bursary by the National Federation in 1936, and a review of the School held in 1937 reported a higher rate of male attendance than usual.[10] If the programme for 1931 is representative of the School for Conductors, then focus was clearly (and perhaps unsurprisingly) on choral music for amateur music-making:[11]

> Wednesday, 11th November *Chairman*: Adrian Boult
> 5.30–7pm *Hints on Taking Rehearsals* by Mr Armstrong Gibbs
> Thursday, 12th November
> > 10am–1pm – Three groups (divided into beginners, intermediate, and more advanced) with one hour sessions on the following:
>
> *The Technique of the Conducting Stick* (with practical work) with Ernest Read
> *Choir Training* (including voice production) with Geoffrey Shaw
> *Sight Reading and Time Values* with Major J.T. Bavin
> 2–4pm – *Conducting* (with demonstration choir) with Ernest Read
> Friday, 13th November
> > 10am–1pm (Three groups – as Thursday morning)
>
> *Learning New Songs* (demonstration with a choir) with Ursula Nettleship
> *Choir Training* with Geoffrey Shaw
> *Sight reading* with Mrs Lampson and *Accompaniments* with Adrian Boult
> 2–4pm *The Principals* [sic] *and Techniques of Conducting* with Adrian Boult
> 9pm *Party at Mrs Wythes' house*
> Short talk on Elizabethan music and a demonstration of madrigal singing.

Although the list of recommended music for preliminary study reveals that the School aimed to cater for beginners, as well as intermediate and advanced conductors, the review of the first School for Conductors, published in *Home and Country* in January 1932, indicates that members of the Women's Institute benefited from the practical sessions on basic technique: 'From Mr Read we began to learn the mysteries of controlling a conducting-stick and by the afternoon, by dint of practice against our neighbour's arms and ribs, were imagining ourselves conducting in fine style.'[12]

---

9 *Music and Drama in the Villages – Report for 1928–31 of the Joint Committee Administering a Fund provided by the CUKT* (1931) merely states that the School held in 1931 was oversubscribed, p. 7.

10 Executive Minutes vol. 13, OFS-C (11 September 1935), p. 194, MDcS-C (4 November 1936), n.p. and MDcS-C (1 December 1937), n.p.

11 Original italics, 'A School for Conductors, 11–13 November 1931' programme. The significance of Elizabethan music being included in the programme will be discussed in Chapter 3.

12 'Conductor's School held in London, November 31st', *Home and Country* (January 1932): p. 32. Parry's *Jerusalem*, Vaughan Williams' arrangement of *My Boy Billie*, Bach's

Indeed, the choice of such figures such as Boult (who at this time was conductor of the newly formed BBC Symphony Orchestra), and Read (who was Professor in Conducting at the Royal Academy of Music until 1930), indicates the seriousness with which the Women's Institute undertook its training.[13]

That said, the recommendations following the Schools in 1937 and 1938 stated that Institute members needed both easier music and longer and less crowded practical sessions. They suggest that the standard of conducting in the organization was generally low.[14] Although these Schools (which were later renamed the Talbot Lampson School for Conductors and Accompanists) continued to be promoted in *Home and Country*, the residential courses on conducting held at Denman College replaced the sessions on conducting that were included at the one-day music conferences.

Denman College provided a focal point for the organization's educational activities, providing residential courses that enabled women to profit from temporary separation from the demands of daily life with their families. Lady Brunner, who later became Denman College's first Chairman and was central in both its instigation and development, highlighted the nature it was to have in her Chairman's speech at the AGM in 1945:

> ... I want you to imagine a place that will be homely and welcoming, where in the pleasantest possible surroundings, away from responsibilities and distractions of our usual lives, we can learn about useful practical crafts, in addition where we can become better informed about the things going on in the world today, where we can learn about our heritage, and consider and discuss our future.[15]

Denman College was a place to meet and talk with others, to learn more about the organization, and a place to continue the work begun in the Institutes. In addition to offering members a taste of independence and education, it also provided opportunities for confidence building, and a promise of what nowadays would be called 'skills enhancement'.

My Heart Ever Faithful, and Howells' *A Croon* were listed for the beginners group, Brahms' *Slumbering Deep The Ocean Lies* and Morley's *I Go Before My Darling* for the intermediate section, and Weelkes' *Strike It Up Tabor* and Holst's *The Swallow Leaves Her Nest* for the advanced group.

13 It is not stated in the NFWI archival material how much these professionals were paid. Ronald Crichton, 'Adrian Boult', *The New Grove Dictionary of Music*, vol. 1, ed. Stanley Sadie, 2nd ed. London: Macmillan Press, 2001, p. 108, and Lynda MacGregor, 'Ernest Read', *The New Grove Dictionary of Music*, vol. 20, ed. Stanley Sadie. 2nd ed. London: Macmillan Press, 2001, p. 894.

14 MDcS-C (1 December 1937), n.p. and (7 December 1938), n.p.

15 Lady Brunner's speech proposing resolution 5 at the Annual General Meeting on 5 June 1945, from Stamper, *Rooms Off the Corridor*, p. 246.

Denman College

In 1948, the National Federation opened its own short-term adult residential college, Denman College in Oxfordshire.[16] The late 1940s was a time of increased enthusiasm for adult education colleges.[17] The publication of the White Paper on 'Educational Reconstruction' in 1945 (based on a government enquiry of 1943 into British institutions of adult education) had highlighted the importance of residential colleges as part of Britain's post-war reconstruction, and specifically recommended the promotion of short-term courses and residential places for women. However, the Educational Act of 1944 (later known as the Butler Act) overlooked adult education, focusing exclusively on issues concerning children's schooling. The education of young adults (up to the age of 18) after leaving school was mentioned only briefly as being the responsibility of LEAs.

The building chosen by the National Federation was a de-requisitioned Georgian house (formerly in Marcham Park) that had been used during the Second World War by the Air Ministry. When it first opened there were 31 beds available, seven double rooms, and four treble rooms (although this has since greatly expanded). In addition, there was a common room, a lecture room, a small dining room and a library named after Grace Hadow. The everyday running of the College was the responsibility of the warden who was appointed by the Executive Committee, the first of whom was Betty Christmas. In addition, a College Chairman acted as the 'hostess' during the period of the course (which was either a weekend or week). In Denman College's early days, this was a member of the National Executive but nowadays is a Federation Chairman.[18]

The courses offered at Denman College comprised two types. 'A' courses were organized by Denman College and open to all members. Among music courses, these included 'Books and Music' (held on 12–16 September 1949), 'Music for the Institute Meeting' (held on 27–31 October 1952), and 'Choral Singers and Accompanists' (held on 26–30 October 1953). 'B' courses were organized by the National Federation and offered specialist training for which representatives from

---

16 Information about Denman College tends nowadays to be limited to the National Federation's official publications, kept at the College's archives. Thomas Kelly, *A History of Adult Education from the Middle Ages to the Twentieth Century* (Liverpool: Liverpool University Press, 1970), for example, which is widely acknowledged and revered amongst historians of education as being a key text, has only one brief references to Denman College (as an example of a residential college that was run by a trust) on pp. 301–304, and p. 394. Historians' attention appears to have been restricted to the top level of a hierarchy of establishments based on academic educational criteria and, as a result, Denman College has been excluded because of its promotion of domestic-based and non-vocational courses.

17 Around 30 short-term adult residential colleges were founded between 1945 and 1951, the first of which was Holly Royde (founded by Manchester University in 1944 to house members of the British and allied forces on short courses). The most recent research on adult residential colleges in Britain appears to be Walter Drews, 'The British Short-Term Residential College for Adult Education, 1941–1995' (unpublished) PhD thesis, University of Ulster, 1995.

18 For further information see Anne Stamper, *Rooms Off the Corridor*, pp. 87–99.

the counties applied, with the idea that the practical skills that individuals had learned would be transmitted on return to their Institutes and the wider community. Conducting, which, along with courses that can also be classed as 'unfeminine' (such as Do-It-Yourself and stage management) because they promote individual self-reliance and decision-making, can be seen to have become more prevalent from the mid-1960s at a time when the second 'wave' of feminism was starting to gain momentum (see Appendix 5).[19]

Conducting Courses at Denman College

The first residential music school was held at Denman College on 23–26 September 1948 and included classes on conducting.[20] The minutes for a meeting of the Music and Dancing Sub-Committee on 7 June 1948 reveal that the works to be studied were all elementary, short settings of choral pieces: *The Lord's My Shepherd* (for four-part female voices), *Sans Day Carol* by Cockshott, Vaughan Williams' *Dinge for Fidele* and *Flowers of Edinburgh* and Cecil Sharp's *O Waly, Waly* and *Crystal Spring*. The inclusion of the hymn *The Lord's My Shepherd*, together with the religious references in the Vaughan Williams commission (which was completed around this time), suggests a relaxing of the Constitutional ruling during the end of the 1940s.

Although there are no archival documents on the second residential music school (held on 5–9 September 1949), the minutes referred to a report by Nancy Tennant, who was Chairman of the course. They state: 'The standard of conducting at the school on the whole had been low, but the standard of singing had been very high.'[21] It appears that members were involved (to some extent at least) in conducting activities, but also that there was a need for their training within the organization.

The first course devoted to conducting at Denman College took place on 22–26 January 1951. There appears to have been a problem with the quality rather than the quantity of students for this course, as the minutes for a meeting of the Music and Dancing Sub-Committee on 13 July 1951 reported: 'It was noted that many of the students had turned out to be not nearly as advanced as they sounded on paper.'[22] Steps were taken to stream students by assessing them at a conducting session on their first evening at Denman College. This first took place in 1952, although it is difficult to gauge whether it became a regular event.[23]

Due to incomplete archival material, it is unclear what music was taught at the conducting courses (or for that matter other music courses) held at Denman College. The only reference is to Britten's *Four Songs for the Audience* from *Let's Make An*

---

19 Ibid., p. 104. Stamper notes that in 1950 'AB' courses were introduced which were of a more academic nature but was only open to members nominated by their Federation. Another publication about the history of Denman College is Barbara Kaye, *Live and Learn*, London: NFWI, 1970. Both publications were written by members of the Women's Institute and are mainly concerned with the construction of its buildings and changes in personnel.
20 Executive Minutes vol. 21, MDS-C (9 June 1947), p. 710.
21 MDcS-C (12 September 1949), n.p.
22 MDcS-C (15 October 1954), n.p.
23 MDcS-C (4 April 1952), n.p.

Opera at a conducting course in 1951.[24] The choice of repertoire is significant, as it would have enabled massed community singing (and was therefore in keeping with the organization's ideological concern for communality) even though attention may have focused on one individual conducting.

It is also unclear who taught the conducting courses. With regard to the teaching of conducting at Denman College, the names Dorothy Erhart and Mrs Kitching as piano accompanist feature the most prominently in the minute books until the 1960s. There is more information about Erhart than about Kitching because of her involvement on the National Federation's Music Advisory Panel. A document in the National Federation's archives entitled 'Music Panel: speakers' WI engagements during the last three years' reveals that Erhart had taken a rehearsal at Hatfield of massed WI choirs for the Mid and West Hertfordshire Festival in 1932, and had also been involved in Schools for Conductors in Ware and Northampton in 1932 and 1933. In addition, she is referred to in a history of the RMSA as being a County Organizer, and a programme of a concert in 1937 of the Society of Women Musicians (SWM) reveals that she also conducted the SWM String Orchestra.[25]

Conducting Outside the Women's Institutes

The topic of women and conducting is difficult to assess, as few publications on conducting refer to women's involvement (discussed later). However, the paucity of references should not lead us to conclude that this is an area from which women have been absent. Examination of *The Musical Directory* reveals that women's involvement in conducting can be traced to the end of the nineteenth century.[26] A Miss Jessie Duks, for example, is listed as conducting the Lyric Society's performances of Sullivan's operas *The Gondoliers* in 1898 and *The Mikado* in 1899 at the National Hall in Hornsey, and a Mrs M. Layton conducted Westbourne Park Choir's performance of Handel's *Messiah* on 14 December 1898.[27] Other references to women's involvement in conducting during the early decades of the twentieth century include a Mrs Whatford conducting Eaglescliffe Vocal Society in 1910[28] and, in 1925, a Mrs Bourne conducting Barrow Madrigal Society and a Miss Olwen

---

24 MDcS-C (12 January 1951), n.p.

25 Dorothy Erhart, is listed as conducting the String Orchestra at a SWM concert on Saturday 10 July 1937 in programme kept in Box 2 (177) in the SWM archives. See also Mary Ibberson, *For Joy That We Are Here: Rural Music Schools*, pp. 42, 64, and 67.

26 I examined the sections entitled 'Choral and Musical Societies' Concerts in London and the Suburbs' and 'Provincial Events' in *The Musical Directory, Annual and Almanack* (London: Rudall, Carte and Co) for the following years: 1900, 1905, 1910, 1915, 1920, 1925 and 1930.

27 'Mrs M. Layton' may be the same Mary Layton who wrote the article referred to in footnote 29. 'Choral and Musical Societies' Concerts in London and the Suburbs', *The Musical Directory, Annual and Almanack* (London: Rudall, Carte and Co., 1900), pp. 70–71.

28 'Provincial Music Events', *The Musical Directory, Annual and Almanack* (London: Rudall, Carte and Co., 1910), p. 76.

Rowlands conducting the Tawelan Choir Society.[29] By 1918 it appears that women were frequently involved in conducting at youth club level. Mary Layton wrote in *The Music Student* in 1918: 'Of course, the great majority of Girls' Clubs, who sing in our modern Festivals, are conducted by women, and one is sorry only to be able briefly to notice this fact, and also the excellence of the women-trained Children's Choirs in the Elementary Schools.'[30]

However, it was not until the mid-1930s that women became officially trained as conductors within the music conservatoire system.[31] The registers at the Royal College of Music refer to Miss Jenny (Christmas 1934 to Midsummer 1935) and Miss Kisch (Midsummer 1936 to Christmas term 1937),[32] attending Constant Lambert's 'senior' class (for second years), Miss Fox-Male (from Easter to Midsummer 1936) and Miss Hambourg (from Easter to Christmas 1936) attending Reginald Jacques's 'junior' class, and Miss Kewish and Miss Donska attending Gordon Jacob's 'senior' classes (Christmas 1939 to Easter 1940). In addition, material in the Royal Academy of Music archives reveals that women won prizes for conducting competitions; winners in the 'mixed' competition include Monica Gillies-Myatt in 1933, Beryl Price in 1936 and Rita Sharpe in 1945 and 1947.[33] This indicates that, to some extent at least, there was a degree of professional acceptance for women in this sphere of musical activity. However, it is difficult to assess what happened to such women once they had left the conservatoires.

Few women though have entered the sphere of professional conducting. An exception appears to be the flamboyant composer Ethel Smyth, who is known to have conducted many musical works in public, in particular performances of her stage works *Fête Galante* (in 1923 and 1925) and *Entente Cordiale* (in 1925).[34] However, there are only a few references to Smyth's conducting in critics' reviews: Smyth's overture to the comedy, *The Boatswain's Mate*, performed at the Queen's Hall was reviewed in *The Times* (on 17 August 1921) and *Fête Galante* was also reviewed in *The Times* (on 5 June 1923 and 25 July 1925), but they provide no more detail other than the fact that Smyth conducted the performance. The most detailed review appears to be of a concert of the Women's Symphony Orchestra held at the Queen's Hall

---

29 'Choral and Orchestral Societies', *The Musical Directory, Annual and Almanack* (London: Rudall, Carte and Co., 1925), p. 59 and 64 respectively.

30 In addition to training children's and female choirs, Layton refers to female organists, who, she states, were often successful in their training of men and boys in church choirs, because of their ability to 'maintain discipline'. Mary Layton, 'Women as Organists and Choir Trainers', *The Music Student* vol. 10 no. 9 (May 1918): p. 336.

31 The only teaching registers available for examination are those of Constant Lambert, Reginald Jacques, Gordon Jacob and Austin Reid, who taught conducting at the Royal College of Music. The others were destroyed by fire in the Second World War.

32 Miss Kisch then studied with Gordon Jacob, intermittently, from the Christmas term 1938 until the Midsummer term of 1941.

33 This information can be found in the prize lists from 1924 to 1949 kept in the archives of the Royal Academy of Music.

34 Guy Warrack, *The Royal College of Music: The first 85 years, 1883–1968 and beyond*, vol. 1. London: Royal College of Music, 1977, p. 158.

in 1924, in a programme conducted by Smyth, Gwynne Kimpton, and an unknown figure referred to as Madame Suggis. *The Times* reported on 27 June 1924:

> One wishes that one could praise unreservedly this admirable organisation [the Women's Symphony Orchestra], but one could not be blind in all to the general lack of vitality. The reason is not far to seek and does not lie with the players, who, in spite of their conductor, imparted some life to the first movement of Beethoven's C minor Piano Concerto ... There is no reason whatever that women should not make good conductors, but Miss Gwynne Kimpton and Mme Suggis, and to some extent, Dame Ethel Smyth, all hindered rather than helped the orchestra by beating in unintelligible jerks, which meant phrasing beat by beat, not even bar by bar, let alone phrase by phrase. The result to the listener was a lack of confidence and of rhythm in the playing.[35]

The references to the orchestra being 'hindered' (rather than led) and derogatory references to the beating as 'unintelligible jerks' reveal the critic's disapproval of these conductors' performances. Furthermore, his concept of musical architecture (based on beats, bars, and phrasing) suggests that he considered conducting even at a basic level to be beyond the ability of female conductors. However, the comment 'There is no reason whatever that women should not make good conductors' raises questions about what sorts of music and ensemble he thought women should conduct.

The 'Gendered' Spheres of Conducting[36]

Examination of the literature on conducting reveals the existence of different spheres of conducting based on gender: whereas histories of the 'art of conducting' (of which there are many) are dominated by key male personalities (such as Berlioz, Wagner, Mahler, Hans von Bülow, Richard Strauss, Toscanini, Nikisch and Furtwängler among others) and specifically concerned with orchestral conducting,[37] literature on the topic of women conductors and choral conducting appears to be severely limited. In fact, Henry Coleman's *Choral Conducting for Women's Institutes* appears to be among only a few publications on the topic (and also indicates the extent of the organization's contribution to this activity).[38]

The spheres of conducting are not mutually exclusive: the male sphere encompasses both orchestral and choral conducting, unlike the female sphere, which is limited to

---

35 [Unsigned]. Review of 'The Women's Symphony Orchestra – A Charity Performance', *The Times* (27 June 1924), p. 12.

36 Broadly speaking, the term 'gendered spheres' draws on the Victorian ideology of a patriarchal society which separated men and women's roles, whereby men were figured as competitors in the economic world while women were positioned as guardians of the domestic realm.

37 For example Peter Pirie, *Furtwängler and the Art of Conducting*, London: Duckworth, 1980, and Rudolph Dolmetsch, *The Art of Orchestral Conducting*, London: Bosworth and Co., 1942.

38 Henry Coleman, *Choral Conducting for Women's Institutes*, London: Oxford University Press, 1932.

choirs and amateur orchestras. The differences between the two is reflected in the use of gendered language: whereas the 'male' orchestral sphere is depicted as comprising skilled interpreters of music, and is associated with 'masculine' qualities such as leadership (exhibited in the use of the baton) and decision-making (in the preparation of the score), the 'female' realm is limited to choral music and the teaching of amateur musicians, and associated with 'feminine' qualities such as expressiveness.[39]

Examination of the National Federation's policy on conducting reveals that it adhered to the 'female' realm of choral music and amateur music-making.[40] Even when courses for string orchestras and orchestral music were introduced at Denman College, the National Federation did not expand its activities to the 'male' sphere of orchestral conducting. Within this context, the decision to invite male conductors (Adrian Boult, Marcus Dods and Antony Hopkins) to conduct at the public national music events (which included orchestral music) does not appear surprising.

It seems that the National Federation was not the only organization that recognized and adhered (at least in public) to the 'gendered' spheres of conducting. The Society of Women Musicians (an organization founded in 1911 by Gertrude Eaton and Marion Scott) also invited men to conduct orchestral items at its public concerts. The first public concert of the SWM, for example, held on 25 January 1912, was based on works by women composers: Smyth, Lucie Johnstone, Katharine Eggar, Maude Valérie White, Ethel Barns, Marion Scott, Mabel Saumarez Smith and Liza Lehmann. But despite there being members such as Emily Daymond (who regularly conducted the SWM choir from 1912 until the early 1920s), the only work in the programme that required a conductor was Lehmann's vocal intermezzo, and that was conducted by Herbert Bedford (an Associate member of the SWM).[41] Although Bedford was Lehmann's husband, the fact remains that the SWM (like the National Federation) did not seek to publicly challenge the gendered spheres of conducting.

It was not until 1960 that an orchestral concert was held at the SWM and conducted by a woman (see Appendix 8). On 8 June, Dr Ruth Gipps conducted a programme of works by Schubert, Brahms, Beethoven, Bax and Rutland Boughton. Indeed, Gipps was one of the first women to enter the male-dominated world of orchestral conducting (although she was first and foremost a composer): she was one of the first female guest conductors of the all-male London Symphony Orchestra and the first woman to conduct at the Royal Festival Hall (in 1957).[42]

---

39 Few publications on conducting deal with both orchestral and choral conducting. Michael Bowles *The Art of Conducting* (New York: Doubleday and Co., 1959), for example, only examines orchestral conducting and issues relating to it; namely the orchestra, interpretation, gesture, instruments, programmes and rehearsal.

40 The only occasion when a female conductor was sanctioned to appear at public National Institute events was to conduct *Jerusalem* at Annual General Meetings.

41 It was the first London performance of Lehmann's Vocal Intermezzo. Programme of the 'First Public Concert of Members' Works' on 25 January 1912 from Box 2 (177) of the SWM archives.

42 [Unsigned]. Obituary, *The Daily Telegraph* (30 March 1999), p. 15.

Conducting – A Feminist Issue?

Although Gipps' achievements in the professional (male) sphere could be interpreted as coinciding with the emergence of the second wave of feminism, conducting has not been widely recognized as a feminist issue. Instead, writings on feminism and music have tended to focus on women's marginal status in the sphere of composition. Marcia Citron, for example, offers a feminist interpretation of the formation of the Western musical canon (as a socially constructed concept). Briefly summarized, she argues that women have been excluded from artistic creativity because of male appropriated beliefs that separate the mind and the body. Citing Elaine Showalter, she writes, 'Creation, which involves the mind is reserved for male activity; procreation, which involves giving birth, is applied to women. Labor [sic] refers to men's production, to women's reproduction'.[43] If Citron's argument is applied to conducting, the role of the conductor can be seen as something of a paradox: on the one hand a 'creative' (and thus masculine) figure who has authority over other performers by interpreting the score, and on the other, a 'feminized' vessel whose detachedness from the (male) composer provides a diluted form of creativity. The 'female' sphere, which facilitates choral learning, remains at the bottom of the 'creative' scale.

In her deconstruction of sexual connections and creativity, Citron refers to feminists' apt use of metaphors. She writes:

> Thus the pen in literature and the paintbrush in art have been termed a metaphorical penis. In music, the pen used to notate music is comparable. Probably more vivid are the phallic performative symbols of the conductor's baton and certain instruments, notably the woodwinds. Predictably, women were prohibited from playing instruments held directly in the mouth. The phallic symbolism of the baton captures the realities of historical male presence at the head of orchestras. All of these symbols may be another indication of male appropriation.[44]

Within this context, the use of the baton in the Women's Institute rather than the hands (which was promoted at the Schools for Conductors and the courses at Denman College) could be interpreted as embodying feminist sentiments, not only in its adoption of phallic symbolism, but also by promoting 'male' leadership (rather than the 'feminine' sphere of enabling group singing). If this is the case, one might view the Women's Institute's promotion of conducting as a mode of feminist empowerment for its members.

Feminism and the Women's Institute

The Women's Institute has only recently been examined from a feminist perspective. Beaumont's research on the concept of citizenship and feminism within Britain's largest women's organizations in the interwar period highlights the Women's Institute

---

[43] Elaine Showalter, 'Creativity and the Childbirth Metaphor: Gender Difference in Literary Discourse', *Speaking of Gender*, New York, 1989, pp. 75–6 cited in Marcia J. Citron, *Gender and the Musical Canon*, Cambridge: Cambridge University Press, 1993, p. 45.

[44] Ibid., p. 51.

as having feminist sentiments in its support of campaigns that enhanced the social and economic position of women. She writes:

> Seeking to represent rural women who embraced domesticity, the Women's Institute leadership constructed a boundary between equal citizenship and feminism. This allowed members to support the extension of social and economic rights to women without risking accusations that they wished to challenge traditional gender roles.[45]

Laverick offers a differing perspective of the organization, but one which also adheres to it being 'feminist' in nature. Her thesis examines living members' perceptions of the Women's Institute based on an adaptation of social science interview technique, ethnography, and poststructuralist theory.[46] In her final chapter (which is concerned with the analysis of her interviews) Laverick discusses her concept of 'the subversive space' – an uncontested female space which, through consciousness-raising, has sparked awareness about (rather than explicitly challenging) the constraints of patriarchy. She writes:

> Moreover, visual signs of femininity, like the ubiquitous WI hat and frock may indicate particular gender roles but, it later became clear that they may also signify a 'disguise', a feminine 'uniform' which is part of the opening of a covert space where plurality of political influences may be discussed.[47]

In *The Acceptable Face of Feminism*, Andrews also refers to the Women's Institute as a feminist organization that has provided an environment where women have been able to contest social constructions of gender.[48] However, in contrast to Beaumont (who argues that through the notion of citizenship during the 1930s, the Women's Institute was able to exert 'feminist' gains for women) and Laverick (whose definition of feminist activity is fundamentally based on her own experiences with the Women's Liberation Movement), Andrews instead interprets the term 'feminism' as a multi-faceted and dynamic concept. Her argument is based on an examination of the ideologies espoused in the 'official' histories of the Women's Institute: three snapshots of the Women's Institute during the inter-war years, Second World War and post-war years; the Women's Institute's campaign for social welfare legislation on housing and rural water supplies; and the establishment of Denman College in 1948.[49]

---

45 Caitriona Beaumont, 'Citizenship and Feminism in England', p. 418.

46 Alyson Laverick 'The Women's Institute: Just Jam and Jerusalem?'. The meanings that current members assign to the organization are examined from 14 taped interviews, although there appears to have been a lack of uniformity in the questions asked at the interviews, which raises questions about her research methods. In addition, she makes the erroneous assumption that a common understanding of the term 'feminism' and what constitutes feminist activity exists.

47 Ibid., p. 37.

48 Maggie Andrews, *The Acceptable Face of Feminism*. The absence of quotations or citations from Laverick in her book suggests that Andrews was unaware of Laverick's dissertation.

49 Andrews appears to be clearer about what she discards in her methodology rather than what she accepts. She states in the Introduction that she wishes to reject Community Studies

Both Laverick and Andrews refer to Denman College as a key site of feminist activity that has provided a 'space' where women have been able to contest social constructions of gender. If their arguments are applied to the 'unfeminine' art of conducting, the Women's Institute's involvement with the Schools for Conductors during the 1930s and 1940s and courses held at Denman College during the 1950s and 1960s can be seen as examples of feminist activity within the 'protected' confines of the organization.

The value of all three accounts is that they look beyond the Women's Institute's veneer of domesticity and recognize that the organization has had a profound influence on the lives of its members in terms of providing 'a space' to challenge societal constructs of gender – a place of personal exploration and empowerment. Although neither Beaumont, Laverick nor Andrews gives much attention to locating their arguments within writings on feminism, it is worth considering where the Women's Institute fits in to broader scholarship on the topic, and indeed whether 'feminism' is an appropriate term to apply to the 'unfeminine' activities within the organization.

'Feminism' and Histories of Women's Organizations

Feminism is not a term that has been widely associated with the Women's Institute. The Women's Institute's exclusion from 'mainstream' discussions of feminism happens partly because, until around the late 1980s, case studies of feminist activity in Britain tended to focus on two defining periods: suffrage and the late 1960s.[50] The interim period (which falls between 1920 to 1967), when organizations such as the Women's Institute flourished, has, until recently, been overlooked by feminist scholars as a period of nominal legislative reform and heightened popularity in women's domestic roles.[51] However, I would argue that the problem lies with how feminism is defined, rather than the attitudes associated with it.

The literature and references that exist about women's organizations tend to be concerned with women's involvement in political clubs. David Doughan, for

---

because it assumes that communities are based on individuals being dependent on one another, and also an organizational history on the grounds that the structure of the organization has not changed greatly since the beginning of the organization, pp. ix–xi.

50 British feminist activity in the twentieth century has been characterized as taking place during two 'waves'; the first located at the end of the nineteenth and beginning of the twentieth century with the women's suffrage movement and the campaign for equal rights for women, and the second from the mid-1960s to the early 1970s with the re-emergence of protests against women's inequality, highlighted by the popular slogan 'the personal is political'. Although the nature of the two waves is fundamentally different (the first stemming from efforts of individuals and the second from consciousness-raising of women's groups), each justifies the importance that has been assigned to the political and often militant aspect of women's activities.

51 The introduction and first chapter of *Votes for Women* provide a useful summary of the recent developments in feminist historiography. June Purvis and Sandra Stanley Holton (eds), London: Routledge, 2000. Caitriona Beaumont's article 'Citizens not Feminists' provides a valuable insight into women's organizations in Britain during the inter-war period.

instance, has written that historians have tended to focus on organizations such as the Six Point Group and the Women's Social and Political, because they had tumultuous leaderships. By comparison, Lady Denman provided the National Federation with a stable Chairmanship from 1916 to 1946. In addition, Doughan notes that historians have focused on organizations that were directly involved in political campaigns, and have overlooked those that lacked an overtly political agenda.[52] Although the Women's Institute's non-political ruling may indeed have blocked the organization's participation in the more radical side of the women's movement, neglect of the Women's Institute purely on the grounds that it is a non-political organization risks unfairly excluding the organization from historical accounts of government measures affecting women. In fact, the Women's Institute has been intimately involved with measures of social policy such as campaigns for housing, water supplies, and women police, to name only a few.

Where the Women's Institute has gained attention is in discussions about a network of leading 'ladies' in women's political organizations. In its early years, it seems that important Officers of the National Federation were visibly active in more than one organization. The National Federation's first Treasurer, Helen Auerbach, was closely connected with Millicent Fawcett until 1917. She was also Treasurer of the National Union of Women's Suffrage Societies (NUWSS), an organization that had been founded in 1898 to co-ordinate suffrage groups and parliamentary supporters in order to help obtain parliamentary franchise for women. A year after the women's franchise section was included in the Representation of the People Act of 1918, the NUWSS became known as the National Union of Societies for Equal Citizenship (NUSEC), an organization that promoted equality of the franchise between men and women. Dame Frances Farrer was Secretary of the NUSEC and later became Secretary of the National Federation.[53] However, it is unclear how these networks worked, and whether such links in personnel were the norm. Indeed, as David Doughan notes, this is an area which to date, remains largely untouched by researchers, possibly due to difficulties in obtaining personal information.[54]

Examination of the biographies of the Women's Institute's early pioneers reveals other links with renowned feminist campaigners and organizations. Helena Deneke's 1946 biography of Grace Hadow, the National Federation's first Vice-Chairman, highlights Hadow's links with the suffrage movement by referring to her as a friend of Fawcett who had been 'engaged in work for women's suffrage'.[55] Gervas Huxley's 1961 biography of Lady Denman, the National Federation's first and to-date longest ruling Chairman, refers to her being elected to the Executive Committee of the Women's Liberal Federation in May 1908 and becoming Chairman of the Women's Liberal Metropolitan Union in 1909. Both organizations campaigned for

---

52 David Doughan and Peter Gordon, *British Women's Organizations, 1825–1960*, London: Woburn Press, p. 3.

53 Sholto Watt (ed.), *What in the Country: What Women Of The World Are Doing*, London: Chapham Hall Ltd., 1932, pp. 183 and 202.

54 David Doughan and Peter Gordon, *Women, Clubs, and Associations in Britain*, London: Routledge, 2006, pp. 3–4.

55 Helena Deneke, *Grace Hadow*, pp. 54–5.

women's suffrage. Lady Denman's role as the founding Chairman of the Family Planning Association (FPA) is also portrayed in this biography as being indicative of her 'feminist' leanings. Although her dual Chairmanship was not easy for the National Federation to swallow (the organization promoted women's 'natural' roles as mothers), it appears that a blind eye was turned to their Chairman's involvement in the FPA, possibly through the fear that if given an ultimatum, Lady Denman would leave the established National Federation to support the new and struggling FPA.[56]

Although examination of the early founders of the Women's Institute reveals an interesting network of membership in women's organizations, it seems unlikely that these women (who were largely drawn from the aristocratic elite and gentry) should be seen as representative of its members. Nevertheless, it does raise questions about whether women perceived membership of the Women's Institute as a natural progression from political clubs following the suffrage victory in 1918, and indicates that the organization has had a feminist face, albeit not always a overt or dominant one.

Definitions of 'Feminist Activity'

Case studies of 'feminist activity' have tended to focus on women's political campaigns to gain equality as evidence of furthering the feminist cause.[57] Although recent scholarship on the women's movement in Britain has explored a more diverse and complex definition of what constitutes 'feminist activity', discussions have tended to focus on the activities of urban-based women. Little is known about the activities of rural women apart from their involvement in the Women's Land Army (with which the National Federation was not officially involved) during the Second World War.[58] Although Lady Denman was Director of the Women's Land Army at the same time she was Chairman of the National Federation, close restrictions were placed on the participation of Institutes in war work in order to uphold the non-sectarian ruling of the Constitution.

Rural women's experience of politics is often assumed to be the same as that of urban women.[59] Since the Women's Institute was (and remains) an overwhelmingly

---

56 Gervas Huxley, *Lady Denman*, pp. 34, 37 and 97 respectively.

57 Examples include Martin Pugh, *Women and the Women's Movement in Britain, 1914–1959*, London: Macmillan, 1972, and Brian Harrison, *Prudent Revolutionaries: Portraits of British Feminists between the Wars*, Oxford: Clarendon Press, 1987.

58 There is scant literature on the topic of rural women. However, see Leonore Davidoff, Jean L'Esperance and Howard Newby, 'Landscape with Figures: Home and Community in English Society', which examines the late nineteenth-century idealisation of rural women as mothers and nurturers. From *The Rights and Wrongs of Women*, Edited and Introduction by Juliet Mitchell and Ann Oakley, Harmondsworth: Penguin, 1976, repr. 1979, pp. 139–176.

59 The importance of rural identity within the Women's Institute is also evident from the Constitution of 1919: 'The main purpose of the Women's Institute movement is to improve and develop conditions of rural life. It seeks to give all countrywomen the opportunity of working together through the Women's Institute organization, and of putting into practice those ideals for which it stands ...' cited from Anne Stamper *Rooms Off the Corridor*, p. 39.

rural association, campaigns to influence government legislation on issues specifically affecting rural women are undervalued. For many rural women, the reality of politics depended more on changes in social policy than the changes in the kind of government legislation for which urban feminists campaigned, such as improvements in working conditions and equal pay. In addition, historical accounts have tended to recognize women's domestic 'work' as housewifery, motherhood and family responsibilities. However, as Sarah Whatmore notes, in addition to domestic household tasks, the reality of rural women's 'work' also often included fulfilling roles as farmers' wives and farm labourers.[60] The division that separate urban women's unpaid work in the private sphere from paid work in the public sphere cannot be applied to many rural women, for whom the physical boundaries that separated work and home were often blurred or non-existent, and where a pre-destined career meant being confined to the home, and the land.

There has also traditionally been an incompatibility between feminism and domesticity. Rosemarie Tong provides a useful summary of the main strands of feminist theory. She states that broadly speaking, liberal feminists argue that women's subordination (and exclusion from the public sphere) is due to constructions of gender and legal constraints; Marxist feminists interpret women's oppression within the capitalist system of production (as originating in the introduction of private property); radical feminists argue that patriarchal dominance of society as a whole needs to be overturned in order for women to gain equality (which includes women's control of reproduction); psychoanalytic feminists examine women's oppression within Freudian theory of the Oedipal complex; existentialist feminists argue that women are oppressed because of their position as 'Other' to men; socialist feminists aim to unite the different strands of Marxist, radical and liberal feminist theory to explain women's subordination; and postmodern feminists interpret the diversity of women's experiences as evidence of resistance to patriarchal domination (by preventing a single definition of women).[61] In each case, feminist activity is assumed to originate from women's dissatisfaction with domesticity, which makes it difficult to place the Women's Institute, an organization that promoted domesticity, within any of these theoretical frameworks.[62]

Although the training of conductors was initially introduced as a means to maintain music-making within the organization (and the community), the fact that conducting continued to be promoted long after the Women's Institute had met its immediate need indicates that it took on another function beyond the pragmatic and, for many, offered a means of empowerment. Although the National Federation's policy on conducting did not seek to challenge the gendered spheres of conducting, it should

---

60 Sarah Whatmore, *Farming Women: Gender, Work and the Family Enterprise*, Basingstoke: Macmillan, 1991, p. 90.

61 Rosemarie Tong, *Feminist Thought: A Comprehensive Introduction*, London: Routledge, 1997, pp. 2–7.

62 The incompatibility of feminism and domesticity is an assumption that underlies Martin Pugh, 'Domesticity and the Decline of Feminism, 1930–50', *British Feminisms in the Twentieth Century*, Harold C. Smith (ed.), Aldershot: Elgar, 1990, pp. 144–64.

not be concluded from this evidence alone that the Women's Institute entirely rejected attitudes and behaviour patterns that might be described as traditionally feminist.

However, the Women's Institute is often overlooked as a site of 'feminist' activity. The image of rural home-based women contrasts starkly with the political activism of the suffrage movement and second wave campaigners that has characterized historians' narratives of feminist women in the twentieth century for so long. But so long as feminism is associated with a narrow group of public and political objectives that are clustered around the waves of 'feminist' activity (a stance that stigmatizes the post-suffrage years as a period of feminist inactivity and overlooks changes in social policy), feminist historians will continue to bypass the Women's Institute. Dismissal of the Women's Institute from discussions not only overlooks its associations with suffrage organizations (such as the network of personnel), but also oversimplifies its relationship to feminism.

The organization's exclusion from so many historians' narratives can be seen to derive from assumptions about the nature of feminist activity (that it only takes place in the public and political sphere) and paid work (as being liberating for women). In contrast, the domestic sphere is regarded as the root of women's subordination and the source of women's dissatisfaction. Despite the diversity of their theoretical underpinnings, the main themes that exist in feminist theory reveal an Essentialist assumption that all women are the same and united in a common aim to overthrow patriarchal domination; this is inadequate for dealing with a case study such as the Women's Institute, which had a clear sense of rural identity and which promoted domesticity.

What is needed therefore is a redefinition of the term 'feminism' – one which has been put forward by Andrews and Laverick – that looks beyond discussions of radical, militant activism and shatters the false universality that assumes all 'feminist' women have the same ideals and are united in their objectives. Examination of the Women's Institute's promotion of conducting (and its music policy more generally) highlights the term's inadequacy for dealing with an organization that did not seek to challenge societal constructs of gender. I propose that the terms 'moderate feminism' or 'empowerment' offer more suitable ways of describing the Women's Institute's promotion of conducting; they not only remove the Essentialist assumptions about 'feminism' and what 'feminist activity' entails, but also allows for women to have fulfilled lives within the traditional social constructions of gender and acceptance of patriarchy.

Chapter 3

The Changing Roles of Folk Song and Part Song in the Women's Institute

Publications of English folk song became popular during the nineteenth century. R. Topliff's 24 popular songs of Tyneside (which included folk songs) appears to have been among the first,[1] whilst others include William Chappell's *National English Airs* in 1838, Reverend John Broadwood's *Old English Songs as Now Sung by the Peasantry of the Weald of Surrey and Sussex* in 1843, and Robert Bell's *Early Ballads and Songs of the Peasantry* in 1877. However, it was the reprint of Broadwood's publication (renamed *Sussex Songs*) in 1889 that historians such as Michael Kennedy state as sparking the widespread methodical collection of folk songs in England.[2] A plethora of folk song collections followed, including the Reverend Sabine Baring-Gould's three-volume *Songs and Ballads of the West* (1889–1901), Frank Kidson's *Traditional Tunes* (1891), and Lucy Broadwood and J.A. Fuller-Maitland's *English County Songs* (1893).[3]

Folk song was identified by the collectors as an important feature of English musical life. It was seen not only to represent the song of the people, but also a vision of England's past before industrialization. Writing in 1907, Cecil Sharp stated:

> The [country] people went on making and singing their own songs unaffected by the growth of art-music amongst the cultivated. Thus, we find, even at the present day, the two streams of art-music and folk-music flowing side by side. In the country, where nowadays the unlettered classes alone survive, the common people still preserve their own music, just as they have kept their own speech.[4]

The mission of the Folk Revivalists was to preserve England's musical heritage before time ran out. As Kennedy notes:

> Sharp's work, and that of his fellow-collectors, was done at the eleventh hour. He estimated that the last generation of folk singers was born about 1840 and he found that it was nearly always useless to obtain a song from anyone who was under the age of fifty. The younger people's songs, even if traditional, were already showing signs of adulteration.[5]

---

1   The publications mentioned in this paragraph are all cited in Michael Kennedy's book. Michael Kennedy, *The Works of Ralph Vaughan Williams*, London: Oxford University Press, 1964.
2   Michael Kennedy, *The Works of Ralph Vaughan Williams*, p. 23.
3   Lucy Broadwood was the niece of the Reverend John Broadwood.
4   Cecil Sharp, *English Folk Song: Some Conclusions*, London: Methuen, 1954, p. 33.
5   Kennedy, p. 24.

Figures involved in the movement include Sharp and Ralph Vaughan Williams (among others), who were actively involved in the English Folk Dance Society (EFDS) – an organization founded in 1911 that was at the forefront in the dissemination of the movement.[6]

Although writings on the Folk Revival have focused on figures such as Sharp and Vaughan Williams, there are a few references to countrywomen who are reported to have provided material for such collectors (and about whom little is known), and figures such as Maud Karpeles, Lucy Broadwood and Mary Neal.[7] Of these three women, Broadwood has had the most scholarly attention, possibly because she was a prominent figure who actively collected folk songs during the early part of the Folk Revival (unlike Karpeles who was Sharp's amanuensis, or Neal who was involved in folk dance).[8]

The Women's Institute's promotion of folk song is discussed in three phases: the 'early' phase from 1919–1938, the 'middle' period from 1939–1950 and the 'late' period from 1951–1969. This structure shows that the position of folk song within the Women's Institute's music-making gradually weakened over the 50 year period, particularly after the premiere of *Folk Songs of the Four Seasons* (discussed in Chapter 4). The shift can be seen to reflect a general change of identity which is reflected in the commissioning of *The Brilliant and The Dark* (discussed in Chapter 5).

Writings on the Folk Revival

Broadly speaking, there are two key publications which have dominated recent writings on the Folk Revival: Meirion Hughes and Robert Stradling's *The English Musical Renaissance 1840–1940*, and Dave Harker's *Fakesong*. Hughes and Stradling's publication locates the Revival within a general interest in 'British' music (as part of growing nationalist sentiment) and examines the role of prominent figures (such as George Grove and Vaughan Williams) who were based in the vicinity of South Kensington.[9] It is essentially a 'top down' approach, focusing on male figures (in particular, composers) involved in the promotion of the English music. No women are mentioned in detail. However, references to W.H. Hadow, Boult, Walford Davies and Hubert Foss, who also feature in the Women's Institute's music-making during this period, not only reveal the involvement of 'outsiders' (who were prominent figures in Britain's music scene) in the National Federation's music activities, but

---

6   The Folk Song Society was founded in 1898 and the English Folk Dance Society in 1911. The EFDS amalgamated with the Folk Song Society (FSS) in 1932 to become the English Folk Dance and Song Society (EFDSS). The Folk Lore Society has remained an independent organization.

7   References to women and folk song in Maud Karpeles, *An Introduction to English Folk Song*, London: Oxford University Press, 1973 include Mrs Reuben Henlsey from North Carolina (pp. 9–10), Mrs Brown of Falkland (p. 77), and Mrs E.M. Leather from Herefordshire (p. 85).

8   References to Neal have (until recently) focused on her disagreement with Sharp over issues of 'authenticity' in the performance of folk dances.

9   Meirion Hughes and Robert Stradling, *The English Musical Renaissance, 1840–1940; Constructing A National Music*, 2nd ed. Manchester: Manchester University Press, 1993.

raise questions about the extent of the organization's involvement in constructing a 'national' music. Does the organization's music policy reflect an overtly 'nationalist' agenda? Was, for example, the Women's Institute's choice of Vaughan Williams for the National Federation's first commission an attempt to uphold a distinctly English musical culture? If this is the case, then what can be gauged about the choice of Williamson, who was of Australian descent and considered a 'modern' composer, for their second music commission?

Harker's *Fakesong* offers a very different interpretation of the Folk Revival.[10] Drawing on concepts of Marxism, Harker argues that the Folk Revival can be viewed as a conspiracy mediated by men such as Sharp (and others) for their own ends, and that the concept of folk song as an expression of the people is false. He states that Sharp and his colleagues were 'mediators' rather than 'collectors', who edited and revised the material and obscured the 'true' nature of folk song to suit their own nationalistic, anti-urban and middle-class values.[11] Although Harker's interpretation has been criticized by A. Lester and C.J. Bearman (among others) for his own political bias and harsh treatment of Sharp,[12] his argument deals with issues of class, which is a topic that has not been discussed in detail in any of the literature on the Women's Institute. In addition, it raises questions about the Women's Institute acceptance of the folk song 'myth'. Did the National Federation edit the folk songs which were promoted within the organization in order to uphold a particular image of rurality?

Early Music-making (1919–1939)

Early responses to the question of what kinds of music should be part of Institute activities reveal that folk songs and part songs were, for some members, the natural choice of repertoire. Two Women's Institute members had first raised the topic in the 'Correspondence' section of *Home and Country* in September 1919. Sylvia H. Drew of Chilworth, Surrey, wrote:

> At a recent meeting in London several of us hailing from different counties felt that more might be done to draw out the musical talent of our Institutes and that possibly some scheme of simple competitions of folk and part songs might be welcomed. We therefore decided, if you will allow us space, to appeal through *Home and Country* for suggestions and opinions on the subject and to see if anything could be done this autumn.[13]

---

10 Dave Harker, *Fakesong: The Manufacture of British 'Folksong' 1700 to the Present Day*, Milton Keynes: Open University Press, 1985.

11 Georgina Boyes also examines the values and ideological processes behind the men who were most prominent in the Folk Revival, and is an off-shoot (although toned-down) version of Harker's argument. *The Imagined Village: Culture, Identity and the English Folk Revival*, Manchester: Manchester University Press, 1993.

12 A. Lester, Review of 'Dave Harker: Fakesong', *Lore and Language* vol. 9 no. 1 (1989): p. 104, and C.J. Bearman, 'Cecil Sharp in Somerset: Some reflections on the Work of David Harker', *Folklore* vol. 113 (2002): pp. 11–34.

13 Sylvia H. Drew, 'Correspondence', *Home and Country* vol. 1 no. 7 (September 1919): p. 2.

Figure 3.1: Angle WI (Pembrokeshire) Ladies' Choir.

In the same edition, an unsigned member of Tysoe Women's Institute requested that the National Federation publish its own song book.[14]

In response, three letters were published in the October edition. Lilian M. Belletti of Stanwell WI, Middlesex, wrote that Institutes should have a choir of their own and that the one at her local Institute sang simple folk songs and part songs. She wrote: 'Folk Songs and Folk Dances should be sung and danced in every village.' Gertrude Lampson of Anstye WI, Sussex, recommended for Institute choirs the *Fellowship Song Book* – which included songs arranged by Walford Davies intended for indoor or open air singing at meetings of organizations such as the National Adult School Union, the Co-operative Holidays Association, the Holiday Association, the Workers' Educational Association, the Home Music Study Union, and other clubs and social unions, as well as public schools.[15] Lampson wrote that this song book contained folk and national songs with simple accompaniment, and described it as 'admirably suited to the efforts of village choirs'. Finally, Alice Crompton of Sutton, Bignor and Barlavington WI, Sussex, recommended that Institutes use *Songs of Faith, Nature and Comradeship* (compiled by the Co-operative Holidays Association) rather than have the National Federation publish its own.[16] Although there does not appear to have been any response to these suggestions, one reason why *Songs of Faith, Nature and Comradeship* was not pursued may have been because the religious songs included would have contravened the non-sectarian ruling of the Constitution.[17]

---

14 An unsigned member, ibid., pp. 2–3.

15 These organizations are specifically mentioned in the preface to part 1 of *The Fellowship Songbook*.

16 Listed under the 'Correspondence' section, *Home and Country* vol. 1 no. 8 (October 1919): p. 2.

17 Nevertheless, examination of *Songs of Faith, Nature and Comradeship* reveals that this song book included folk songs, some of which were later included in the National Federation's own song book (including *Sweet Afton* and *Come Lasses and Lads*).

Cecil Sharp and the Folk Song Ideology

Although the first major article on folk song was not published in *Home and Country* until 1950, early editions included references to Sharp and his collections of folk songs and dances.[18] An article of 1920 made a connection between Sharp and the Institutes by citing East Harptree as the second Women's Institute to be established in Somerset, and pointed out that this was where Sharp first started his collection of folk songs and dances.[19] M.E. Hobbs also made indirect reference to Sharp by describing music in England's Tudor period as 'a nest of singing birds' (a term used by Sharp in *English Folk Song: Some Conclusions*),[20] and in a later article wrote:

> ... Cecil Sharp's lasting memorial is in the hearts of the common people of this country whom he loved and for whom he laboured, in his own words, 'to restore to them their lost heritage'. It lies with us who follow to see that the final achievement of his efforts is accomplished.[21]

Such references raise questions about the organization's relationship with Sharp – did the Women's Institute serve as an outlet for his ideology? If so, was it intentional or a naïve acceptance of the doctrines espoused at the time?

The Revivalists stated that folk song was totally different from contemporary popular song: unlike 'art' music which was associated with the urban and was a product of individual (rather than mass) creation, folk song was the product of isolated rural communities that had been sung by peasants and evolved through oral transmission. In his Introduction to *English Folk Song: Some Conclusions*, Sharp wrote:

> The main thesis of this book is the evolutionary origin of the folk song ... The claims ... made by those who advocate the re-introduction of folk songs into our national life, all hinge upon the question of origin. They rest upon the assumption that folk music is generically distinct from ordinary music; that the former is not the composition of an individual and, as such, limited in outlook and appeal, but a communal and racial product, the expression in musical idiom, of aims and ideals that are primarily national in character.[22]

The absence of 'popular' music from the National Federation's song books and song lists suggests that the organization shared Sharp's rejection of a genre associated with the 'urban' music scene. Indeed, apart from an article published in *Home and*

---

18 The first article solely on the topic of folk songs was Hubert Foss, 'Our English Folk Song: A Great Possession', *Home and Country* vol. 32 no. 2 (February 1950): pp. 32–3.

19 J. Nugent Harris, 'A Village in Somerset', *Home and Country* vol. 2 no. 4 (June 1920): p. 5.

20 Sharp wrote: 'The evidence is overwhelming that, as recently as 30 or 40 years ago, every country village in England was a nest of singing birds', *English Folk Song: Some Conclusions*, p. 105.

21 M.E. Hobbs, 'Dancing and Music II', *Home and Country* vol. 7 no. 7 (June 1925): p. 232.

22 Cecil Sharp, *English Folk Song: Some Conclusions*, p. x.

Country in 1958 about the fashion amongst teenagers for 'rock 'n' roll', popular music did not feature in the National Federation's music policy until the preparations for the 1969 Music Festival, and then it was only briefly considered (discussed in Chapter 5).[23] When a jazz course was introduced at Denman College in 1965, it was promoted for its associations with 'folk' music. The review published in *Home and Country* stated:

> Much confusion exists in the public mind regarding the word 'jazz' – there are those who think that beatleism [*sic*] and pop are a part of it, and to some people jazz serves as a whipping boy for juvenile delinquency. But a new generation has arisen which is anxious to learn of the roots and growth of this fascinating folk music.[24]

Otherwise, the National Federation can be seen to have distanced itself from popular music in an attempt to be faithful to Britain's rural music traditions.

Sharp wrote that the role of adults in the Revival was to 'Flood the streets ... with folk-tunes, and those who now vulgarize themselves and others singing coarse music-hall songs will soon drop them in favour of the equally attractive but far better tunes of the folk'.[25] However, he believed that the future of England's folk song not only depended on its long-term cultivation, but also on being included in the education of England's younger generation. Sharp outlined his ideology on folk song and education in his publication *Folk Singing in Schools*, in the final chapter, 'English Folk Song'. He argued in both that folk songs could be integrated into the essence of everyday life through the education of children, which would benefit the future of English music and stimulate the growth of patriotism.[26] Writing in 1907, he stated:

> Our system of education is, at present, too cosmopolitan; it is calculated to produce citizens of the world rather than Englishmen. And it is Englishmen, English citizens that we want. How can this be remedied? By taking care I would suggest, that every child born of English parents is, in its earliest years, placed in possession of all those things which are distinctive products of its race ... The discovery of folk-song, therefore, places in the hands of the patriot, as well as of the educationalist, an instrument of great value. The introduction of folk songs into our schools will not only affect the musical life of England; it will also tend to arouse that love of country and pride of race the absence of which we now deplore.[27]

In view of the educational value of folk songs, it raises the question whether the Women's Institute saw its role in the Revival in reaching the next generation by educating women (as mothers) in England's musical traditions. The fact that the National Federation's *First Song Book* (discussed later) was to be used by the Parents' National Education Union indicates that the National Federation recognized

---

23 Atherton Harrison, 'Our Rock 'n' Rolling Teenagers', *Home and Country* vol. 40 no. 7 (July 1958): p. 157.
24 'Introduction to Jazz', *Home and Country* vol. 47 no. 2 (February 1965): p. 55.
25 Sharp, *English Folk Song*, p. 137.
26 Cecil Sharp, *Folk Singing in Schools*, London: EFDSS, 1912, p. 2.
27 Cecil Sharp, *English Folk-Song*, p. 135–6.

the organization as having some responsibility in the promotion of folk song outside the Institutes.[28]

Part Songs and the 'Golden Age'

Folk songs were not the only type of music promoted within the Institutes. Part songs also featured in the organization's repertoire, although they never achieved the same degree of prominence as folk songs. But the two repertoires were presented as being closely linked. The Revivalists saw folk song as synonymous with indigenous rural peasant music and part songs as also being part of England's musical past. Geoffrey Shaw, who at the time was a government Inspector on the Board of Education, wrote, 'In almost every line of the Madrigal you can find the folk-song spirit in the tunes'.[29] Although it is difficult to gauge how widespread such an opinion was, it appears that despite being fundamentally different in their origin and nature, links were made between folk songs and part songs.

The Revivalists depicted music-making in the late sixteenth- and early seventeenth-centuries as a nostalgic time when part songs and madrigals were sung as part of everyday English life. Sharp wrote that the fashion for foreign musicians in the eighteenth-century had created the 'habit of self-depreciation' and the 'ingrained belief that nothing of musical value can come out of England' which had hampered native musical growth. He continued:

> Under such conditions no art could flourish. It is not surprising, therefore, that we have had no musician of the first rank since the death of Purcell in 1695. And even Purcell was not uninfluenced by the prevailing beliefs of his day, for he found it necessary to look abroad ...[30]

This view of music-making in 'Merrie England' during the Elizabethan era was one replicated in the articles on music in *Home and Country*. Indeed, it is within this context that W.H. Leslie's promotion of descant singing in the Institutes during the early 1920s should be understood – as a means of reviving both the music and the techniques of England's 'golden age'.

The first major article on madrigals and part songs in *Home and Country* was by Lilian Belletti in November 1923, and traced the origins of the madrigal, and discussed its modes and polyphonic textures.[31] Between 1931 and 1932, Teresa Berwick published three essays entitled 'A Short History of Music' in *Home and Country*, which similarly revered the 'golden age' of the Tudor and Elizabethan rule for the patronage that was bestowed upon English music. The success and

---

28 Recorded in the Executive Minutes vol. 7, ELPS-C (7 December 1925), p. 416. I have been unable to find any information about the Parents' National Education Union apart from its having published a journal (the dates for which are unknown).

29 Response to G.H. Clustam by Geoffrey Shaw, 'Classicism and False Values', *Proceedings of the Musicological Association* vol. 44 (1917–1918): p. 141.

30 Sharp, *English Folksong*, p. 128.

31 Lilian Belletti, 'Madrigals', *Home and Country* vol. 5 no. 11 (November 1923): p. 304.

proliferation of music composed by Byrd, Wilbye, Weekles, Morley, Bennett and Bateson during the sixteenth- and seventeenth-centuries is shown to have resulted not only from native talent, but also from the monarchical nurturing and support of the arts. Berwick wrote: 'The Court had continuously given its support and patronage to national music and several of our sovereigns, Henry V, Henry VI, Richard III, Henry VII, Queen Mary and Queen Elizabeth were remarkable musicians.'[32] The organization's support for the monarchy is also evident in Esther Neville-Smith, 'Singing Across the Centuries' and Joan Bernard, 'The Queen's Musick', that were other articles published in *Home and Country* (discussed later).[33]

In view of the few articles that were published on the topic of madrigals and folk songs in academic journals during this period, namely in *Music & Letters* and *The Musical Times*, questions arise about who were the authors of the articles that appeared in *Home and Country* and what informed their writings on the topic.[34] Was it a case of blindly accepting and replicating the Revivalists' writings, or were the articles opportunities for the National Federation to espouse a particular ideology? Indeed, what was the organization's relationship with the EFDSS, which was at the forefront of the Revival?

On first inspection, it might appear that the relationship between the two organizations was mutually beneficial: whilst the EFDSS collected, preserved and, in many cases, published folk songs, ballads and tunes, the National Federation distributed and popularized them by promoting them to be sung at Institute meetings.[35] However, more detailed examination reveals that that the relationship between the organizations was somewhat one-sided. The EFDSS provided a representative to serve on the Music Sub-Committee from 1924 (until 1952), and advertisements in *Home and Country* reveal that the EFDSS invited Institute members to local folk dance classes.[36] In addition, it provided the National Federation with at least two articles for *Home and Country* that promoted folk songs and folk dancing as the

---

32 Teresa Berwick, 'A Short History of Music I', *Home and Country* vol. 13 no. 11 (November 1931): p. 567.

33 It should be noted that Queen Mary, the late Queen Mother and Elizabeth II have all been members of Sandringham WI.

34 The first major article on madrigals in the EFDSS journal was John Horton, 'Some Folk Elements in the Elizabethan Madrigal', *Journal of the EFDSS*, vol. 4 no. 5 (December 1944): pp. 197–203.

35 Although there is a reference in the minutes to the encouragement of Institutes actively collecting folk song, there is no evidence to suggest that this became part of the National Federation policy on music. Executive Minutes vol. 19, MDS-C (5 October 1943), p. 750.

36 C.J. Gaskell, 'The English Folk Dance Society and the Institutes', *Home and Country* vol. 14 no. 7 (July 1932): p. 328. The EFDSS Executive Minutes for a meeting held on the 17 July 1924 state that Miss [Helen Dorothy] Kennedy (sister of Douglas Kennedy, also known within the EFDSS as 'Kenny' in order to avoid confusion with Douglas Kennedy's wife, Helen Karpeles) was asked to represent the Society on the Music Sub-Committee of the NFWI (p. 136–7). Mrs Penn, who was representative for the EFDSS on the NFWI Music Sub-Committee, served from 1949 until mid-1952, does not appear to have been replaced.

essence of English music-making.[37] The National Federation offered the EFDSS little (if anything) in return apart from an invitation for members of the Executive to attend the National Music Festival in 1950. It seems most likely that the National Federation fostered links with the EFDSS primarily as a means to enable Institutes to interact with branches in their music and dancing activities, rather than serve as an outlet for EFDSS ideologies.[38]

Folk Songs and Amateur Music-making

Folk songs, then, provided a means to assert the Women's Institute's identity as a British organization for countrywomen, and offered opportunities to interact with other music-making organizations on a local level. Along with part songs, they were also considered to be the most suitable repertoire for amateur music-making. An article in the *Journal of The English Dance and Song Society* referred to the value of folk song in the training of village choirs. K. Marshall Jones wrote:

> The first business of anyone trying to help village musicians must be to bring out, encourage and develop that which lies hidden in all of us, whether we know it or not, namely the feeling for rhythm and melody. Folk music, being the creation of the folk, is the national embodiment of rhythm and melody, and from that point of view is a very suitable medium, in which to experiment in the early stages of musical training.[39]

Examination of works by composers involved in the promotion of amateur music-making during the early decades of the twentieth century also reveals that folk songs and part songs were also used in the training of school choirs. Gustav Holst, for example, wrote a number of arrangements of folk songs or part songs during his time as a teacher at James Allen's Girls' School (1903–1905), Head of Music at St Paul's Girls' School (1905–1934) and Director of Morley [Adult] College (1907–1924). His vocal music includes a three-part arrangement of the madrigal *How Merrily We Go* that Holst used to teach singing at both the girls' schools, and numerous folk song arrangements which were first performed at Morley College and the Central High School for Girls.[40]

---

37 Articles include D.N. Kennedy, 'Singing and Dancing in the Village', *Home and Country* vol. 15 no. 8 (August 1933): p. 390, and Hubert Foss, 'Our English Folk Song: A Great Possession', *Home and Country* vol. 32 no. 2 (February 1950): pp. 32–3.

38 Joan Brocklebank appears to have been closely involved with the EFDSS as her name is listed as one of the editors (along with Biddie Kindersley) of *A Dorset Book of Folk Songs* London: EFDSS, 1948.

39 The author considered part songs which involved humming and had difficult inner parts as being 'impossible for rural singers'. K. Marshall Jones, 'The Use of Folk Song in Village Choir Training', *English Dance and Song Journal* vol. 3 no. 2 (November and December 1938): p. 19.

40 Cited from Imogen Holst, *Thematic Catalogue of Gustav Holst's Music*, London: Faber Music Ltd., 1973. Number 85 refers to the folk song arrangements first performed by Morley College (on 19 December 1908 and 27 May 1933) and number 136 to the choral folk song that was first performed at the Central High School for Girls on 27 May 1916.

Vaughan Williams' compositions for amateurs also include part songs and folk songs. In addition to *Folk Songs of the Four Seasons*, these include an arrangement of part songs for unaccompanied mixed chorus called *Three Shakespeare Songs*[41] and an arrangement of the folk song *The Jolly Ploughboy* which featured in song books for use in schools (for example *Folk Songs for Schools*) and publications intended for amateur music-making (for example *The Motherland Song Book*).[42] Indeed, there appears to have been little (if any) differentiation between the folk songs and part songs recommended for schools and those considered suitable for communal amateur music-making, which may have been a contributory factor in Institutes' later rejection of the repertoire (discussed later).

The National Federation's Song Books

The National Federation published two song books in the 1920s: *The Women's Institute Song Book* in 1925 (Appendix 7) and *The Women's Institute Second Song Book* in 1926 (Appendix 8). Their circulation was confined to Institutes.[43] The National Federation did not involve itself directly in another song book until 1957, *Singing for Pleasure: A Collection of Songs* (for female voices), which was edited by Imogen Holst.[44] This was followed by the *Book of Carols* published in 1968 (discussed in Chapter 5).[45] In the meantime, Oxford University Press published *Songs for All Seasons* in 1937 edited by Brocklebank (then the National Federation's Music Adviser).[46] This, together with *Singing for Pleasure* and the *Book of Carols*, was made available for use both within the Institutes and outside the organization.

The National Federation also issued song lists to Institutes which supplemented the song books; the first was published in 1938, followed by another in 1958. In 1939, a separate list for Welsh Institutes (which consisted of songs available in Welsh translation) was compiled in collaboration with the National Council of Music for Wales as part of a scheme (led by the South Wales Council of Social Service and the National Council of Music for Wales) to help Welsh County Federations in their

---

41 *Three Elizabethan Songs* were premiered on 23 June 1951 by choirs of the British Federation of Music Festivals, conducted by Cecil Armstrong Gibbs.

42 *The Motherland Song Book: Songs for Unison and Mixed Voices*, London: Stainer & Bell, Ltd., 1919. This was a four-volume collection of songs published in collaboration with the League of the Arts for National & Civic Ceremony.

43 Although the 'Music Review' section of *Home and Country* sometimes included arrangements for unison or choral voices (as well as music for instrumental music-making), it was predominantly concerned with newly composed repertoire for women's voices rather than arrangements of folk songs or part songs.

44 Imogen Holst, *Singing for Pleasure: A Collection of Songs*, London: Oxford University Press, 1957. Imogen Holst's role was to edit the songs for female voices and give advice on suitable publishers. MDcS-C (11 February 1954), n.p. An Ad Hoc Committee was set up in October 1955 for the organization of this song book, consisting of Miss Darling, Mrs Strode, Mrs Sanderson, Imogen Holst, and a representative from Oxford University Press. The Committee also decided on the song book's contents and title.

45 *Book of Carols*, London: NFWI, 1968.

46 Joan Brocklebank, *Songs for All Seasons*, Oxford: Oxford University Press, 1937.

music-making activities.[47] The lists provided little more than a guide to recently published music that was deemed suitable from a range of choral repertoire, grouped by genre and level of difficulty (ranging from easy unison songs to four-part songs for combined singing, and Welsh translations of stage works by Gluck and Purcell).[48]

Plans for the National Federation's first song book were initially based on a list of songs prepared by Dr Marion Arkwright, a Women's Institute member who had been one of the first women to gain a Mus.Doc. from Durham University. However, it is unclear whether these were included in the final version.[49] The minutes reveal that following difficulties gaining copyright clearance for the folk songs, Leslie carried out negotiations with the publishers Novello for a new Institute song book containing 13 songs.[50] At first, 10,000 copies of the song book were ordered, 4000 of which were paid for by Leslie as a gift to the National Federation. The idea was that once the first song book had sold out, the profits could be used for the National Federation to issue a second.[51] Indeed, it appears that sales went well, as little over a year later the minutes for a meeting of the Music Sub-Committee reported that members were asked to submit suggestions for a second song book to W.H. Leslie.[52]

However, unlike the contents of the first book (which appear to have been chosen on the basis of an agreement with Novello),[53] those of the second were decided at a meeting of the Music Sub-Committee.[54] It appears that once the National Federation was left to its own devices, it chose a repertory that catered for a wider range of choral tastes (rather than abilities). Whereas the first song book consisted of mainly English folk song arrangements, a few rounds and part songs (with an optional descant), the second also included Welsh folk songs (such as *The Blackbird* arranged by Nicholas Gatty), an American sea-song (*Shenandoah* arranged by Leslie Woodgate), and a Scottish song (*Afton Water* arranged by C. Stanford Terry), an excerpt from an opera by Sydney Nicholson called *The Music-Makers*, and Florence Hoare's setting of

---

47 The scheme consisted of talks being given at group meetings, providing instruction in conducting, and meetings being held with members of county music committee. MDcS-C (6 January 1937), n.p.

48 *Golyfeydd o Orpheus'* (Scenes from *Orpheus*) by Gluck, and *Y Lloer* (The Moon) by Purcell. The latter work may refer to either *The World in the Moon* (1697) or *The Emperor of the Moon* (1700), both of which were stage works by Purcell.

49 Executive Minutes vol. 7, MS-C (7 January 1924), p. 27. Arkwright's obituary states that she had also been involved in conducting choral and orchestral societies in Hampshire. *Home and Country* vol. 4 no. 5 (May 1922): p. 9.

50 Executive Minutes vol. 7, MS-C (9 February 1925), p. 262.

51 Executive Minutes vol. 7, ELPS-C (9 March 1925), p. 277.

52 Executive Minutes vol. 7, MS-C (11 May 1925), p. 308.

53 The two song books consist of a selection of folk songs and part songs each of which had previously been published as sheet music by either Novello and Company or Stainer and Bell, apart from Dr Arne's *A-Hunting We Will Go* in *The Women's Institute's Second Song Book* which was published by Curwen & Sons (1908).

54 The minutes reported that it was to consist of three folk songs three shanties, two part songs, two or three rounds, and two songs in Welsh and English. Executive Minutes vol. 7, MDcS-C (7 December 1925), p. 407.

Pedlar Jim to a sixteenth-century tune *The Carman's Whistle* (which was the only work or arrangement by a female composer included in the song books).

The music in both the National Federation's song books consists of simple settings of folk song sung in unison, rounds, and part songs with optional descants, which indicates that the standard of choral ability within the Women's Institutes during the mid-1920s was of an elementary nature. There does not appear to have been any attempt at regional representation as far as the songs' provenance was concerned. Those with a declared 'origin' were either from Somerset or Warwickshire or based on one of Sharp's collections. The majority of songs are on the topic of love (for instance, *Just As The Tide Was Flowing*) or they depict an idyllic rural scene (such as *The Lark in the Morn* and *The Plough Boy*), and there is little evidence to suggest that the National Federation altered any of the words.[55]

Examination of other song books published during the early decades of the twentieth century for amateur music-making reveal that folk songs were included but did not dominate the repertoire. *The Pocket Sing-Song Book* for example, included the folk songs *Summer Is A-Coming In* and *Widdicombe Fair* as well as hymns, national songs and nursery rhymes.[56] Similarly, the *News Chronicle Song Book* includes folk songs and part songs in its 'general section', as well as sea shanties, 'Negro spirituals', a section on children's songs, and hymns and carols.[57] Apart from a few part songs, the National Federation's song books are dominated by folk song repertoire which highlights the importance of being associated with 'the folk' in the organization's early identity.

Unlike the National Federation's first two song books, *Songs for All Seasons* and *Singing for Pleasure* were distributed outside the organization. Although it is unclear how many were published or whether they were targeted at specific organizations outside the Institutes, it seems likely that they were recommended to the NUTG and the RMSA, which also promoted amateur music-making and would have been obvious candidates. *Songs for All Seasons* consists mainly of folk songs (which include songs from Sharp's song book *English Folk Songs*, and a few part songs and carols).

Published 20 years later, the proportion of folk songs in *Singing for Pleasure* is considerably smaller: of a total of 80 songs, 13 are folk songs. Instead, there are more part songs and new compositions (including ones by Imogen Holst) which feature in the more difficult sections of three- and four-part settings (for accompanied and unaccompanied voices). The hymn *Let Us Now Praise Famous Men* (for unison

---

55 It is a possibility that 'Hes gone to fight the *French* for King George' was changed to 'Hes gone to fight the *foe* for King George' in *The Blue Bell of Scotland*. Comparison with other editions of the songs suggests that cuts were made, namely the third verse of *The Blue Bell of Scotland*, a verse in *Afton Water*, and two verses in *Come Lasses and Lads*. It seems most likely that such decisions were made for practical rather than political reasons: the verse omitted from *The Blue Bell of Scotland* is about the clothes worn by a Highlander; the verse cut from *Afton Water* describes birds in flight; and the two verses missing from *Come Lasses and Lads* are about dancing and payment of the violinist.

56 *The Pocket Sing-Song Book for Schools, Homes and Community Singing*, New Edition. London: Novello and Co., undated.

57 *News Chronicle Song Book*, words edition, London: News Chronicle Publications Department, undated.

female voices) is the only work in the collection by Vaughan Williams, who, seven years earlier, had written the National Federation's first music commission based on an arrangement of folk songs. No excerpts from this work are included.

Examination of *Singing for Pleasure* not only indicates that by the mid-1950s a wide range of musical abilities existed within the organization, but also that the prominent position of folk songs within the organization's music-making was in decline. This was part of a general drift away from folk song in Britain, both in composition and in musical debate. In *Music & Letters*, an academic journal that had been sympathetic to folk songs in the 1920s, for example, interest in the genre began to wane in the early 1930s.[58] Only two articles appeared on the topic of English folk song during the 1940s: R. Nettl's 'What Happened to Folk Song', and a tribute to the journal's first editor, A.H. Fox Strangways.[59] It seems that the National Federation was somewhat behind the times in its promotion of a genre that was increasingly becoming regarded as old-fashioned. Nevertheless, the Women's Institute eventually cut somewhat looser from these particular rural roots, and followed the general trend.

A Growing Dissatisfaction (1940–1950)

Although the non-political and non-sectarian ruling of the organization's Constitution prevented the Women's Institute from being 'officially' involved in the war effort of the Second World War, many Institutes participated in the preservation and bottling of fruit, which made an important contribution to the production of food during this time. In addition, there were articles in *Home and Country* on ways in which members could 'do their bit' (which included assisting in home safety services and looking after evacuees from the cities), during a time of national crisis. The fact that Lady Denman held a dual Chairmanship of the National Federation (1919–1946) and the Women's Land Army (1939–1945) also suggests that the issue of the organization's involvement in the war effort was by no means clear cut.[60]

The Second World War brought with it a renewed importance for music within Women's Institute activities. In an article published in *Home and Country* in July 1940, Elsie Rigg referred to a remark made by Malcolm Sargent: 'Hitler may make us go short of our butter, bacon and sugar – but thank goodness, he can't make us go

---

58 Articles in the 1920s include A.H. Fox Strangways, 'English Folksongs', *Music & Letters* vol. 5 no. 4 (October 1924): pp. 293–301; Donald Attwater, 'English Folk-Song', *Music & Letters* vol. 9 no. 2 (April 1928): pp. 129–39; and Jeffrey Marks, 'The Fundamental qualities of folk music', *Music & Letters* vol. 10 no. 3 (July 1929): pp. 287–91. The only article in *The Musical Times* during this period is Robert Hull, 'The Folk-Song Movement' (1 August 1929): pp. 711–12.

59 R. Nettl, 'What Happened to Folk Song?', *Music & Letters* vol. 26 no. 1 (January 1945): pp. 28–30 and a tribute to A.H. Fox Strangways, *Music & Letters* vol. 29 no. 3 (July 1948): pp. 229–37.

60 Lady Denman resigned as Chairman of the Women's Land Army in January 1945 in protest at the government's policy which gave post-war benefits to men and women in the Forces and to Civil Defence workers, but not to the Women's Land Army. For further information Gervas Huxley, *Lady Denman*, pp. 174–5.

short of our music.' As well as encouraging patriotic fervour, music was promoted during wartime as a recommended diversion for Women's Institute members, to unburden the weary mind. In the same article, Rigg continued: 'The other day without any special preparation we had a really stirring rendering of *Land of Hope and Glory*, with voices and percussion. "Not music", a critic might say – but I know we all felt better for it.'[61]

Home and Country encouraged members to be as enterprising as necessary during wartime in order to continue their music activities within their communities. In particular, Institutes were encouraged to co-operate with other local organizations: in addition to inviting neighbouring Institutes to singing rallies, Rigg recommended more community singing at Institute meetings, and collaboration with local branches of the RMSA.[62] However, it is difficult to gauge whether these recommendations were carried out and how successful they might have been, since the 'News from the Institutes' section of *Home and Country* was suspended during wartime.

Only a few articles dedicated to the topic of music were published in *Home and Country* during the Second World War. These included a series of snapshots that celebrated the lives and achievements of three of the nation's greatest musical heroes: Sir Arnold Bax, Sir Henry Wood and Sir Arthur Sullivan. The publication of each of these articles was well timed. Bax had been recently appointed to the prestigious and distinctly British office of Master of the King's Musick; the year 1942 was also the centenary of Sullivan's birth; and Wood had died on 19th August 1944.[63] A few paragraphs in *Home and Country* listed new choral music for different groupings of voices, but apart from that, articles recommended that music and drama activities should be combined, in view of the lack of resources. In particular, folk songs were recommended as being suitable for combination with drama activities. Joan Brocklebank's suggestions included combining sequences of mimes with folk songs such as *The Brisk Young Widow*, *I'm Seventeen Come Sunday* and *William Taylor*.[64]

A heated discussion on the use of music in the Institutes occupied the 'Correspondence' section of *Home and Country* during 1943. Although the initial objection appears to have been about the nature of the Social Half Hour, members' responses reveal a growing dissatisfaction with the role of folk songs within the organization. One 'country member' wrote: 'The complete fatuity of the Social Half Hour has to be experienced to be believed. In these days it is pathetic that busy women should be expected to waste their time singing infantile nursery rhymes, tinkling triangles, and shaking bell sticks.'[65] The responses that followed were

---

61 Elsie Rigg, 'Music in Wartime', *Home and Country* vol. 22 no. 7 (July 1940): p. 159.
62 Ibid., p. 159.
63 Edwin Evans, 'Master of the King's Musick', *Home and Country* vol. 24 no. 3 (March 1942): p. 41, Anonymous, 'Centenary: Arthur Seymour Sullivan', *Home and Country* vol. 24 (April 1942): p. 75, and Edwin Evans, 'Sir Henry Wood', *Home and Country* vol. 26 no. 10 (October 1944): p. 147.
64 Joan Brocklebank, 'Choosing Music for Women's Institutes', *Home and Country* vol. 21 no. 3 (March 1939): p. 92.
65 'Country Member', 'Letters to the Editor', *Home and Country* vol. 25 no. 11 (November 1943): p. 179.

clearly fuelled by concerns about women's roles during a time of national crisis. An unidentified 'South-Eastern member' wrote:

> I went to our monthly meeting to hear, as I thought, a talk on Music. I found the members sitting idle handed, singing childish songs, and after about half an hour of that we were invited to play 'Ring of Roses'. Contrast that with the women of Stalingrad. When one thinks of the privations, it seems awful that some women here can footle away an afternoon, not even knitting.[66]

The responses reveal that members questioned the suitability of singing folk songs in the Institutes for essentially two reasons. Firstly, references to 'infantile nursery rhymes' and 'childish songs' indicate that some members were aware of folk songs' associations with music-making in children's education, and questioned whether this was a suitable repertoire for adult music-making. And secondly, members questioned whether a repertoire that was associated with a bygone age of innocence had a role within a country that had been blighted by the atrocities of war, and an organization whose members included those who had suffered tremendous personal losses.

In view of the questions being raised about folk songs in the Social Half Hour, it may seem surprising that it was the National Federation's decision (rather than that of Vaughan Williams) to choose this repertoire as the basis of the National Federation's first music commission. However, *Folk Songs of the Four Seasons* should not be seen as an attempt to contribute to the Revivalists' preservation of England's musical traditions, but as a celebration of the organization's past involvement with the folk song tradition and achievements in music. The National Federation's first music commission was part of the organization's scheme of national events, the first of which was a Handicrafts Exhibition held in 1929 (and further exhibitions followed in 1935, 1952 and 1960). Other events included an exhibition of members' home produce in 1948, and an art exhibition (entitled 'Painting for Pleasure') in 1963, to name only a few (see Appendix 9). In each case, they were intended to be retrospective (rather than prospective) celebrations of the organization's achievements in a particular field for both members and outsiders.

The commissioning of *Folk Songs of the Four Seasons* coincided with the first in a series of four articles in *Home and Country* written by Hubert Foss on the topic of singing and the history of song. In the first article Foss outlined the 'naturalness' of song, which he described as a 'more regulated form of expressive speech'; in the second he presented a history of sacred and secular song; in the third he surveyed the different forms of communal singing; and in the final article he traced the history of German *Lieder*.[67] Whilst the core of each article was concerned with describing

---

66 A 'South-Eastern member', 'Letters to the Editor', *Home and Country* vol. 26 no. 1 (January 1944): p. 15.

67 Hubert Foss, 'The Singer in Our Music – 1', *Home and Country* vol. 32 no. 4 (April 1950): p. 88; Hubert Foss, 'The Singer in Our Music – 2', *Home and Country* vol. 32 no. 4 (May 1950): p. 119; Hubert Foss, 'The Singer in Our Music – 3', *Home and Country*, vol. 32 no. 5 (June 1950): p. 153; and Hubert Foss, 'The Singer in Our Music – 4', *Home and Country*, vol. 32 no. 8 (July 1950): p. 179.

the function of singing and song, Foss contrasted the notion of folk song's 'natural' existence with the art songs of Schubert and Wagner in his final article. He wrote:

> The trend of vocal music had many years been either German or Italian. For a long time, everybody sang the Italian way, and then they sang the German way – or both! Except, of course, the folk singers, who went on singing their charming native songs. Certain composers were not content with foreign ways, and wanted to sing in music as their own people sang.[68]

Whilst Smetana, Grieg and Moussorgsky are described as examples of 'foreign' composers who used native folk songs in their compositions during the nineteenth century, Foss's English equivalent is saluted in the figure of Vaughan Williams. These articles, together with a profile of Vaughan Williams, provided readers of *Home and Country* with the opportunity to understand the historical and national significance of their first major musical commission.

A Broadening of Musical Interests: 1951–1969

Links with the Folk Revival were by no means immediately severed after the premiere of *Folk Songs*. In 1952, Diana Darling wrote that English family music originated from the folk tradition, a time 'when those working together sang as they planted, hoed, reaped, threshed, or tended to their animals – *The Merry Haymakers, One Man Shall Mow, Sheep Shearing* …'.[69] She contrasted scenes of domestic music-making from Jane Austen's novels with the orchestral music of the towns. Darling's history of England's family music-making concluded with the image of the Victorians saving amateur music-making (which she writes, had been blighted by industrialization during the eighteenth century) through their love of the upright piano. In addition to providing an historical account, Darling's message to readers of *Home and Country* is clear in the final sentences. She wrote:

> Children are taught singing at school, their mothers learn it at the Institute meeting, and school and Institute choir may meet at the same Musical Festival; is it too much to hope that the family which has gathered only to look or to listen – reminded perhaps by the wireless of some song which they have learnt – will turn again to singing as they sit round the fire …?[70]

Darling's article suggests that in 1952 the National Federation still recognized that the Institutes had a role with the next generation in their music activities.

Links with the Folk Revival loosened further during the 1950s. One reason why the National Federation chose to break away from the folk movement may have been as a means to distance the organization from the trade unionism and political demonstrations with which folk music was increasingly being associated. Niall

---

68 Hubert Foss, 'The Singer in Our Music – 4', p. 179.

69 Original italics. Diana Darling, 'Music in the English Family', *Home and Country* vol. 34 no. 8 (August 1952): p. 235.

70 Ibid., p. 235.

Mackinnon's *The British Folk Scene* provides a valuable insight into the promotion of folk music in Britain during the second half of the twentieth century. He writes:

> The aim [of the second Revival] was not to reconstruct the past from its songs and music but to change the social role of music from one where music-making was in the hands of the music industry to one where the control of music-making was restored to ordinary people.[71]

Mackinnon reveals how organisations such as CND used folk music during the 1950s and 1960s for political purposes, as well as individuals, such as Myra Abbott (a Communist and active trade unionist) who set up folk clubs as hotbeds for political activism.[72] Although there are no references in the archival documents that openly state that the National Federation was aware of associations between folk music and Left-wing politics, a change to the non-sectarian and non-party ruling in 1950 may have been timely reaffirmation of the organisation's stance. The minutes state:

> That the NFWI Executive Committee re-affirms its adherence to the non-sectarian and non-political principles on which the Institutes were founded. The Committee reminds members of the all-embracing character of the movement and of the wide and charitable outlook which it is desirable to maintain. The Committee further emphasises the fact that all members who so wish have an opportunity of expressing their religious and political loyalties through the appropriate party-political and religious organisations and stresses the importance that they should in fact do so.[73]

It was at this point that the Executive Committee deleted the clause that had previously allowed Institutes to co-operate with other organizations without contravening the Constitutional ruling.

The articles published in *Home and Country* after the premiere of *Folk Songs of the Four Seasons* reflect a widening of musical interests within the organization, as activities expanded beyond singing and the promotion of a wholly English heritage of music.[74] Among the first articles were profiles of Mendelssohn, Chopin, J.S. Bach and Mozart, each celebrating either a centenary or bicentenary of the composer's death.[75] In the profile of Mendelssohn, Peter Grant focused on the composer's early prodigal years and the neglect which his music suffered during the later Victorian era (despite his enjoying great fame whilst he was alive).[76] His article on Chopin emphasized that it was a misconception to see the composer as 'a meek consumptive

---

71 Niall Mackinnon, *The British Folk Scene: Musical Performance and Social Identity*, Buckingham: Open University Press, 1994, p. 30.

72 Ibid., 25–7. Abbott set up The Hoy Club at Anchor, Southend in 1961.

73 'Rulings Files: Re–affirmation on non-sectarian and non-party rules' (dated September 1950).

74 The only major article on folk music published after *Folk Songs* is Paul Green, 'Music for Folk Dancing', *Home and Country* vol. 42 no. 2 (February 1960): pp. 43–5.

75 When the articles were published, it was 100 years since the deaths of Mendelssohn and Chopin, and 200 years since the deaths of J.S. Bach and Mozart.

76 Peter Grant, 'Felix Mendelssohn Bartholdy, 1809–1847', *Home and Country* vol. 29 no. 11 (November 1947): p. 192.

angel, politely coughing from keyboard to grave', and instead depicted him as a self-taught composer typical of his time, writing music for the drawing rooms of his noble patrons.[77] Finally, in his articles on J.S. Bach and Mozart respectively, Grant focused on their 'amazing' musical families, prolific musical output, and dedication to music.[78] What is particularly interesting about the profile of Mozart is the importance given to the women in his life. Although Grant described them as being 'rather less interesting than those of his operas', it is implied that Constanze's ability to keep her husband happy had considerable influence on his prolific output. Indeed, it is interesting that Constanze is portrayed as Mozart's muse, rather than Aloysia Weber whom biographers have tended to refer to as having a closer affinity with him in their shared love of music.[79]

In addition, articles on listening to music began to feature more prominently in *Home and Country*. The topic had been introduced during the 1930s following the technological developments that made it possible for the music of the concert hall to be brought into the homes of countrywomen. J.W. Robertson Scott wrote in *Home and Country*, 'There is no listener more appreciative than the countrywoman and there is none more deserving ...'.[80] Although the wireless and gramophone were credited for their educational and emotional value, Gertrude Lampson's article outlined their proper use for readers of *Home and Country*. She wrote:

> The wireless programmes should be read with care and the times noted of those items that have special attraction for us. Before listening in, it is worth while to read about the music we are going to listen to in one of the many books now published for that purpose and, if followed would obviate the lament (often quite unfounded), that the BBC programmes are dull. A good gramophone in the hands of a music lover might well serve the whole village as a valuable friend. By its means the whole community might be introduced to the boundless realms of music ...[81]

Listening was promoted as a means to an end – the idea was that listeners should become 'doers as well as hearers'.[82] As Andrew Blake has shown, this is also what the BBC wanted listeners to do.[83] However, it was not until 1964 that there was a clear attempt to educate *Home and Country* readers about listening to the 'great'

---

77 Peter Grant, 'Frederic François Chopin, 1810–1849', *Home and Country* vol. 31 no. 10 (October 1949): pp. 216–7.

78 Peter Grant 'Johann Sebastian Bach', *Home and Country* vol. 32 no. 7 (July 1950): p. 176; 'A Mercurial Genius', *Home and Country* vol. 38 no. 1 (January 1956): p. 7.

79 For further information about the muse paradigm in biography see Christopher Wiley, 'A Relic of an Age Still Capable of a Romantic Outlook: Musical Biography and The Master Musicians Series, 1899–1906', *Comparative Criticism* vol. 25 (November 2003): pp. 161–202.

80 J.W. Robertson Scott, 'The Cottage Housewife's Earphones', *Home and Country* vol. 9 no. 1 (October 1932): p. 422.

81 Gertrude Lampson, 'The Gramophone', *Home and Country*, vol. 12 no. 1 (January 1930): p. 19.

82 Ibid., p. 19.

83 For a useful discussion of the BBC's educational role see Andrew Blake, *A Land Without Music: Music, Culture and Society in Twentieth-Century Britain*, Manchester: Manchester University Press, 1997, pp. 54–8.

works. In the first of a series of articles, George Barker encouraged readers to start a record library and recommended music that ranged from J.S. Bach to Stravinsky and Bartók.[84] In the following article, he listed various settings of music inspired by Shakespeare, favouring Elgar's *Falstaff*, Mendelssohn's and Britten's settings of *A Midsummer Night's Dream*, Berlioz's *Beatrice and Benedict* and Verdi's *Othello*.[85]

The most significant development in the National Federation's music policy after *Folk Songs of the Four Seasons* was the formal introduction of instrumental music at Denman College. Prior to this, music courses had been dominated by conductors' schools and courses such as 'Folk Music and Folk Dancing' (held from 28 May to 1 June 1950), and 'Music for the Institute Meeting' (held from 1 to 5 October 1951) which were periodically repeated (see Appendix 5). Although there was a course titled 'Choral Singers and Accompanists' (held from 26 to 30 October 1953) which is likely to have included sessions on piano techniques, instrumental music was not formally introduced until a course titled 'For those who play stringed instruments' (held from 27 September to 1 October 1954).[86] The decision to promote ensemble rather than solo performance is significant, as, like choral singing, it was in keeping with the organization's ideology to enable communal music-making. Iris Lemare's review in *Home and Country* provides a valuable insight into the first instrumental course held at Denman College. She wrote:

> All the guide there had been was contained in notes of their previous experience in playing which each student had been requested to send in advance. According to their own evaluations, there were twelve back desk second fiddles, two violas, three 'cellos and a bass, all very firmly described as 'rusty!'[87]

The course consisted of morning sessions based on string orchestral ensemble work, evening sessions of demonstrations and recitals, and individual coaching from Sybil Eaton (who led the first course). It concluded with an orchestral concert. The course appears to have been successful: a similar one was held each year until 1959, and was extended to include wind players from 1960. However, woodwind and brass instruments were not widely performed within the organization, which may have been due to issues of gender: wind instruments (in particular brass) being associated with the 'masculine'.[88]

However, it was ultimately opera that was to replace the prominent position held by folk song within the National Federation's music policy. Articles on opera became more prominent during the 1960s in *Home and Country* as the preparations

---

84 George Barker, 'On Record', *Home and Country* vol. 46 no. 2 (February 1964): p. 49.

85 George Barker, 'Shakespeare and Music', *Home and Country* vol. 46 no. 4 (April 1964): pp. 125–6.

86 Such courses included 'For Recorder Players and Accompanists', 'Folk Music and Folk Dancing' and 'Madrigal Singers and Elizabethan Music.'

87 Iris Lemare, 'For Those Who Play Stringed Instruments', *Home and Country* vol. 36 no. 12 (December 1954): p. 439.

88 For a detailed discussion of women playing instruments and issues of gender see Lucy Green, *Music, Gender and Education*, Cambridge: Cambridge University Press, 1997, pp. 53–81.

for the second music festival started to take shape.[89] Before that, the only real operatic focal point was Britten's *Gloriana*, commissioned by the Queen to celebrate her Coronation. An article had featured in *Home and Country* in 1953, but even that was mainly concerned with the ceremonial aspect that accompanied the gala performance, rather than the work itself.[90] Esther Neville-Smith wrote:

> Its first performance took place before her [Queen Elizabeth II] at the Royal Opera House, Covent Garden, on June 8, an occasion which was marked by due ceremony. A Royal Box immediately opposite the stage was specially constructed for the night and garlanded with gay flowers and drapery. Yeoman of the Guard lined the foyer and the floor of the house and before the overture six State trumpeters sounded a fanfare in front of the curtain. The guests were asked to do honour to the Queen and to music with ceremonial dress and badges of distinction; dark clothes glowed with ribbons, medals and orders: bright jewels glittered on hair and gowns.[91]

Two months earlier, Joan Bernard's article 'The Queen's Musick' had been published in *Home and Country*, and listed in detail the programme that accompanied the Queen's Coronation ceremony.[92]

Phyllis Olive's article 'Towards Opera' highlights some of the reasons why opera was seen to hold the key for the Women's Institute's music and drama activities in the early 1960s. She wrote that Institutes' interest lay within a general national revival in opera (following the premiere of Britten's *Peter Grimes* in 1945), and that opera provided the Women's Institute with a new direction since it enabled the communal spirit to be promoted within Institute activities. She continued:

> ... there is a feeling that Music and Drama in our organisation require a new sense of direction. They have, or had, become too dependent on the competitive spirit. Choirs often reach a creditable standard, and rarely fall below an acceptable one; but this is usually at the price of rehearsing a restricted repertoire for a long time. This seriously limits the musical experience, if not the enjoyment, of the members, and they are unable to offer a programme of sufficient length and variety to the community as a whole. The music which they sing is usually chosen by a knowledgeable committee, nor do adjudicators normally find occasion to criticise the choice of pieces.[93]

In addition, opera embraced the participation of outsiders at a time when recruitment was at an all-time low, thus upholding the ideology of communal music-making within the organization: husbands, brothers and sons were encouraged to join in Institute operatic productions of works by composers such as Arne, W. Vaughan

---

[89] These articles include George Baker, 'The Lure of Opera', *Home and Country* vol. 46 no. 9 (September 1964): pp. 301–302 and 'The Beggar's Opera', *Home and Country* vol. 47 no. 2 (February 1965): p. 51.

[90] Esther Neville-Smith, 'Singing Across the Centuries', *Home and Country* vol. 35 no. 8 (August 1953): pp. 255–6.

[91] Ibid., p. 255.

[92] Joan Bernard, 'The Queen's Musick', *Home and Country* vol. 35 no. 6 (June 1953): p. 191.

[93] Phyllis Olive, 'Towards Opera', *Home and Country* vol. 44 no. 2 (February 1962): p. 42.

Jones, Purcell, Hugo Cole and Armstrong Gibbs. However, preliminary examination of the 'News from the Institutes' section of *Home and Country* indicates that few Institutes managed to do this.[94]

It is significant that apart from Mozart's *The Magic Flute* (which is referred to as *Papageno*) and *Bastien and Bastienne*, Olive limited her recommendations to works by British composers. Within this context it could be argued that the organization upheld Sharp's nationalist ideal of promoting a distinctly English musical tradition (in both English folk songs and operas by British composers). Indeed, were it not for Britten recommending Williamson, it seems unlikely that an Australian-born composer would have been chosen for the National Federation's second commission.

Examination of the Women's Institute's promotion of folk song reveals that the organization had a role in the dissemination of the Folk Revival. The National Federation had links with the organization at the forefront of the movement, but examination of its relationship with the EFDSS indicates that this was to enable community-based music-making rather than a union of ideologies. The articles on music in *Home and Country* reveals that until the 1950s the organization subscribed to the Revivalists' notion of England's musical past and the nature of folk songs. Furthermore, the National Federation can be seen as an outlet for Sharp's theory about the future of the English folk song, especially as an educative tool. Although the National Federation did not actively follow Sharp's ideology, their policies can be seen to have been in harmony with it.

The role of folk songs (and to an extent part songs) within the organization waxed and waned over the 50-year period covered by this study. From the 1920s until the premiere of *Folk Songs of the Four Seasons*, the promotion of folk songs dominated the organization's music policy. The National Federation's first music commission was a celebration of the Women's Institute's 'heritage' of singing folk songs, but left a void in music policy. This was reflected in the array of articles published in *Home and Country* during the 1950s and 1960s: biographies of composers, articles on listening to music and the introduction of instrumental music-making at Denman College.

After over a decade of expansion in the organization's music activities, the void was finally filled with the National Federation's second music commission from Williamson: *The Brilliant and The Dark*. This work, a mixed-genre work for female voices, drew on the organization's promotion of combining music and drama and provided a much-needed sense of direction in music policy. It also was part of a wider shift in the organization's identity away from a genre formerly associated with rurality yet now increasingly being utilized for political activism, towards up-to-date 'modern' music which it was hoped, would increase membership figures by attracting younger members to the organization.

---

94 The few references I have found to Institutes performing operatic works mostly pre-date these articles. They include Mrs G. Penman's report that Sudbury WI (Middlesex) performed an Elizabethan period play and an unnamed opera. *Home and Country* vol. 51 no. 1 (January 1951): p. 17; and Mrs Hughes' report that Aldbury WI (Hertfordshire) performed a 'home-made ballad opera' called 'Polly Oliver'. *Home and Country* vol. 33 no. 6 (June 1951): p. 176.

Chapter 4

Folk Songs of the Four Seasons and the First National Singing Festival

Commissioned for the National Federation's first Singing Festival, Ralph Vaughan Williams's cantata for female voices, *Folk Songs of the Four Seasons*, was premiered at the Royal Albert Hall on 15 June 1950, with a choir of nearly 3,000 members of the Women's Institute accompanied by the London Symphony Orchestra under the baton of Sir Adrian Boult. Not only was the premiere of *Folk Songs* the National Federation's first national musical event, but it was also the first time that the organization had commissioned a work for a specific occasion.

However, the composer's biographers have paid little attention to *Folk Songs*, focusing instead on the *Antarctic Symphony* which Vaughan Williams began composing around the same time. Information about the work has become dependent on anecdotes that draw on stereotypical images of Women's Institute members, or else the work is ignored altogether.[1] There is a detailed description by Frank Howes[2] and a stylistic analysis by Elsie Payne (in an unpublished thesis).[3] Otherwise, the sources that provide the most detailed background information about *Folk Songs*, by Ursula Vaughan Williams and Michael Kennedy respectively, date from 14 years after its premiere and focus on the singing of the Women's Institute members. The music is presented as being rather peripheral.

In her biography, *R.V.W.*, Ursula Vaughan Williams described the premiere of *Folk Songs*: 'The Albert Hall was packed, and when the choirs rose to their feet it was strange to find that the audience seemed far fewer than the performers – mostly not good-looking, all in their best clothes, so unlike the uniform black or white of the usual choir.'[4] Published in the same year, Michael Kennedy's 1964 biography described the work as 'a labour of love, an old and practised hand returning to his first enthusiasm'. Kennedy continues: 'His [Vaughan Williams's] private joke during the composition was that he was delighted at the thought of all those matronly women singing "I wish I was in that young man's arms that once had the heart of

---

1   In many biographies there is no reference to *Folk Songs*, such as in the most recent biography by Simon Heffer, *Vaughan Williams*, London: Weidenfeld and Nicolson, 2000.

2   Frank Howes, *The Music of Ralph Vaughan Williams*, London: Oxford University Press, 1954, pp. 196–204.

3   Elsie Payne's discussion of *Folk Songs* focuses on Vaughan Williams's treatment of folk song themes in the cantata. 'The Folk-Song Element in the Music of Ralph Vaughan Williams', PhD dissertation (unpublished), University of Liverpool, 1953, p. 389–98. I have been unable to find any other publications by this author.

4   Ursula Vaughan Williams, *R.V.W.: A Biography of Ralph Vaughan*, London: Oxford University Press, 1964, p. 299.

mine'".[5] The absence of references to the work in secondary literature since 1964 and the fact that Payne's and Howes' contributions date from only three and four years respectively after its premiere, suggest that *Folk Songs* suffered a short shelf-life.

Music Policy and the *Folk Songs* Commission

A request for the National Federation to hold a Singing Festival was first made in 1928. Although details of the proposed event are unclear from the minute books, possible reasons why plans were abandoned can be gleaned from a small amount of correspondence belonging to the General Secretary, Ignez Ferguson. In a letter dated 18 October 1928 sent to a member of the Music Sub-Committee (Gertrude Lampson), Ferguson requested that she contact the Warwickshire Music Adviser, Mr Walker, who, at a conference recently held in Buxton, had offered to help with the preparations for a Music Festival.[6] Ferguson also stated in the letter that Walker was of the opinion that the Women's Institute was not ready to undertake a National Music Festival, and urged Lampson to find out the reasons why from him. The decision to seek opinion from 'outside' the organization suggests that uncertainty about the venture was also shared by the Executive Committee. The proposal was turned down in favour of a 'Demonstration Festival', which was an exhibition of handicrafts held in 1929. The Executive Committee's decision may have been influenced by Walker's comments, or that from competing requests such as the Worcester Federation's Organizing Secretary to hold an annual Handicraft Exhibition.[7] Indeed, the popularity of handicraft exhibitions within the organization may account for their frequency in the overall scheme of the National Events (see Appendix 9).[8]

A Music Festival had thus been rejected in 1928 although it is not clear why. However, there is no doubt that Institute music was better organized and livelier in 1948 than it was in 1928, and so, exactly 20 years later, the Executive Committee accepted the proposal. A National Singing Festival had not been on the Music and Drama Sub-Committee's initial agenda for 1948–1949, which broadly speaking did not extend beyond its usual role: making recommendations to the Executive Committee as to the best means of encouraging music, drama and dancing in the Institutes, helping county federations in their activities and assisting in the drafting of publications concerning the Sub-Committee's work.[9]

---

5   Michael Kennedy, *A Catalogue of the Works of Ralph Vaughan Williams*, London: Oxford University Press, 1964, repr. 1966, p. 306. Kennedy fails to cite the source of this quote.

6   Letter to Gertrude Lampson from the Assistant Secretary [Ignez Ferguson] (dated 16 October 1928).

7   Letter to Miss Turner which is unsigned (but probably from Ignez Ferguson) (dated 17 November 1928).

8   The National Federation's National Handicraft Exhibitions were held in 1929, 1935, 1938, 1952 and 1960.

9   Executive Minutes vol. 21, 'Scheme for NFWI Sub-Committees 1948–49', p. 1051.

In February 1948, Tennant, then Chairman of the Music and Dancing Sub-Committee, put in a request for the National Federation to hold a Music Festival in 1950.[10] The proposal must have been well received by other Committee members, as details about the Festival's format, timing, preliminary costing and possible composers had been agreed by the next meeting. These plans included holding the Festival in June 1950, the Chairman (Lady Albemarle) making an announcement at a Consultative Council meeting in January 1949, planning for the county festivals to be held in the spring of 1950 (followed by area festivals in March and April), and the final London event comprising of three choirs from each area.[11] Vaughan Williams is listed as the preferred choice of composer for a commission, with Imogen Holst and Christopher Le Fleming in reserve.

Ralph Vaughan Williams and the Women's Institute

Beyond her initial proposal, Tennant was to remain central to the organization of the Singing Festival. However, it was Dame Frances Farrer, primarily in her capacity as General Secretary of the National Federation but also as daughter of the Dowager Lady Farrer (and a fellow student of Vaughan Williams during his time at the Royal College of Music), who appears to have started the negotiations with the composer for a commission.[12] Links between the Farrer family and the composer had been forged over many years. It is likely that Vaughan Williams knew the family before his student years, as Ursula Vaughan Williams recalls in her biography that he played chamber music in their home when he was a schoolboy.[13] The firm friendship that developed between these two families was based on their love of music and their involvement with the annual Leith Hill Music Festival held in Dorking.[14] Indeed, it was at the Leith Hill Festival that Vaughan Williams's *Three Children's Songs* (for unison female voices) was premiered on 1 May 1930, with words written by Frances Farrer.

Vaughan Williams had composed only two works for female voices before the National Federation's commission: *Sound Asleep* for three female voices with piano accompaniment, and the *Magnificat* for contralto solo and women's choir accompanied by orchestra.[15] *Sound Asleep* features in the National Federation's

---

10 Executive Minutes vol. 21, MDS-C (9 February 1948), p. 1014.
11 Executive Minutes vol. 21, MDS-C (5 April 1948), p. 1097.
12 Dame Frances Farrer is the only individual member of the Women's Institute referred to in Ursula Vaughan Williams's account of the commission; she wrote that she 'asked him [Ralph Vaughan Williams] for a work for women's voices for their National Singing Festival when they proposed to have a concert at the Albert Hall, in 1950', *R.V.W: A Biography of Ralph Vaughan Williams*, p. 292.
13 Ibid., p. 74.
14 Vaughan Williams's sister Margaret and Frances Farrer both held the position of Secretary of the Leith Hill Music Festival.
15 *Magnificat* was premiered at the Three Choirs Festival at Worcester Cathedral on 8 September 1932, and *Sound Asleep* on 27 April 1903 as a test piece for the East Lincolnshire Musical Festival, Spilsby.

song lists, but the *Magnificat* does not, possibly in accordance with the non-sectarian ruling of the Constitution.

Vaughan Williams's arrangements of folk songs featured strongly in the National Federation's publications on music. The first song book includes *Farmyard Song* and *The Jolly Plough Boy*. The second includes *Just As The Tide Was Flowing*. Although none of his other folk song arrangements appeared in *Songs for All Seasons* or *Singing for Pleasure*, ten were included in the National Federation 1938 song list. The music reviews section of *Home and Country* also recommended Vaughan Williams's folk songs, as well as his other choral works, such as *Thanksgiving for Victory* and an arrangement of *Greensleeves*. Only a limited amount of space in *Home and Country* was given to instrumental music.[16]

The image of Vaughan Williams as the intellectual descendant of Sharp (an idea which he himself mentioned in *National Music*) was not one propagated by the National Federation.[17] However, examination of the profile of Vaughan Williams published in *Home and Country* reveals that he was presented to readers as typifying Englishness in a Sharp-esque manner.[18] The first main paragraph begins:

> Born in Down Ampney in Gloucestershire, this 'grand old man of British music' is now in his 77th year. He is essentially an English gentleman, loving his country and the countryside, kindly, humorous, incredibly hospitable and completely unassuming.[19]

The first half of the article refers to Vaughan Williams's links with the countryside, which are presented as being the source of his Englishness; for example his rural birthplace, his interest in agriculture, and his collection of folk songs from the countryside. However, according to his wife, it seems unlikely that Vaughan Williams saw himself in this way. In a private letter, Ursula Vaughan Williams wrote:

> I do think that it is a mistake to think of Ralph as a countryman – he wasn't. Certainly born in Gloucestershire – but who can choose where they're born? Brought up in his grandparents' house at Leith Hill – but, he moved to London as soon as he could, and lived there till Adeline's [his first wife] ill health made their tall Cheyne walk house impossible. He was enchanted to return to London in 1953. He said that his London Symphony should be called 'Symphony by a Londoner'. He certainly loved some country halls and walking, but he had no other country pastimes. (War-time vegetable growing doesn't really count,

---

16 Elsie Rigg, 'New Music for WI Choirs', *Home and Country* vol. 27 no. 12 (December 1945): p. 187. Vaughan Williams's *Suite for Pipes* for treble, alto, tenor and bass pipes was recommended by Rigg in 'New Music', *Home and Country* vol. 30 no. 4 (April 1948): p. 61.

17 Ralph Vaughan Williams, *National Music*, London: Oxford University Press, 1934, pp. 107–108 and pp. 113–130.

18 Alain Frogley links the popularity of Vaughan Williams during the composer's lifetime with his associations of 'Englishness' in 'Constructing Englishness in music: national character and the reception of Ralph Vaughan Williams' in *Vaughan Williams Studies*, Alain Frogley (ed.), Cambridge: Cambridge University Press, 1996, pp. 1–23.

19 Mona Tatham and Mrs Tylor, 'Ralph Vaughan Williams', *Home and Country* vol. 31 no. 2 (February 1949): p. 23.

I think.) And, if you look at his hands you will see that they are not all country hands – I think that is very important to remember.[20]

The profile in *Home and Country* also refers to Vaughan Williams's support for amateur music-making, which by 1948 had obtained him celebrity status. In addition to his involvement in local music-making (such as the Leith Hill Music Festival), Vaughan Williams voiced his enthusiasm for amateur music-making in his published writings.[21] His article 'The Composer in Wartime' called for composers to think of the 'needs of the modest amateur'. He argued that high art had its roots in the humble origins of amateur music-making:

> ... to write for the amateur may limit the scope but it need not dim the inspiration of composers. The amateur player, also, has his duty toward the young composer. Let him welcome and encourage him. In doing so who knows that he may not entertain an angel unaware?[22]

Although Vaughan Williams did not address the issue of amateurs (or folk songs) in his writings of the mid-1940s, his 'The Making of Music' essays, which were based on a series of four lectures given at Cornell University in 1954, indicate that his ideologies on the promotion of amateur music-making and the folk song movement had not changed during this period: they correspond to those promoted in *National Music* and 'The Composer in Wartime'.[23]

The Commission

Decisions regarding the date, budget and organization of the Singing Festival had been arranged before Vaughan Williams's accepted the commission. The format was based on the three-tiered system of competition that had been used for the Combined Arts Festival in 1946: county festivals, followed by area festivals, culminating in a final London event for the winners.[24] A Singing Festival Ad Hoc Sub-Committee

---

20 Letter from Ursula Vaughan Williams to Mr [Lionel] Pike (dated 30 September 1989).

21 An entry in 'News in the Institutes' refers to Vaughan Williams leading a Music Festival in Surrey. *Home and Country* vol. 26 no. 6 (June 1944): p. 93.

22 Ralph Vaughan Williams, 'The Composer in Wartime, 1940'. From *Heirs and Rebels: Letters written to each other and occasional writings on music by Ralph Vaughan Williams and Gustav Holst*, Ursula Vaughan Williams and Imogen Holst (eds), London: Oxford University Press, 1959, pp. 92–3.

23 Vaughan Williams's writings in the 1940s include *Gloria, Sanctus, and Agnus Dei from Mass in B minor – Bach* (1947), *A Minim's Rest* about eighteenth-century music and entertainment as a luxury for the privileged, *Gustav Theodore Holst* (1949) and *First Performances* in the preface to the prospectus of the Henry Wood Promenade Concerts (1949). Cited from Michael Kennedy, *A Catalogue of the Works of Ralph Vaughan Williams*, London: Oxford University Press, pp. 303–305.

24 Articles that refer to the Combined Arts Festival include Mabel Osborne, 'A National Festival of Combined Arts', *Home and Country* vol. 27 no. 3 (March 1945): p. 35, and [Anonymous] 'Combined Arts Festival', *Home and Country* vol. 27 no. 11 (November 1945): p. 169.

was set up to deal solely with matters concerning the Festival, thus enabling the Music and Drama Sub-Committee to focus on the promotion of drama during the two years of preparations for the Music Festival. It comprised only four members of the Music and Drama Sub-Committee, each of whom were recommended for the posts: Mrs Beale (elected Chairman), Nancy Tennant, Mrs Tylor and Mona Tatham. Other Sub-Committee members attended meetings, in particular Elsie Rigg (then the National Federation's Music Adviser) who reported on the preparations for the Festival in the counties, and those from the Office and Finance Sub-Committee.

Although the Ad Hoc Committee was formed to deal with issues and preparations for the Singing Festival, the minutes reveal that the Executive Committee was consulted regarding 'non-musical' issues such as the timing of the event. An entry in the minutes states:

> It was noted that the Executive Committee had not endorsed the recommendation of the Music and Drama Sub-Committee that the Festival be held either immediately following or preceding the AGM. After discussion, it was agreed to recommend that in view of the fact that the office would have special help for the Festival, the Executive Committee be asked to reconsider their decision and should it be decided that the AGM in 1950 is a one day meeting the Festival be held the previous day.[25]

Musical matters, on the other hand, were largely left to the Singing Festival Sub-Committee, and beyond Farrer's initial contact, negotiations with Vaughan Williams were placed in their hands.[26]

It is difficult to gauge the exact nature of the National Federation's contract with Vaughan Williams. Mona Tatham's report refers to Vaughan Williams agreeing to compose a 'special arrangement of "Folk Songs for the Festival"' lasting approximately half an hour and consisting of songs for massed singing and others organized into three types that catered for different abilities and different sized Institutes. Class one was for Institutes with membership of under 50, class two for Institutes of between 50 to 100 members (of moderate difficulty), and class three for choirs of over 50 members (more advanced).[27]

The choice of conductor appears to have been Vaughan Williams's decision.[28] Although Boult had been previously involved with the National Federation through the Schools for Conductors, he had also conducted many first performances of Vaughan Williams's works: *The Lark Ascending* (1921), *A Pastoral Symphony* (1922), the *Piano Concerto* (1933), *Fourth Symphony* (1935), *Five Variants of Dives and Lazarus* (1939), *Thanksgiving for Victory* (1945), *Sixth Symphony* (1948) and

---

25 SFS-C (15 July 1948), n.p.

26 The fact that Vaughan Williams later donated his fee of 50 guineas to the National Federation indicates that he supported the organization's broader ideologies. SFS-C (19 January 1949), n.p.

27 Ibid., n.p. The songs for massed singing were *Wassail Song*, *In Bethlehem City* and *God Bless the Master*.

28 At the time of the premiere of *Folk Songs*, Boult had recently become music director of the London Philharmonic Orchestra (a post which he held until 1957), having spent almost 20 years as conductor of the BBC Symphony Orchestra.

the *Partita* (1948).[29] In addition to conducting the premiere of *Folk Songs*, Boult was involved in the arrangements for the performers' seating and in finalizing the programme of the Singing Festival.[30] It was on Boult's recommendation that Holst's *The Perfect Fool* (which required an orchestra larger than the regular London Symphony Orchestra) was dropped from the Festival programme, in favour of Vaughan Williams's arrangement of *Greensleeves* and Leslie Woodgate's arrangement of Purcell's *Trumpet Tune and Air*.[31]

The National Federation was unwilling to interfere with the composer's decisions. The minutes state:

> A request from Wales for the inclusion of a Welsh Folk Song in the Suite was received but it was agreed to inform Wales that apart from the fact that the Suite was now complete we could not in any way dictate to Dr Vaughan Williams on his choice of songs.[32]

However, the inclusion of Arnold Foster's arrangement of Vaughan Williams's *Prelude on the Welsh Hymn Tune Rhosymedre*, and *Land of our Fathers* sung in Welsh in the second half of the Festival's programme, reveals that the request was not completely ignored. Furthermore, the National Federation turned a blind eye to the references to Christianity in *Folk Songs* (namely in *Maysong, The Unquiet Grave, In Bethlehem City* and *God Bless the Master*), which contravened the non-sectarian ruling. A possible reason may have been to ensure Vaughan Williams's involvement and co-operation beyond the submission of the score until the work's premiere.

In *Folk Songs*, Vaughan maximized his use of different types of vocal combinations by including a large proportion of unison songs with a descant semi-chorus, such as *To the Ploughboy* and *May Song*, as well as two-part songs such as *The Lark in the Morning*, three-part songs that include *Early in the Spring*, and the four-part *Summer Is A-Coming In*. In addition, he wrote songs for unaccompanied voices such as *The Sheep Shearing* for two voices (which is perhaps the most difficult of the songs), and *Early in the Spring, The Unquiet Grave* and *In Bethlehem City* for three unaccompanied voices.

Folk Songs also reveals striking similarities with the *Concerto Grosso* for string orchestra which the RMSA commissioned from Vaughan Williams to celebrate the organization's twenty-first birthday at the same time.[33] The *Concerto Grosso* has five movements (Intrada, Burlesca Ostinata, Sarabande, Scherzo and March and Reprise) and, like *Folk Songs*, is scored for three levels of ability; the 'concertino'

---

29 Boult had also conducted premieres and repeat performances of works by other composers such as Elgar, Bax, Walton, Holst, and Tippett, helping to nurture a flourishing British musical scene. There is no mention of the National Federation commission in Boult's autobiography, *My Own Trumpet*. London: Hamish Hamilton, 1973.

30 Boult declined the National Federation's invitation to attend the Preparatory Conductor's Day because of a prior engagement in America. SFS-C (21 March 1949), n.p. References to Boult's involvement include SFS-C (21 November 1949), n.p.

31 SFS-C (5 May 1950), n.p.

32 SFS-C (2 December 1948), n.p.

33 The *Concerto* was premiered on 18 November 1950 at the Royal Albert Hall, performed by members of the RMSA and conducted by Boult.

part is scored for skilled players, 'tutti' sections for all those who can play in third position and double stops, and 'Ad Lib.' for less experienced players and those who are able to only use open strings. Indeed, it is possible that *Folk Songs* provided the model for the *Concerto*; Ursula Vaughan Williams's biography refers to Vaughan Williams beginning to plan the concerto in 1949 (by which time *Folk Songs* had been completed) and its first run through taking place on 15 April 1950 (which was two months before the National Federation's final London event).[34]

Furthermore, it appears that links between Vaughan Williams's two commissions for amateurs were evident at the time. In an article published in the RMSA's souvenir programme, Scott Goddard noted the similarities between Vaughan Williams's orchestration for the concerto and the vocal writing of *Folk Songs*. He wrote:

> This is the second work that has come within a short time from Vaughan Williams, designed for special occasions. The one I have in mind is the cantata for women's voices *Folk Songs of the Four Seasons* where trained choirs do the more expert work and 'All Voices' are given their chance with singable unison tunes, much in the way the Ad Lib band is treated in this Concerto Grosso.[35]

In the absence of information about Vaughan Williams's opinion of Women's Institute choirs, the music for *Folk Songs* indicates that he and Goddard regarded the standard of the choirs as more sophisticated than the instrumental abilities of the string players of the RMSA.

Preparations for the Festival

On 18 July 1949, a 'Preparatory Conductor's Conference' was held at the Wigmore Hall for county representatives who had been appointed by their County Music Committees. The aim was to ensure that there was a uniform approach to *Folk Songs* amongst choral leaders within the Institutes during the months of preparations before the area festivals took place. It also provided an opportunity for delegates to quiz both the members of the Singing Festival Sub-Committee and Iris Lemare, which the Executive hoped would stem the flood of questions (such as a query about tempo from the Derbyshire Federation) being sent by post.[36] The summary of comments from representatives at the conference indicates that the majority of the time was devoted to demonstrations of how each song was meant to be sung.[37] However, there was also a session at which Institute representatives aired their views. It seems that some Institutes were unhappy about the method of grading choirs according to the size of the Institute. Despite such requests for the ruling to be changed, no alterations were made.[38]

---

34 Ursula Vaughan Williams, *R.V.W.: A Biography of Ralph Vaughan Williams*, p. 290 and 299 respectively.

35 Scott Goddard, 'Concerto Grosso for All Comers'. Souvenir Programme of the Rural Music Schools Association 21st Birthday Festival on 18 November 1950, p. 12.

36 Executive Minutes vol. 22, SFS-C (2 May 1949), p. 260.

37 'Summary of Comments given to representatives at the Conductor's Conference held at the Wigmore Hall on 18 July 1949' (dated 9 August 1949).

38 SFS-C (25 July 1949), n.p.

The county festivals appear to have been adjudicated by members of the National Federation's Music Panel and local music advisers, and it seems likely that the method of selection was based on personal choice rather than a set list of criteria sent by the National Federation.[39] The minutes reported that there were more entries for class two than for the other classes – which suggests that either choirs of between 50 and 100 members were the average size of Institute choirs, or that Institutes preferred the music which Vaughan Williams wrote for choirs of 'moderate' ability.

The adjudicator for the area festivals was Iris Lemare, who was chosen by the Singing Festival Sub-Committee primarily for her work on the panel for the British Federation of Music Competition Festivals.[40] With only a list of the number of choirs that should be chosen at each area festival, Lemare had the ultimate responsibility for selecting the choirs to perform at the Albert Hall for the official premiere of *Folk Songs*. She received little guidance apart from the stipulation that she should choose the best choirs irrespective of which counties they came from, and that she comment on (rather than grade) each individual choir.

Lemare's report of the area festivals not only reveals wide regional differences in the standard of choral singing in the Institutes, but also suggests that Vaughan Williams had over-estimated the musical abilities of Women's Institute members. She wrote:

> I had started with the idea that all these 'picked' choirs would be note perfect, and all very good, that a detailed adjudication would be unnecessary, and that it would be a matter of choosing between perfection and lesser perfection! These illusions were quickly dispelled by Class One at the first London Festival. It soon became apparent that the choirs were not necessarily even note perfect, and many were making elementary mistakes in singing and interpretation that called for some detailed comment. The choirs on this side showed an overwhelming keenness that spelt woe to an adjudicator, who, through pressure of time, omitted to comment on even one of the three songs sung!
>
> The only general comments could be that the choirs appear to have loved the music, that with only a few exceptions, it had remained fresh to them; again with only a few exceptions, they had triumphantly overcome its difficulties, although we had to wait a long time for any real gem performance to appear … The standard, rather surprisingly did not <u>necessarily</u> hinge on the number of county festival entries from which the choir had been chosen. There were some poor choirs who had been the product of keen competition in a large county class, and some good choirs who had come forward as a result of being practically unopposed.[41]

---

39 SFS-C (21 November 1949), n.p.

40 Executive Minutes vol. 21, SFS-C (10 January 1949), p. 18. The Area Festivals that were finally decided (at a later date) were London (Wigmore Hall on 12 April 1950), London 2 (St Pancras Hall on 13 April 1950), Colwyn Bay (Church House on 18 April 1950), York (The Co-operative Hall on 20 April 1950), Cambridge (Guildhall on 14 April 1950), Birmingham (The Friend's Institute on 25 April 1950), Exeter (The John Stocker School Hall on 29 April 1950), Cardiff (The Assembly Room on 27 April 1950) and Preston (The English Martyr's Hall on 22 April 1950).

41 Original underlining. Iris Lemare, 'Area Festivals Report' (dated 30 May 1950).

Lemare wrote that the reasons some had achieved low marks were due to their either failing to grasp the style of a folk song (the Middlesex choir in the second London Area), not knowing how to set about the work (many choirs in the Cambridge Area), or lacking confidence (a trait which she stated prevailed in the York Area). The two London Area Festivals appear to have had the least successful choirs, obtaining a 'poor' in all three classes. The best choirs were East and West Sussex, West Suffolk and Northumberland, followed by Wiltshire and Worcestershire, with the best folk song singing from Sussex, Northumberland and Somerset. The overall impression of Lemare's report is that *Folk Songs* was greatly liked throughout the country, but that the work had suffered due to a lack of musical advice and inadequate choir training. Although Lemare's findings did not report a rosy picture of the standards of choral singing in the Institutes, it did provide the National Federation with evidence of members' needs in terms of the standard of music to be recommended and the kinds of training required, which was useful for directing future music policy.

Publicity

Publicity was not an issue raised until January 1949, which suggests that the National Federation had not initially intended the Singing Festival to attract attention outside the organization. Although the Singing Festival Sub-Committee had allocated £300 for an orchestra,[42] it was Vaughan Williams's request for a large professional orchestra for the premiere of *Folk Songs* that launched the commission into the realm of the British public.[43] The minutes reported:

> The Committee hoped that if the BBC broadcast the concert from the Albert Hall they would finance the orchestra. It was agreed however to explain this difficulty to Dr Vaughan Williams and to tell him that failing a broadcast, the provision of a large orchestra might prove to be financially embarrassing.[44]

Although the Arts Council had provided financial aid for the Singing Festival by ensuring a guarantee against financial loss and covering costs for increased expenditure for office staff and clerical assistance, it did not include provision for a large symphony orchestra. The National Federation's policy, which required that National Events were financially self-supporting, put added pressure for an agreement with the BBC for a recording of the premiere.

Negotiations between the Head of BBC, Sir Steuart Wilson and Mona Tatham, occupied a great deal of the Singing Festival Sub-Committee meeting's time in 1949. On the 4 October 1949 Wilson wrote to Farrer:

> The BBC Symphony Orchestra can no longer be lent as a co-operative gesture, but must be hired and a rebate allowed for the broadcast. The nature of the programme, however, is taken into consideration, and we agreed that for an 'accompanying programme' our

---

42 The cost of the orchestra is stated in a document entitled 'Singing Festival – Amended Budget, Sept. 1948'.
43 Executive Minutes vol. 22, MDS-C (6 March 1950), p. 920.
44 Executive Minutes vol. 22, SFS-C (2 May 1949), p. 260.

Symphony Orchestra is not suitable, and we suggested that an outside orchestra would be better. The whole question of a broadcast, i.e. time, place of programme and suitability of programme content, etc. has been put to Miss Evelyn Gibbs of 'Woman's Hour' on Light Programme.[45]

Wilson's letter indicates that the decision not to allow the BBC Symphony Orchestra to perform at the premiere of *Folk Songs* was because involvement with an amateur music festival threatened to demean the BBC Symphony Orchestra's professional status. The Singing Festival Sub-Committee investigated the price of other professional London orchestras (namely the Philharmonia Orchestra and the New London Orchestra) but chose the LSO, primarily it seems, for financial reasons.[46]

Once arrangements for the broadcast of the premiere during the 'Woman's Hour' programme had been finalized, the Singing Festival Sub-Committee requested that the BBC record *Folk Songs* so that the premiere could be re-broadcast during an evening programme. Clearly the Sub-Committee felt that more listeners would be able to tune in to an evening's programme than the late morning 'Woman's Hour', which raises questions about who they envisaged these additional listeners to be – Women's Institute members who had missed the first broadcast? Performers from the premiere? Or was it hoped to attract further attention from the British public?

Publicity for the Singing Festival started with the first press release on 8 March 1949 which gave details about the forthcoming premiere.[47] Soon after, the minutes reported:

> The Secretary [of the Singing Festival Sub-Committee] reported that press cuttings had been received from fifteen provincial newspapers protesting against an element of professionalism which, it was claimed, was likely to spoil the true spirit of the festival. The Committee agreed that the criticism was totally inaccurate and unfounded and that the statements should be disregarded. No protest had been received by Headquarters and it seems most likely that the paragraphs have been written by an outsider.[48]

In view of the fact that the use of a professional orchestra was not mentioned in this press release, it appears that journalists' criticism stemmed from the means of selection, which excluded some members from participating in a national music event. In January 1950, a second press handout was released which highlighted the format and scope of the Women's Institute's undertaking. It stated: '1,230 country women's choirs, comprising 22,185 singers in 55 counties have entered for the Festival, and 20,000 copies of the vocal score, published by the Oxford University Press, have been distributed to WI singers.'[49] Although it was hoped that this might encourage women's monthly magazines to allocate space in their June editions for articles about the Singing Festival, none appear to have been published.

---

45 A letter to 'Fanny' Farrer from Steuart Wilson (dated 4 October 1949).
46 SFS-C (1 November 1949), n.p.
47 'Dr Vaughan Williams Composes Cantata for National Festival of Song' (undated).
48 The minutes do not report which newspapers included articles or the content of them. SFS-C (20 June 1950), n.p.
49 'National Federation of Women's Institutes 1950 Singing Festival'. Press Release (dated January 1950).

A member of the Office and Finance Sub-Committee, Miss Mundy, dealt with all of the National Federation's press and publicity. The minutes reveal that she had a hectic schedule during the preparations for the Singing Festival. In addition to attending press conferences, supplying broadcasting information and photographs, her other engagements included answering numerous telephone queries on behalf of all the Sub-Committees and publicizing the National Federation's other events.

However, it appears that gaining media support for the Singing Festival did not trouble Miss Mundy. The minutes refer to an incident concerning a journalist from the housekeeping magazine *Illustrated*, who arranged to visit the Cambridge Area Festival for a special feature in the June edition to coincide with the premiere.[50] The minutes reported that 'the photographer sent by *Illustrated* had been a nuisance' and Miss Mundy was 'requested [by the Executive Committee] to take up the matter with the paper'.[51] Needless to say, no article or photograph about the Singing Festival appeared in the magazine, although this may have been influenced by a decision made in July 1949 not to accept the magazine's proposal for a regular space in the magazine for WI news.[52] Beyond the handouts and a press tea party (held on 24 May 1950), news of the premiere of *Folk Songs* was limited to entries in the publications of kindred organizations, such as the EFDSS and the RMSA.[53]

Publicity for the Singing Festival was not given priority even in the vital months leading up to the premiere. Instead, media attention focused on the National Federation's Chairman, Lady Albemarle, who had not only featured in the television series 'Women in Britain' and 'Designed for Women', but also in numerous newspaper and magazine articles on the topic of adult education.[54] In addition, Miss Mundy's attention was distracted by an attractive offer from the BBC to contribute material for a new feature in the Woman's Hour programme that dealt with news items from women's organizations.[55]

The Premiere

On the day, the Royal Albert Hall was filled mainly with Women's Institute members who made up the winning choirs. The remaining seats were allocated to the runner-up choirs, accompanists and conductors of participating choirs, and a proportion of tickets for sale in the counties (depending on the number of their entries at the final

---

50 Executive Minutes vol. 22, OFS-C (21 February 1950), p. 890.

51 Executive Minutes vol. 22 (27 April 1950), p. 941.

52 Apart from it being a housekeeping magazine printed by Odhams Press, I have been unable to find out much information about *Illustrated* as there are no copies kept within the British Library's collection. OFS-C (27 July 1949), n.p.

53 Frank Howes, Review of '*Folk Songs of the Four Seasons* by Ralph Vaughan Williams' in the *Journal of the English Folk Dance and Song Society* vol. 6 no. 1 (December 1949): p. 56. An advertisement appeared in the Rural Music School's Association journal, *Making Music* vol. 13 (Summer 1950): p. 15 which reiterated the press release of March 1950.

54 Executive Minutes vol. 22, OFS-C (21 September 1949), p. 491.

55 Executive Minutes vol. 22, OFS-C (9 March 1950), n.p.

event).[56] The grand tier boxes were reserved for special visitors who included members of the Executive Committee and Music Sub-Committee, 40 County Organizers and members of the press. Christopher Le Fleming and Miss Ibberson of the RMSA were also present.[57] In addition to the Queen Mother, Vaughan Williams, members of Oxford University Press, and Michael Mulliner and Phyllis Thorfold (both of whom had been involved with the Preparatory Conductor's Conference) were also sent special invitations to the premiere.[58] Being aware of the Queen's commitments during Ascot Week (which co-incided with the Festival), the Singing Festival Sub-Committee hoped that another member of the Royal Family might attend the premiere in her place, although this request also appears to have been declined.

The Festival began with massed singing of Parry's *Jerusalem*, followed by Vaughan Williams's *Fantasia on Greensleeves*, and the premiere of *Folk Songs*. The second half completed the programme of music by English composers and consisted of predominantly orchestral music: Leslie Ashgate's arrangement of Purcell's *Trumpet Tune and Air*, Butterworth's *Idyll Banks of Green Willow*, Elgar's *Introduction and Allegro for Strings*, Arnold Foster's arrangement of Vaughan Williams's *Prelude on the Welsh Hymn Tune Rhosymedre*, and massed singing of *Land of Our Fathers* (in Welsh) and the National Anthem.[59] However, only the first half of the programme was broadcast live on 'Woman's Hour'.[60]

Reception

The National Federation was disappointed with the paucity of reviews that followed the premiere of *Folk Songs*. The minutes stated: 'It was felt that on the whole, the response from the national press had not been very great.'[61] Part of the problem was a clash with that year's AGM, at which eleven resolutions were passed during a two-day meeting that grabbed the headlines.[62] The *Daily Graphic* and *The Evening News* printed articles on the discussions on the conditions in British villages, whilst the *Daily Telegraph* reported on the contents of Lady Albemarle's speech on the importance of home life.[63] The *Daily Herald*, *Daily Mirror*, *Reynolds News and Sunday Citizen* and

---

56 SFS-C (1 November 1949), n.p.

57 MDcS-C (6 March 1950), n.p.

58 SFS-C (27 February 1950), n.p.

59 Programme for the Women's Institute's National Singing Festival at the Royal Albert Hall on 15 June 1950.

60 The programme was introduced by Olive Shapley and the premiere preceded by Monica Mugan's review of events at the Women's Institute's AGM. Apart from a script of the radio broadcast of 'Woman's Hour: No. 33' on 15 June 1950 and a letter (dated 15 September 1949) from J.H. Davies (Music Librarian) to Miss E. Peel, there is no information about *Folk Songs* at the BBC Written Archives Centre.

61 Executive Minutes vol. 22, SFS-C (10 July 1950), n.p.

62 The AGM was held at the Royal Albert Hall from 13–14 June 1950. There do not appear to have been any reviews of the National Singing Festival published in any women's magazine.

63 *Daily Graphic* (14 June 1950): p. 10. *The Evening News* (13 June 1950): p. 3. *Daily Telegraph and Morning Post* (14 June 1950): p. 8.

News Chronicle all had features on the discussion that surround the resolution about whether mothers should have visiting rights to their children in hospital.[64]

Unlike the secondary literature on *Folk Songs*, reviews of the premiere tended to focus on Vaughan Williams's music rather than on the performance of the Women's Institute choir. In particular, critics were united in admiration for Vaughan Williams's ability to compose a work for all female voices and to create variety where there was apparently little to be had. The unnamed music critic for *The Times* wrote: 'in a word, the greatest ingenuity has been employed to avoid the total monotony of unrelieved female voices.'[65] Similarly, the *News Chronicle* reported:

> The composer's part has been [*sic*] the arranging of these songs and to obtain the greatest possible effect from the voices of women only. This he has done to perfection and has decorated the songs with an orchestral accompaniment of the utmost tact and charm.[66]

Few critics went beyond referring to the 'remarkable achievement'[67] of having 3,000 voices packed into the Royal Albert Hall, and marvelling at the National Federation's organizational efficiency. *The Times* reported: 'there must have been a great deal of staff work which reduced the number of participating choirs to a fractional representation of the total number of Institutes.' The critic concluded: 'The result was astonishing for its accuracy, homogeneity of tone, and what adjudicators miscall 'diction', confidence of attack, and precision of ensemble.'[68] *The News Chronicle* similarly praised the overall quality of the Women's Institute's performance and described it as 'admirable'.[69]

The most favourable review was in the journal *Music and Education*. An unnamed author described *Folk Songs* as 'a truly stupendous work', and recommended it as a suitable for senior schools and teachers' training colleges. The review states:

> They [Women's Institutes] are honoured by this magnificent work, and they in their turn will honour it. As a musical force in our country they are now to be regarded seriously: they are no longer novices. They deserve the recognition they have been accorded in London. Their musical organisers, led by Miss Iris Lemare, have done work the value of which can hardly be properly grasped and estimated in our time; but it will be recorded in the musical history of the country.[70]

---

64 Cicely Fraser, 'Mothers Place is in the Home', *Daily Herald* (15 June 1950): p. 3. Joyce Chesterton, 'Cruel to Keep Us Away Plead 438,000 women', *Daily Mirror* (15 June 1950): p. 7. Clive Graham, 'Let These Mothers See Them', *Reynolds News and Sunday Citizen* (11 June 1950): p. 6. [Unsigned] 'Should Mothers Visit Their Children in Hospital?' *News Chronicle* (15 June 1950): p. 3. Other articles in the *News Chronicle* included [unsigned] 'More Sugar Plea by 438 000 Housewives' which was another resolution discussed at the AGM (14 June 1950): p. 2.

65 [Unsigned]. *The Times* (16 June 1950): p. 719.

66 S.G., 'WI Choirs in New Cantata', *News Chronicle* (16 June 1950): p. 3.

67 [Unsigned]. *The Times* (16 June 1950): p. 719.

68 Ibid., p. 719.

69 S.G. 'WI Choirs in New Cantata', *News Chronicle* (16 June 1950): p. 3.

70 [Unsigned]. Review of 'Oxford University Press', *Music in Education* (July–August 1950): n.p.

However, it seems that few reviewers shared such optimism. Indeed, despite representatives of the organizations being present at the premiere, reviews of the premiere were not featured in publications of organizations such as the RMSA or the EFDSS, which also promoted folk songs and amateur music-making. *Folk Songs* received only one review in a leading academic music journal. An author signed as 'I.K.' described *Folk Songs* in *Music & Letters* as being 'designed for performance – more important, for rehearsal – by Women's Institute choirs', which suggests that it has not been taken seriously by reviewers within and outside of academia because it was commissioned for amateur musicians (rather than for professionals).[71]

Critics' responses to the premiere also raise questions about the extent to which their comments can be attributed to disparaging treatment of works for women's or high voices. Britten's *A Ceremony of Carols* op. 28, which was composed for treble voices and harp, provides a useful comparison.[72] Following its first London performance on 21 December 1942, an unsigned critic for *The Times* wrote:

> The original numbers, settings of medieval words, are eight, skillfully disposed to allow the composer varied expression in handling the all-pervading theme of the mystic birth. The danger is that in avoiding monotony the composer may sink into artificiality …[73]

Reviewers' criticism therefore was not restricted to works composed for women's voices, but concerned with the limitations of composing for treble-clef registers.

Within the organization, the Singing Festival was hailed as a success. The minutes reported that the Singing Festival Sub-Committee had received a very large number of letters of thanks and congratulations from the choirs and counties that had competed in the Festival.[74] The Festival clearly meant a great deal to the Women's Institute members, not only by providing what was for many the opportunity to work for the first time with professional musicians, but also the opportunity to gather together the best of its musical talents. One member of the Pickering Women's Institute described her experience of the Festival:

> Words fail to do full justice to the experience shared by all who were privileged to share the inspiration and uplift of this great occasion. The longed for television to place on record that colourful and amazing sight. The selected choirs arranged on each side of the mighty organ, the massed singers in the arena all in summer dresses turned the Albert Hall into a gigantic and magnificent flower garden. The atmosphere of keen anticipation as we awaited Sir Adrian Boult preceded the long looked for performance of our own special Vaughan Williams cantata. Standing in absolute silence to sing *Jerusalem* the effect was overwhelming and vivid. This intensity of feeling continued throughout to the marvellous climax when Sir Vaughan Williams took over and we repeated under his baton *God Bless the Master* – an echo which no space of time can destroy. The happy and

---

71 I.K., 'Reviews of Music – Choral Music', *Music & Letters* vol. 31 no. 4 (October 1950): pp. 373–4.

72 Britten's *Ceremony of Carols* was premiered at Norwich Castle on 5 December 1942. It was first performed in London by the Fleet Street Choir, conducted by T.B. Lawrence (with Gwendolen Mason on harp), at the National Gallery in London.

73 [Unsigned], *The Times* (22 December 1942): p. 8.

74 SFS-C (10 July 1950), n.p.

inspired performance accompanied by London's wonderful orchestra is a lasting memory for which all concerned will never fail to be deeply thankful. Not least are we thankful for our own particular conductor's guidance and patience and wonderful and complete organisation of the National Federation which made the whole event possible.[75]

Indeed, Pickering Institute choir must have competed successfully at the county and area festivals and performed at the London premiere, as a member, F. Gertrude Lax, sent her poem, 'A Song of Pickering' (which was to be sung to the tune of 'Sing a Song of Sixpence') to the National Federation, about the choir's experience of singing at the premiere.

In the aftermath of the premiere, the final meeting of the Singing Festival Sub-Committee was held on 10 July 1950. The issues discussed included why empty seats in the arena and stalls had been sold to massed singers who had then not attended, how to distribute the £381.15 profit to the 59 winning choirs, how much it would cost to issue certificates to the winning choirs, and whether another performance during the Festival of Britain in 1951 should be organized.[76] In general, the National Federation appears to have been generally satisfied with the final London event.

The After-Life of Folk Songs in the Institutes

Various schemes for a repeat performance were considered, including a proposal from the Arts Council to perform *Folk Songs* at the Festival of Britain. However, the National Federation rejected the idea not only on the grounds of finance, but also because it was felt that music would start to dominate the Institutes' activities. It was also proposed that a performance take place during the International Folk Music Council Annual Meeting in July 1951 – a three day folk dancing event organized by the EFDSS held at the Royal Albert Hall. However, there is no evidence that this in fact took place.[77]

Although it is difficult to gauge whether it had been Vaughan Williams's intention for *Folk Songs* to have an existence in the Institutes beyond its premiere, reports listed in the minutes reveal that performances in the Institutes did indeed take place. Mrs Bateson reported a performance was to take place on 8 November 1950 and Mrs Jessel referred to a Music Day and a concert being held by Hertfordshire County Council.[78] Even a year after its premiere, performances of *Folk Songs* continued to take place in the Institutes. In May 1951, the minutes reported, 'Arising on the Committee members' reports, it was noted that far from being tired of the Cantata, Institutes were constantly asking to sing and hear it again and new choirs were learning it'.[79]

---

75 Document entitled 'National Singing Festival as experienced by Pickering Choir' (undated).
76 SFS-C (10 July 1950), n.p.
77 MDS-C (14 July 1950), n.p.
78 MDcS-C (15 September 1950), n.p, MDcS-C (12 January 1951), n.p., and MDcS-C (11 May 1951), n.p. respectively.
79 MDcS-C (11 May 1951), n.p.

The 'News in the Institutes' section of *Home and Country* also provides an insight into Institutes' performances of the cantata. Miss W.M. Comber's review of Cheshire Federation's activities, which appeared in June 1950, referred to plans for a performance at the Autumn Council Meeting in Wimslow.[80] Mrs Hughes reported that the Hertfordshire Federation were planning a combined choral and orchestral concert for 5 December 1950 at Hitchin, the first half of the programme consisting of *Folk Songs*, and the second half of carols.[81] In December 1950, *Home and Country* reported that Bishop's Cleeve WI in Gloucestershire also performed *Folk Songs* at the Cheltenham Festival Concert.[82] However, reports of performances of *Folk Songs* in 'News in the Institutes' disappeared after the end of 1950 which suggests that either county press reporters did not regard it as being important enough to be included in their summaries, or that interest in the cantata had dwindled.

Folk Songs did not become the 'new' *Jerusalem* or anthem for the Women's Institute. Within the history of music in the organization, *Folk Songs* represents the pinnacle of the Women's Institutes' involvement with the folk song tradition, in its commissioning one of England's most important composers of folk song settings of the twentieth century, and it sparked a new confidence in the Women's Institutes' abilities, both musical and organizational.

The National Federation's first National Singing Festival was essentially an exercise in assessing the standard of music and needs for development within the organization. It also provided an opportunity for the organization to unite in music beyond the singing of *Jerusalem* and to work towards a common goal that culminated in a display of their musical achievement. For Vaughan Williams, the commission was not only a chance to compose a new folk song work, but also provided an opportunity to foster his involvement with amateur groups. However, Vaughan Williams's aspirations for the premiere essentially changed the nature of the commission from one that the Women's Institute organization intended to be relished privately, to one that, due to the pressure of finance, was pushed into the public sphere.

Beyond the Women's Institute, *Folk Songs* failed to make a significant impact. Examination of its reviews highlights the fact that the media failed to grasp that the Singing Festival was not initially intended as a public display of musicianship to outsiders. In her role as Head of the National Federation's press and publicity, Miss Mundy could have increased publicity for the premiere of *Folk Songs* and clarified the nature of the Singing Festival to outsiders. However, the decision not to attempt to win public support or draw attention to their efforts, or at least to do so only modestly, highlights the essence of the National Federation's Singing Festival, which had been for its members' enjoyment rather than to present a WI music debut to the British public.

---

80 Miss W.M. Comber, 'News in the Institutes – Cheshire Federation', *Home and Country* vol. 32 no. 6 North-western counties supplement (June 1950): p. 154.

81 Mrs Hughes, 'News in the Institutes – Hertfordshire Federation', *Home and Country* vol. 32 no. 8 (August 1950): p. 210.

82 'News in the Institutes', *Home and Country* vol. 32 no. 8 (December 1950): p. 326.

Apart from references to letters of appreciation, there is little information about what it meant for the numerous country women's choirs who entered in the first National Singing Festival. What motivated such an overwhelming response from Women's Institute members to participate in the Festival? Did it result from intense competition between Institute choirs? Or was it the opportunity to participate in the premiere of a musical work? Although questions about members' personal fulfilment cannot be answered, *Folk Songs* was responsible for increasing members' involvement in music in the Institutes, despite its having only a short shelf-life, and it spurred Women's Institute choirs to greater heights.

Chapter 5

The Brilliant and The Dark and the Second Music Festival

On 3 June 1969, over 1,300 members of the Women's Institute took part in the premiere of *The Brilliant and The Dark* at the Royal Albert Hall. The piece is an operatic sequence composed by Malcolm Williamson, and saw Institute members accompanied by the English Chamber Orchestra and conducted by Marcus Dods.[1] Commissioned by the National Federation for their second national music festival in 1969, *The Brilliant and The Dark* was the third national festival to include a commissioned premiere. Following Vaughan Williams's *Folk Songs* in 1950, the National Federation commissioned a play from Robert Gittings entitled *Out of This Wood* for the National Drama Festival in 1957.[2] However, unlike its predecessors, *The Brilliant and The Dark* combined music, drama, dance and handicrafts, and represented the first public performance at a national event that incorporated so many activities promoted within the organization.

The Genesis of *The Brilliant and The Dark*

It was seven years after the 1950 Singing Festival that the idea of holding another national music event was discussed by the National Federation. At a Music and Dancing Sub-Committee meeting in February 1957, it was proposed that a music festival be held in 1963, to include both vocal and instrumental music, a possible theme being a history of the music of Britain.[3] Discussions regarding the details of the festival (such as its organization and finance) took place at Sub-Committee meetings over the next year. In June 1958, the Music and Dancing Sub-Committee put forward its official proposal to the Executive Committee for a festival that would include different kinds of choir, each singing a short commissioned work.[4] The overall plan was to produce an evening in which various historical periods were evoked. The reason why instrumental music was later withdrawn from the festival is unclear.

---

   1   John Cox directed the drama and Peter Rice designed the settings for the premiere of *The Brilliant and The Dark*.
   2   Briefly summarized, *Out of This Wood* is a set of six plays that run continuously, and are set on the Welsh border: 'Out of This Wood', 'Thomas Tusser's Wife', 'Parson Henrick's Parishoners', 'William Cowpers' Muse', 'The Bronte Sisters' and 'Our Clouded Hills'.
   3   Executive Minutes vol. 27, MDcS-C (15 February 1957), p. 195.
   4   Executive Minutes vol. 27, MDS-C (9 June 1958), p. 302.

It was left to the vote of the Executive Committee to decide what would be the national event in 1963. Other proposals had been submitted: a travelling exhibit to illustrate activities in the Women's Institute (submitted by the Organization Sub-Committee), an exhibition of costume (submitted by the Royal Show Sub-Committee), and an agricultural competition (submitted by the Agricultural Sub-Committee). However, none of these was discussed at length. The Executive Committee was left with the choice of either a music festival or an art exhibition. The minutes summarize the Executive Committee's discussion as follows:

> ... [there was] some feeling that an Art Exhibition would be a forward move on new ground and in line with our desire to cater for the younger members, many of whom were showing an increased interest in Art; others feeling that a Singing Festival would draw in a greater number of Institute members, particularly the more rural members, and that it would lead to a greater variety to hold a Singing Festival as the next National Event to a Handicraft Exhibition [*sic*], rather than an Art Exhibition.[5]

It appears that whereas the Executive Committee considered art as a 'new' activity within the organization that could attract younger members, singing was associated with rurality and (like handicrafts), regarded as a 'traditional' activity that would cater for a wider range of members. This may explain why a music festival that included other arts (rather than another singing festival) was later chosen as a means to cater for both younger members and existing members alike.

The Executive Committee voted in favour of an art exhibition (later entitled 'Painting for Pleasure') rather than a music festival, a decision that may have been influenced by the inclusion of music in the National Drama Festival that had been held the previous year. Although the incidental music to accompany Gittings' six plays (which was performed by a small orchestra of auditioned Institute members) formed only a small part of the National Drama Festival, the instrumental element (which included works by Byrd, Purcell, Handel, Finzi, Karl Rankl and Arnold Foster) may have dissuaded the Executive Committee from hosting another festival, so soon, with a musical element.

The Golden Jubilee Festival

The celebrations to mark the National Federation's Golden Jubilee provided the next opportunity for the Music and Drama Sub-Committee to suggest a national music event.[6] Gabrielle Pike, who was Chairman of the National Federation at the time and was reputed to know Britten, pursued negotiations for a commissioned song, opera or choral work.[7] On 24 May 1962, Britten wrote to Pike: 'Thank you very much for suggesting I should write something to celebrate the Golden Jubilee of the WI Movement. Although this is as far away as 1965 I am rather hesitant to agree at

---

5 Executive Minutes vol. 27 (24 July 1958), p. 312.
6 Executive Minutes vol. 29, GJS-C (23 March 1962), p. 327.
7 An unpublished letter (dated 16 May 1962) from Gabrielle Pike to Britten in a file marked 'Pike, 1of 2' at The Britten-Pears Library.

this moment, since I have a very heavy schedule of work indeed.'[8] Britten did not, however, reject the National Federation's proposal completely: he requested that another composer be approached for the major work and offered to dedicate a short piece to a friend who had been involved with the organization for a number of years.[9] Several unpublished letters now kept at Britten's residence in Aldeburgh reveal that the friend to whom he referred was Cecily Smithwick, a member of East Coker Women's Institute in Somerset. His arrangement of Hardy's poem, 'The Oxen', which is dedicated to 'Cecily Smithwick and the Somerset Women's Institutes', was included in the National Federation's *Book of Carols* published in 1968.

The second choice of composer was Imogen Holst, who was approached to compose both an original work and arrangements of existing songs for the Golden Jubilee celebrations. However, she also declined the National Federation's request, stating that she had a very heavy schedule for the next two years.[10] Other composers listed in the minutes include Elizabeth Lutyens, Elizabeth Poston and Phyllis Tate. Only Lutyens would have been unknown to Institute members, as Poston and Tate had had numerous works published in the National Federation's song books.[11] Negotiations appear to have taken place only with Poston, who agreed to be the Musical Director in a drama production that had written by an ex-member of the Music and Drama Committee, Cherry Vooght.[12] It was hoped that Poston would compose arrangements of songs and original compositions to accompany the drama.[13] However, following advice from Poston and drama advisors (who included Mr Boweskill, Pamela Ratliff and Kathleen Doman), the Executive Committee rejected the script as being too costly and impractical. Poston's involvement with the National Federation ended soon afterwards.[14]

Plans for a large festival of music and drama in 1963 were further hindered when Lady Brunner (then Chairman of the National Federation) proposed to increase the AGM (which was originally intended in 1963 to be a one day event) to two days, which severely limited available time for music and drama activities to be rehearsed and performed. An exhibition, 'The Countrywoman Today', which showed various Institute activities for a year of monthly meetings, was held instead.[15] The display for music was a photograph showing an Institute choir singing at a children's hospital,

---

8 An unpublished letter (dated 24 May 1962) to Gabrielle Pike from Britten in a file marked 'Pike, 2 of 2' at The Britten-Pears Library.

9 Ibid., an unpublished letter (dated 24 May 1962) to Pike from Britten.

10 Executive Minutes vol. 29, MDS-C (13 February 1964), p. 620.

11 Elizabeth Poston's *The Ladybird, Song of Wisdom, The Dormouse's Carol, O Bethlehem, Praise Our Lord, The Magi*, and her collection of songs titled *Songs of the Women of Britain* were recommended in the NFWI's song list of 1958. Phyllis Tate's *The Sailor and Young Nancy* and *The 12 Days of Christmas* also featured in the same publication. The decision to approach these three female composers was recorded in Executive Minutes vol. 29, EC (28 February), p. 643.

12 Executive Minutes vol. 29, MDS-C (10 April 1963), p. 699.

13 A letter to Elizabeth Poston from the Principal Assistant Secretary of the NFWI. [M.R. Withall] (dated 4 March 1963).

14 Executive Minutes vol. 29, MDS-C (12 June 1963), p. 687.

15 Executive Minutes vol. 29 (27 June 1963), p. 773.

fronted by a representation of a conductor and accompanied by tape recordings of women's voices.[16]

The 1969 Music Festival

By 1964, 14 years after the premiere of *Folk Songs*, the Music and Drama Sub-Committee was eager to commission another musical work. On 5 August 1964, Pike wrote again to Britten:

> The [Music and Drama] Committee has asked me to approach you, and find out if there is any possibility that you would be willing to compose a work to provide the principal part of the performance on this occasion. The members were so sad that you were unable to help us for our Jubilee celebrations, and hope that this time we shall be more fortunate. In discussing the matter, our Music and Drama Committee had many tentative ideas and suggestions, but perhaps it will suffice to say that it is hoped that the whole event will be forward looking, appealing to those interested in modern music and popular music as well as those with more conservative tastes. While the main part of the programme would need to be a choral work, for which WI Choirs would probably be selected through eliminating Festivals of some kind, the inclusion of individual professional performers, at least at the London Festival, is not excluded.[17]

Whereas the National Federation's first music commission in 1950 was a celebration of the organization's past music activities and its heritage of singing folk songs, the 1969 Music Festival was an attempt to look forward by embracing 'modern' high culture and 'popular' music.[18] Whilst a commission from Britten would cater for the former, it was hoped that hiring John Lennon of 'The Beatles' would serve the latter.[19] The idea that such a famous rhythm guitarist as John Lennon, whose band's successes in the previous year had included the songs *She Loves You*, *Can't Buy Me Love*, and *Do You Want To Know A Secret*, not only highlights the sheer scope and popular appeal which it was hoped the Festival would achieve, but also the amount of money that the National Federation was willing to spend on its second national music event. In 1964, the band was at its height of popularity. Dale Cockrell writes:

> Tours of Britain in early 1963 gave rise to The Beatles' sudden popularity which had reached unprecedented heights by October that year, precipitating the 'Beatlemania' phenomenon when teenagers screamed, wept and became hysterical at the glimpse of them.[20]

---

16 Executive Minutes vol. 29, MDS-C (11 December 1963), n.p.

17 An unpublished letter signed Gabrielle Pike to Britten (dated 5 August 1964) from the file marked 'National Federation of Women's Institutes' at The Britten-Pears Library.

18 During the years that separate the two music commissions society had changed dramatically; the rations of the Second World War and National Service had ended, and for many, standards of living had improved. The 1960s also saw both advances in technology as well as rise in youth culture.

19 Executive Minutes vol. 29, MDS-C (6 May 1964), p. 1114.

20 Dale Cockrell, 'Beatles', *The New Grove Dictionary of Music*, vol. 2, ed. Stanley Sadie, London: Macmillan, 1980, p. 321.

The prospect of a member of 'The Beatles' performing at the festival appears to have quickly disappeared soon after it was proposed: there is no mention of it again in the minute books, which probably indicates that it was quickly recognized as being an unrealistic option.

Examination of the National Federation's Annual Reports reveals why a second music festival was regarded as a valuable opportunity to widen the organization's appeal. Although membership within the Institutes had grown steadily during the early 1960s, the organization had been in financial difficulty in 1963 and had borrowed £6,000 from reserve funds.[21] Gaining the membership fees of new recruits was part of the scheme to repay the organization's debt, which also included increasing the existing membership fee, promoting sales of *Home and Country*, and using the revenue from the National Federation's investments and income from Denman College, as well as gifts from members (which totalled over £5,000).[22]

Britten again declined the National Federation's request for a commission, stating that he had other commitments, but recommended Williamson and Arthur Oldham as possible composers for a commission.[23] In an unpublished letter to Pike, Britten described Williamson as already having great operatic successes and being 'very brilliant and well on the way to becoming very famous'. He described Oldham as 'a much more serious and reticent composer but with perhaps greater knowledge of choirs …'.[24] Oldham had substantial experience of writing both choral and vocal music; by 1964 his choral output, which was predominately sacred, included *My Truest Treasure* for SATB (1951), four anthems (1952), *Missa in Honorem Santi Thomae Mori* for SATB (1958), *Missa Sanctae Mariae Virginis* for congregation, chorus and organ (1960), two carols for SA and organ (1961), *Laudes Creaturanum* for soprano solo, children's chorus, chorus, organ and strings (1961), *Hymns for the Amusement of Children* for soprano solo, chorus and organ (or chamber orchestra) (1962) and *Remember, O Thou Man* for SSATBB (1962). Williamson's choral music comprised only the *Symphony for Voices* for SATB choir and *Wrestling Jacob* for soprano and SATB choir (both 1962).

Other composers considered by the National Federation were Gordon Jacob, Herbert Howells or Poston for the main work, with Williamson composing for 'a short supplementary part of the programme', and an arrangement by Roger Fiske or Mary Chater.[25] In view of his extensive number of vocal works, the most likely choice (excluding Chater, about whom little is known) would have been Howells.[26]

---

21 In December 1962 the membership figure was recorded as 442,729, compared to 432,321 in 1963. The NFWI Annual Reports listed the membership figures on 31 December for each year as follows: 461,153 in 1967, 456,230 in 1968, and 436,819 in 1969.

22 For detailed information about the accounts see the 48th Annual Report for 1964, pp. 24–5.

23 Executive Minutes vol. 29, MDS-C (9 September 1964), p. 1267.

24 An unpublished letter to Gabrielle Pike from Britten (dated 8 August 1964) from file marked 'National Federation of Women's Institutes' at The Britten-Pears Library.

25 Executive Minutes vol. 29, MDS-C (9 September 1964), p. 1267.

26 Howells' vocal works by this time included 5 part songs op. 11 (1915–17), *A Golden Lullaby* (c.1920), *Piping Down The Valleys Wild* (1938), *The Key of the Kingdom* (1948) and *Pink Almond* (1957), among numerous other songs for female voices.

The prospect of securing a work from Williamson who was thought to be a young composer on the verge of fame most probably influenced the National Federation's decision.

In view of the Women's Institute being an all-women's organization, and been rejected by Britten twice, the question arises as to why the Music and Drama Sub-Committee did not take the opportunity to commission a work from a female composer. After all, the National Federation's song list of 1958 included songs by Imogen Holst, Poston, Grace Williams, Shena Fraser and Phyllis Tate, among others, which indicates a familiarity with some of the music of contemporary female composers. Indeed, in comparison with the National Federation's song list of 1938, which only included songs by Imogen Holst, Evelyn Sharp, Ann Megary and Mary Manson, the 1958 list indicates an attempt not only to include songs by a greater variety of composers, but also to include lesser known female composers such as Muriel Dawn, Eva Forvargue, Evelyn Sharpe, Susan Perrin, Linda Chesterman, Ann Driver, Carol Besancon and Marjory Harrison.[27] Furthermore, the decision not to re-establish negotiations with Poston after the rejection of Vooght's script for the Golden Jubilee celebrations appears curious, particularly in view of a compositional output that included songs for female voices (*Salve Jesus Little Lad* and *Balulalow* among others) and the publication of her collection, *Songs of the Women of Britain* (1956), which had been recommended in the NFWI's Song List of 1958.

Since Williamson was Australian, it is also implausible that there was a desire to commission an English composer (which might otherwise have explained the decision not to propose female composers such as the Northern Irish composer Dorothy Parke, Scottish composer Shena Fraser, or the Welsh composer Grace Williams). The reason may rather have been to either the personal preferences of Sub-Committee members, or a matter of convenience. The majority of composers who were proposed at the Sub-Committee meeting on 9 September 1964 appear to have either lived close or had institutional affiliations in London, where the National Federation had its Headquarters: Jacob was on the teaching staff at the Royal College of Music (a position he held from 1924–1966), Fiske was a broadcaster for the BBC and based in London, Williamson was living in South West London, Howells retired as Director of Music at St Paul's Girls' School in 1964, and apart from brief stints abroad, Poston was based in Hertfordshire.

The Choice of Williamson

When the National Federation approached Williamson for a commission, he was increasingly in demand as a composer.[28] He had had his first operatic success, *Our Man in Havana*, which had premiered in London on 2 September 1962 (continuing

---

27 Apart from Dorothy Parke, there are no entries for these composers in *The New Grove Dictionary of Music* or Sophie Fuller's *The Pandora Guide to Female Composers: Britain and the United States, 1629–Present*, London: Pandora, 1994.

28 Apart from contemporary reviews of his works, there is scant detailed literature on Williamson and his works. The most detailed discussion to date appears to be Christopher Austin's 'To Be a Pilgrim – Malcolm Williamson at 70', *British Music* vol. 23 (2001): pp. 5–9.

to 13 May 1963); and in 1964 alone first performances of his commissions included four separate works (compared with only two the previous year, and seven in 1965): *Mass of Saint Andrew* (commissioned by the churches of St Andrew for the festival of the City of London), *English Eccentrics* (commissioned by the English Opera Group), *A Young Girl* (commissioned by the Thames Concerts Society) and incidental music to Shakespeare's *The Merry Wives of Windsor* (for the Royal Shakespeare Theatre).[29] However, it seems unlikely that Williamson would have been chosen for the National Federation's second music commission had it not been for Britten's recommendation. He was an entirely new name to the National Federation: there is no mention of Williamson's music in the articles on 'modern music' or in the recommended music in *Home and Country* during the late 1950s and none of his music had featured in the National Federation's song books or song lists prior to the premiere of *The Brilliant and The Dark*.

The Libretto

Britten, it seems, also had some influence on the choice of the librettist. A report of a meeting with a representative from the music publishers Weinbergers[30] stated:

> The need for a Librettist was also mentioned and he [Williamson] said that he had discussed this with Benjamin Britten and the latter did not feel that Myfanwy Piper, who had been mentioned at the last interview, was necessarily the right person. He was now considering Ursula Woods (Mrs Vaughan Williams) and as it was felt that it was so much a matter for him to choose someone with whom he could work, it was suggested that he sound her [out] about the proposition and let the NFWI know the rest.[31]

In view of his own use of Piper's libretto for *The Turn of the Screw* (1954) and later collaborations in *Owen Wingrave* (1971) and *Death in Venice* (1973), one wonders why Britten did not consider her suitable for the National Federation's commission. Was it because of the type of work (which had quite 'dark' subjects) that Piper was involved with?[32] Was she intolerant of amateurs? Or were his comments motivated by self-interest in order to safeguard the delivery of librettos for his own operas?

Ursula Vaughan Williams provided what was described in the National Federation's publicity material as a 'happy link' with the last national music event. Not only had she been involved behind the scenes with the *Folk Songs* commission,

---

29 Honor Wyatt's profile, 'Malcolm Williamson,' referred to his success as an operatic composer. *Home and Country* vol. 48 no. 7 (July 1966): p. 267.

30 Weinbergers is a publishing company (founded in 1885), which specializes in music composed for the stage.

31 Report of interview with Weinbergers, 10 December 1964. From the 'Addendum to a report' following MFS-C (26 November 1964), n.p.

32 Briefly summarized, *The Turn of the Screw* is about a ghost who haunts and possesses two children, *Owen Wingrave* is about a man who sleeps in a haunted room in order to prove his bravery and is later found dead, and *Death In Venice* is about the unrequited love of an artist for a young boy. For detailed synopses see Stanley Sadie ed. *The New Grove Dictionary of Opera*, Vols. 1–4, London: Macmillan, 1992.

collecting textual variants from the British Museum, but she had conveniently married Ralph Vaughan Williams in 1953, just three years after the National Federation's first musical commission received its premiere. In her biography, she fondly recollects the *Folk Songs* commission:

> ... there were so many lovely tunes, so many versions of each song, that he [Ralph] had an enjoyable time, bringing down volume after volume of the *Folk Song Journal* from the gallery and playing through the possible melodies while I was sent to the British Museum to look for variants of words.[33]

Williamson's choice of librettist was not based on Ursula Vaughan Williams's status as the widow of the famous English composer, but on her capacities as a leading literary figure, who, by the Music Festival in 1969, had published five books of verse, a biography, two novels, and libretti for cantatas by Vaughan Williams and Anthony Milner, and for one-act plays set by Elizabeth Maconchy, Charles Camilleri and David Barlow.[34]

In the 'First Notice to Counties' which was issued to the Institutes on 10 December 1965, Ursula Vaughan Williams explained the background to her libretto:

> Except for Agnes Strickland's *Lives of the Queens of England*, published in 1851, there is not, as far as I know, any history book written about women from a woman's point of view. When Malcolm Williamson asked me for a libretto for the choral work commissioned for the Federation of Women's Institutes, he very generously left the choice of subject to me and I thought it might be interesting to explore the centuries from this angle.[35]

The libretto is based on a series of episodes about the lives of British women during the previous 1000 years, starkly contrasting women's achievements and sufferings. The work comprises eight sections grouped by type of event (rather than chronology), and which provide glimpses into the lives of ordinary women. A chorus of embroiderers links the work together.

The Brilliant and The Dark opens with 'Landscape', which tells of the lives of rich and poor women in the nineteenth century and the Peasants' Revolt of 1381. 'Seascape' is two stories, the first of which is about women in the sixteenth century who watched their husbands and sons set sail to the New World, and the second about a girl whose man had been kidnapped by the Press Gangs in the eighteenth century. 'Dark Scherzo' tells of the Dissolution of the Monasteries in 1536, the Plague in 1665, witch-hunting in 1612 and martyrdom by fire in 1555. The fourth section is titled 'The Educationist' in which a contralto solo sings of greater opportunities for women outside the confines of the home. The fifth section, 'Summer Dance of

---

33 Ursula Vaughan Williams, *R.V.W.: A Biography of Ralph Vaughan Williams*, pp. 92–3. The term 'happy link' is used in a document entitled 'The Story of *The Brilliant and The Dark*, National Music Festival 1969', n.p.

34 These are referred to in the biography of Ursula Vaughan Williams in the programme to *The Brilliant and The Dark*, London: Novello and Co. Ltd., 1969, p. 21. The one-act play Ursula Vaughan Williams wrote for Maconchy is the comic-opera, *The Sofa*, which was premiered on 13 December 1959.

35 'First Notice to the Counties' (dated 10 December 1965).

the Old and Young' recalls old legends, and is followed by 'Double Lament' about the Wars of the Roses. The penultimate episode, 'Spring Dance', celebrates May Days in the seventeenth century and twelfth-century songs of the troubadours. In 'Lachrymae' the Embroiderers sing about the futility of war:

> War is our enemy,
> War is our enemy above all others.
> Wars of attrition,
> Wars of desolation binding the wealth and talent of a nation to fight at once on earth, sea and air.
> There is no safety left for any creature,
> Man makes himself an enemy of nature.
> Why should he waste the world, and why despair?[36]

The work ends with a series of events, recalling the Battle of Hastings in 1066, the Crusades of 1250, the Civil War in 1640, the Crimean War of 1854–1856, and the two World Wars. Only two women are named in the libretto: King Harold's mistress, Edith Swan-Neck, who searched for his body after the Battle of Hastings and Florence Nightingale, who campaigned for medical supplies during the Crimean War. Ursula Vaughan Williams wrote that these two historical figures were symbolic: Edith Swan-Neck represented women who have lost their loves through war and Florence Nightingale represented women who have comforted and helped others through skill and courage.[37] The choice of these two women appears significant. They both adhere to women's 'traditional' roles as wives and caregivers, rather than being powerful decision-makers such as Cleopatra, Bodeccia, or Elizabeth I, who, despite being key figures in the history of women, actively challenged female 'traditional' roles (and therefore threatened rather than adhered to patriarchal domination). Other (unnamed) women in the libretto also celebrate their 'traditional' roles. The 'poor women' in 'Landscape' refer to Eve spinning to clothe her children, and the 'abbesses' in the 'Dark Scherzo' celebrate women's roles as providers of charity.

Although the sentiments of these women can be seen to correspond to the concept of 'moderate feminism', there is a sense that *The Brilliant and The Dark* embodied the strongest form of feminism experienced in the National Federation so far over the 50-year period. This can be seen, for example, in the 'Aria' (sung by an alto soloist called 'The Educationist'), which overtly questioned whether women's roles would ever be recognized. 'The Educationist' sings:

> We are one half of the nation, still in bondage:
> A whisper, a hope, a promise, after so long a bondage may we not be heard?
> We have endured, may we not speak for life?
> Fulfil our talents, share and be set free?
> A hope, a promise, a truth.
> We who are life givers shall stand between life and death,
> From hearth and garden, bed and board, lovers, wives, widows,

---

36 Malcolm Williamson, Vocal score of *The Brilliant and The Dark*, London: Josef Weinberger Ltd., 1966, pp. 107–109.

37 'The story of *The Brilliant and The Dark*. National Music Festival 1969', n.p.

From life and death or wisdom has been learned,
Let loving kindness light the world and shine for war deceives and breaks all hopes,
All lives.
A hope, a promise, a light,
After such long endurance set us free and let us speak for life.[38]

Although Ursula Vaughan Williams chose the topic of the libretto, the image of womanhood in *The Brilliant and The Dark*, which promoted women's 'traditional' roles and their empowerment within them, was one that mirrored the articles on women in *Home and Country*. To celebrate the journal's fiftieth anniversary, it published a series of articles titled 'Woman in a Man's World' in 1969 about members who had created or risen to positions in the community that would have been unimaginable 50 years before. The profiles included Doreen Wright (of Chenies and Latimer Institute, Buckinghamshire), who was a garage business owner, Anne Hennar (of Lilbourne Institute, Northamptonshire), who was a qualified electrical engineer and Ann Scampton (of Chew Magna Institute, Somerset), who was an architect, among others.[39] These articles and the libretto of *The Brilliant and The Dark* indicate that by 1969 there was a heightened sense of women's achievements within the organization, and the National Federation recognized itself as having a prominent role relating to the promotion and empowerment of women.

The Music Festival Ad Hoc Committee

The Music Festival Ad Hoc Committee was established on 25 September 1964 to deal exclusively with the planning and organization of the 1969 national event. It did not include any members who had played a role in the 1950 Singing Festival Ad Hoc Committee, and was five times the size: 30 members, as opposed to six. The majority of the members of the Music Festival Ad Hoc Committee were members of the Executive Committee who had previously served on other Sub-Committees before being elected or co-opted to the higher office. In addition to the four Officers of the National Federation (comprising the Chairman Gabrielle Pike, Vice-Chairmen Sylvia Gray and Lady Hemingford and Treasurer Pat Jacob), there were eight other members of the Executive Committee: Lady Anglesey, Joan Battle, Mrs M.A. Brooke, Miss Buddug-Jones, Olive Farquharson, Mrs Travers, Cherry Vooght and Miss Withall. The Music Festival Ad Hoc Committee also included members who had served on the Music and Drama Sub-Committee, as well as existing members: Mrs May, Mrs Powell, Mrs Payne, Mary Lake, Miss Bower and Mrs Hudson. The remaining 12 members were neither members of the Executive Committee nor of the Music and Drama Sub-Committee. Apart from Mrs Mounsey, Miss King and Mrs Barling, little detail is known about the remaining members: Mrs Bowers, Mrs

---

38 Malcolm Williamson, Vocal score of *The Brilliant and The Dark*, pp. 59–62.
39 'Woman in a Man's World', *Home and Country* vol. 50 no. 1 (January 1969): p. 11; vol. 50 no.2 (February 1969): p. 54; and vol. 50 no. 5 (May 1969): p. 189 respectively. Others included an officer for nature conservation, an administrator in the civil service, a prize-winning dairy farmer, and an undertaker.

Braine, Mrs Burnham, Lady Chaplin, Mrs Hackett Paine, Mrs Joslin, Mrs Vincent, Miss Unwin and Mrs Wells.

Williamson was invited to discuss the commission before any contracts were signed. His ideas for the commission, which were discussed at a meeting on 26 November 1964, are summarized as follows:

a) A piece either lasting about 40 or 45 minutes in length, or in two parts of 40 or 50 minutes.
b) Might have a dramatic quality and a theme which might be allegorical, historical or idealistic.
c) It could comprise four part, three part, two part and unison items to allow for choirs of varying standards and interest.
d) He suggested a small orchestra and the possibility of four pianos with eight pianists selected or auditioned from WI members also the inclusion of a very limited number of solo parts since he felt that there must be trained singers in the movement.
e) He suggested having some choirs in the gallery and that colour and interest could be added by the use of various colours and lighting.[40]

However, the National Federation hoped he would compose a longer work and offered a fee of £3000 for a choral opera lasting about 90 minutes. Williamson rejected the offer but, rather than lose the commission, was willing to negotiate another fee, which indicates that he was not motivated primarily by financial gain but by genuine interest in the organization's undertaking. It seems most likely the National Federation reconsidered its financial arrangements and offered Williamson a higher fee, as the possibility of a shorter work of 50 minutes, which it was hoped would allow a reduction in the proposed fee, was only briefly considered by the Music Festival Ad Hoc Committee.[41]

It seems that Williamson had ultimate authority over the work. Although the minutes state that during the early plans for the commission he had been 'glad to consider suggestions for themes, as much thought and research would be needed to find just the right idea', there is no mention of members of the Sub-Committee or Executive Committee opposing any of his ideas.[42] Indeed, his active involvement with the commission during the planning of the festival is symptomatic of Williamson's commitment to the event as a whole. This enabled the Music Festival Ad Hoc Committee to make decisions quickly and in the confidence of having his agreement and support. Furthermore, it enabled the Committee to turn the situation to its advantage in its application to the Arts Council for a grant, even though the Council did not normally provide financial assistance for commissions. As part of their flexible approach, the Council was apparently prepared to consider making some contribution towards the cost of a performance for which the composer had been actively involved in the preparations.[43]

---

40   MFS-C (26 November 1964), n.p.
41   'Addendum to Report' on 10 December 1964 recorded after MFS-C (26 November 1964), n.p.
42   MFS-C (26 November 1964), n.p.
43   MFS-C (10 March 1965), n.p.

The Preparatory Conference, November 1966

At an early stage in the festival's preparations, the Music Festival Ad Hoc Committee held a preparatory conference in London which introduced *The Brilliant and The Dark* to official county representatives, 'observer visitors' from the village Institutes, county music advisers, LEA representatives, and members of the Executive Committee. The conference began with an overview of the festival's organization with questions and discussion led by the Chairman of the Music Festival Ad Hoc Committee, Mrs Travers. This was followed by Ursula Vaughan Williams's description of the libretto, then a play-through of the work sung by the Ambrosian Singers[44] with the soprano Nancy Evans and mezzo-soprano April Cantelo (accompanied by Williamson on the piano).[45] The motivation behind the use of such eminent soloists was to produce a good recording that could be used in the village Institutes to help conductors and the training of choirs during the county and area festivals.[46] Dods, who had been chosen by Williamson to conduct the premiere, led a session on the structure and selection of choirs, and the conference concluded with a discussion on the possibilities of producing the work in village Institutes after its premiere.[47]

Whereas the preparatory conference for the Singing Festival in 1950 had highlighted problems felt at local level with the organization of the event, the London conference for *The Brilliant and The Dark* revealed delegates' uncertainties about the music. In particular, the official report refers to comments made by the Cornwall Music Adviser who questioned the suitability of the work for the organization and whether it should finish on such 'a note of depression'. The report of the conference cites Williamson's reply:

> It would have been quite easy to write a lighter piece and not stir people up. Although it was a serious ending as opposed to a 'pretty pretty' ending there was a hope of peace, but to make people think, it seemed necessary to put the tragedy and loss at the end. It was not difficult to write something much lighter and less worthwhile but he had understood that the Committee wanted something with meat in it. It was not a sermon, it was not a tract. It was a work of art related to life. It was intended to make people think and to leave something with them after the performance had ended …[48]

---

44 I have been unable to find out much about the Ambrosian Singers, apart from their being a London choir formed in 1952 by John McCarthy, *The New Grove Dictionary of Music Online*, L. Macy (ed.) (Accessed 1 September 2004), <http.www.grovemusic.com>.

45 MFS-C (20 September 1966), n.p. Williamson dedicated his *Six English Lyrics* (1966) to Nancy Evans.

46 However, due to technical difficulties, a recording could not be made at the London Conference. It was re-recorded (using the same performers) a month later. MFS-C (28 February 1967), n.p.

47 The choice of Marcus Dods as conductor was wholly Williamson's, and based on his previous experience of working with him and amateur musicians. MFS-C (6 May 1965), n.p. 'Agenda' for the London Conference on 1 November 1966.

48 'Report of the Conference Tuesday November 1st, 1966.'

Ursula Vaughan Williams also responded to criticism about the ending, saying that members of the Women's Institute were 'serious people and serious minded' and therefore, she felt, required a thought-provoking libretto.[49]

Conductors' Conferences, November 1967

As part of the festival's preparations, the National Federation also hosted two Conductors' Conferences in November 1967. It was originally envisaged that a single day event would be held in London (to which representative conductors would be invited), but Dods recommended that a series of regional days be held, as both he and Williamson were keen to reach as many choirs as possible. On both practical and financial grounds, the Music Festival Ad Hoc Committee decided to have events on two days: the first in Leeds with Williamson and the second in London led by Dods.[50] Scheduled to coincide with the preparations for the county festivals, and linked to the new Conductor's Training Scheme, these conferences were intended to allow conductors from the village Institutes the opportunity to be helped and advised by the professionals, as well as to provide feedback from the Institutes about attitudes to the work. The minutes reported that the 120 people who attended the London conference knew the work better than the 72 who had attended the Conductor's Day in Leeds, which indicates that either interest in the festival was southern-based, or that the standard in musicianship was lower in the north.[51] There do not appear to have been any adverse reports of *The Brilliant and The Dark* from the Institutes at these conferences. This suggests that Jersey Institute, which did not enter the Festival partly because it did not have enough members for a choir but also was reported not to like the music, was an exception.[52]

The County and Regional Festivals

Like the Singing Festival, the preliminary rounds for the 1969 Music Festival first took place in the counties, followed by regional festivals; and choirs were able to choose the sections that they entered depending on their level of ability, ranging from the part of the Embroiderers, to unison, two-part, three-part, or four-part settings. The selection of choirs at county level was carried out by adjudicators recommended by Williamson: Lionel Nutley, Iris Lemare (who had adjudicated the area festivals of the 1950 Singing Festival), John Churchill, Hubert Dawkes, John Aldin, Stanley Vann, William Llewellyn, Ronald Surplice and R.A. Smith. However, unlike the position in 1950, the adjudicators were given guidelines. The minutes reported: 'County Adjudicators will be asked to work on the basis of *an average* of five choirs to go through, though the figures may be lower where there is a very small entry or

---

49 'Report of the Conference Tuesday November 1st, 1966.'
50 Executive Minutes vol. 30, MFS-C (19 October 1965), p. 328.
51 MFS-C (5 December 1967), n.p.
52 Executive Minutes vol. 30 (27 April 1967), pp. 1284–5.

where there are insufficient choirs of a high enough standard.'[53] Although the criteria for selection are unclear, it appears that the Music Festival Ad Hoc Committee hoped to achieve representation for all counties at the final London event.[54]

It seems that choirs entered for the Music Festival rather slowly. The Music Festival Ad Hoc Committee stated in December 1967 that to date only 181 choirs had signed up. The Committee did not consider this to be enough, and attempts were made to encourage Institutes to enter the festival, which included issuing a notice of 'an encouraging nature' in *Home and Country*.[55] Williamson and the Music Festival Ad Hoc Committee members also visited a number of Institutes in an attempt to popularize the festival.[56] Entries in the minute books suggest that such visits had positive effects: following Joan Battle's visit to Devon, it was reported that 'there seemed to be much more interest in the Festival as entries [for the county festivals] had been received'.[57] Furthermore, four months later the minutes recorded that the number of choirs entering for the county festivals had almost doubled, to a total of 345.[58]

Unlike the Singing Festival, the regional rounds of the 1969 Music Festival allowed supporters and members of the public to attend (with the exception of the Taunton Festival which had limited space). Although no press invitations were sent out and photographers were discouraged because they might distract the performers and conductors, it appears that the Music Festival Ad Hoc Committee was keen for the work to be promoted not only amongst Institute members, but also as much as possible on a local level.[59]

It is likely that Williamson was not involved with the regional festivals due to a full compositional schedule and recent premieres of his works, which included *Quintet* premiered on 23 March 1968, *From A Child's Garden* on 24 April 1968, *Knights in Shining Armour* and *The Snow Wolf* on 29 April 1968, and *The Growing Castle* on 13 August 1968. He appears to have delegated the task to Dods, who adjudicated all of the regional and metropolitan competitions (held in Leicester, Chester, Leeds, Cambridge, Cardiff, Taunton, Solihull and two in London). There is little detail about these festivals apart from Dods's hectic timetable, in which he was allocated an average of ten minutes per entry and adjudicated around 30 choirs per day. At the end of each set he listed those who had been selected to perform at the final London event, gave constructive criticism on the work each day, and conducted a session on massed singing.[60] The minutes for a Sub-Committee meeting on 28 February 1969 reported that the eliminating rounds had all been completed.[61]

The most significant difference between the National Federation's two national music events was the inclusion of soloists and pianists in the 1969 Music Festival.

---

53 Original underlining. MFS-C (31 May 1967), n.p.

54 MFS-C (31 May 1967), n.p. refers to Joan Battle working on the notes for adjudicators, and that Dods had agreed to assist in preparing them.

55 MFS-C (5 December 1967), n.p.

56 Ibid., n.p.

57 MFS-C (6 February 1968), n.p.

58 MFS-C (2 April 1968), n.p.

59 Letter to all County Press Officers from Mrs M. Millard (dated 18 October 1968).

60 MFS-C (9 July 1968), n.p.

61 MFS-C (28 February 1969), n.p.

Candidates who were considered suitable were recommended by county music representatives and auditioned at county, regional and national levels, with the final selection being made by Williamson at an audition held in London on 7 March 1969. The soloists' test pieces were based on Williamson's works; for pianists, he listed two of the pieces from *Travel Diaries* for the county round and one of the *Five Preludes for Piano* for the regional festival; and for singers he chose one piece from his *Six English Lyrics* and a song of the entrant's own choice for the county rounds and a short piece from *The Brilliant and The Dark* chosen by the entrant for the regional festival. It is unclear what music was required at the final London audition.

Most of the vocal soloists selected had a musical background: Sylvia Campbell (who sang A Sister in the Civil War in *Lachrymae*) trained at the Webber-Douglas School of Singing and Dramatic Art; Anne Gee (who sang The Unwilling Novice in the *Dark Scherzo*) had studied singing and performed in operas and oratorios both in Britain and abroad; Audrey Hughes (who sang Edith Swan-Neck in *Lachrymae*) had spent two years in Sadler's Wells Opera Chorus; and Barbara Justham (who sang the part of the Lancastrian wife in the *Double Lament*) had sung with the Carl Rosa Company and at the Royal Opera House. Enid Lloyd Roberts (who sang the part of the Yorkist mother in the *Double Lament*), Patricia Viles (who sang Johnnie's Lover in *Seascape*), Margery Would (who sang The Last Survivor of the Plague in the *Dark Scherzo*) and Elizabeth Lamb (who sang The Educationist) had little previous singing experience. All of the eight pianists chosen were accomplished musicians: Marjorie Blackburn had trained at the Leipzig Conservatoire, Janet Cannetty-Clarke, Hilda Evans, Margaret Payne and Isabel Thompson at the Royal Academy of Music, and Shena Neame and Felicity White at the Royal College of Music. Doris Catheside appears to have been the only pianist who had not trained at a conservatoire.[62]

Although Williamson could have chosen professional soloists such as Cantelo and Evans to perform at the premiere, he decided instead to have members of the Women's Institute perform as vocal soloists and pianists – a decision that highlights his commitment to the amateur nature of the festival. However, his amateur commitment did not extend to the use of a WI Orchestra or a WI conductor, despite the fact that a members' orchestra was included in the initial plans for the 1969 Music Festival and that the national scheme for the training of conductors within the organization had been launched at the music conference held on 16 March 1967.

Publicity

The publicity campaign for *The Brilliant and The Dark* was somewhat different from that for the Singing Festival, which suggests that valuable experience had been gained from the national events which separated the two Music Festivals: the 1957 Drama Festival, the 1960 Handicrafts Exhibition, the 1963 Art Exhibition, and the 1965 Golden Jubilee celebrations. It is clear from the minute books that the Executive Committee had become forward planners, thinking up to five years in

---

62 Programme to *The Brilliant and The Dark*, performed on 3 June 1969 at the Royal Albert Hall.

advance with regard to their next national event. During the peak of the preparations for *The Brilliant and The Dark*, a meeting of the Executive Committee reported:

> ... as it was agreed in June the Committee would consider what form a National Event would take in 1972 or 1973, and, should the subject have an impact on the Countryside, the Committee would think very carefully of what might be said at the Countryside Conference with regard to WI contribution to European Conservation Year 1970.[63]

The publicity of *The Brilliant and The Dark* was similarly well planned, with a trio of articles for *Home and Country* arranged at the first meeting of the Music Festival Ad Hoc Committee on 22 February 1966 – a full three years before the work's premiere. Honor Wyatt's interviews with Ursula Vaughan Williams and Williamson were published in *Home and Country* in May 1966 and July 1966 respectively, followed by Williamson's own article in September 1966 in which he explained the aims behind the work.[64] Other articles that appeared in *Home and Country* included progress reports, such as Battle's 'Taking Shape', that reported on the Festival's developments, and news of activities in the counties.[65]

Whilst *Home and Country* was used as a means to stimulate interest within the organization, plans to launch the publicity campaign outside the organization, which included specifically targeting music journals, were recorded in the minutes of 31 May 1967.[66] However, arrangements for *The Brilliant and The Dark*'s publicity campaign were severely hampered by Williamson's restrictions. The minutes state:

> Miss Unwin reported that she had discussed this [i.e. publicity] with Mr Williamson and he was adverse to any form of statement which could be interpreted as a review or criticism of the work until after the Festival Performance. It was agreed therefore that any information supplied to the Musical or National Press must be of the nature of 'Coming Events' rather than a description of the work.[67]

Although Williamson's motivations are unclear, in view of the harsh treatment which some of his works had received from critics, it is likely that he wanted to avoid anything that could have had a detrimental effect on the impact of the premiere.[68] However, reports of activities in the counties suggest that before its premiere, Institutes publicized *The Brilliant and The Dark* by other means, which included

---

63 Executive Minutes vol. 31, EC (23 May 1968), p. 355.

64 Honor Wyatt, 'Ursula Vaughan Williams', *Home and Country* vol. 48 no. 5 (May 1966): p. 179, and 'Malcolm Williamson', *Home and Country* vol. 48 no. 7 (July 1966): p. 267. Malcolm Williamson '*The Brilliant and The Dark*', *Home and Country* vol. 48 no. 9 (September 1966): p. 315.

65 Joan Battle, 'Taking Shape', *Home and Country* vol. 49 no. 9 (September 1968): p. 311.

66 MFS-C (31 May 1967), n.p.

67 Original capitals. MFS-C (10 July 1967), n.p.

68 Articles which refer to reviews of Williamson's works include Colin Mason's 'The Music of Malcolm Williamson', *The Musical Times* vol. 103 (1967): pp. 757–9; and Stephen Walsh's 'Williamson the Many-Sided', *Music and Musicians* (July 1965): pp. 26–9, continued p. 55.

musical extracts being performed at an Agricultural Exhibition, the Denman Cup Exhibit, and the 1968 Royal Show.[69]

Whereas the publicity for the 1950 Singing Festival had been the responsibility of one individual, it appears that the campaign for the 1969 Music Festival not only involved the aid of other Sub-Committees (such as the *Home and Country* Sub-Committee), but also a member of the Music Festival Ad Hoc Committee, Miss Unwin. Although Mrs Millard (Head of the Press and Publicity Department) and Miss Unwin played a vital role in writing press releases, contacting the press and organizing photographs, it was Lorna Moore who secured the greatest external publicity for *The Brilliant and The Dark*. Moore had a long involvement with the organization, having been editor of *Home and Country* (a position from which she resigned in December 1944 on account of ill health).

Moore's involvement with the BBC as Chief Producer of Arts Talks proved useful for the National Federation's publicity department. It was she who led negotiations with the then Dr Brian Trowell (Chief Assistant of Opera at the BBC) for a recording of the Festival's performance[70] and Godfrey Baseley (then Producer of the radio programme *The Archers*), who even worked in references to Ambridge WI being eliminated at the regional festival into one episode of *The Archers*.[71] Other radio publicity included an interview between Thea Musgrave, Ursula Vaughan Williams and Williamson on 'The Lively Arts' programme, which was broadcast on 18th November 1966 (on the BBC's Home Service). It covered the background to the libretto and Williamson's musical setting for amateur voices. In addition, the BBC broadcast a 'Woman's Hour' report by Nancy Wise (on 15 May 1969) which included brief interviews with Ursula Vaughan Williams, the Director John Cox and Institute members who were participating in the Festival (Joan Battle, Mrs Somerset, Kathleen Locke, Elizabeth Lamb and Jean Read). Interspersed were excerpts of the music.[72]

Negotiations with the BBC for a radio broadcast were pursued for a number of reasons. Firstly, the National Federation was unwilling to provide a guarantee of 2,000 record sales, which the publishers Weinbergers had demanded as part of a recording deal.[73] A year earlier the Music Festival Ad Hoc Committee had pointed out to a representative of Weinbergers, Mr Benson, that in their opinion, a record of the festival 'was not likely to have great sales to WI members who were not on the whole great buyers of expensive long-playing records'.[74] Secondly, a television programme was regarded as 'undesirable' because of the limited rehearsal time. And

---

69 MFS-C (22 September 1967), n.p. refers to the agricultural show and the Royal Show (the latter used Peter Rice's designs). MFS-C (2 April 1968), n.p refers to the Denman Cup Exhibit.

70 MFS-C (9 July 1968), n.p.

71 MFS-C (6 February 1968), n.p.

72 'Women's Institute, Malcolm Williamson, TLO 45 TF 245H' transcript of 'The Lively Arts' Programme, 11–12.30pm (dated 4 November 1966), and TLO 46 F 241H (dated 18 November 1966), both from LIV T297 Talk Scripts, 'Item from "Woman's Hour" *The Brilliant and The Dark*' transmitted 15 May 1969 from 'Woman's Hour, M101/102' at the BBC Written Archives Centre.

73 MFS-C (25 April 1969), n.p.

74 MFS-C (2 April 1968), n.p.

thirdly, enquiries about making a film had proved that it would be too expensive and difficult to produce.[75]

The BBC agreed to broadcast the Festival. On 19 August 1968, Trowell wrote to Battle: 'Though I can make no promises at this stage, the project looks attractive; I would expect Radio 4 or Radio 3 (Music Programme) to take quite an interest in a venture such as this, with a vast ready-made radio audience.'[76] In addition to the potential audience of 700,000 listeners, the publicity it had received in *The Archers*, and the amateur status of the choir (which meant that only the professionals needed to be paid) enabled a contract between the BBC and the National Federation to be secured. *The Brilliant and The Dark* was recorded at its premiere (rather than broadcast live) so that gaps could be edited, explanatory narrations could be inserted into the programme and members who had participated in the premiere could tune in.

The Premiere and its Reception

The premiere of *The Brilliant and The Dark* took place after the National Federation's AGM at the Royal Albert Hall. But unlike the 1950 Singing Festival, additional music was not included in the programme (apart from Dods's arrangement of the National Anthem which was specially written for the event) and two performances took place on the same day: one at 5.30pm and the other at 8pm. Although it is unclear who attended the performances, Williamson's list of celebrities included Sir William Walton, Yehudi Menhuin, Flora Robson, Frederick Ashton, Margot Fonteyn, Dame Eva Turner, Sybil Thorndike and Hugh Casson, Sir Laurence Olivier, Edith Evans and Peggy Ashcroft. It is likely that Sir Arthur Bliss attended the 5.30pm performance in his capacity as a representative of the Royal family, having been appointed Master of the Queen's Music in 1953. The Duchess of Kent attended the 8pm performance.[77] The fact that two performances were included in the early planning of the Festival, and that celebrities were invited to both, highlights the attention and publicity that the Festival organizers hoped to attract.[78]

The four resolutions passed at the AGM on 2 June 1969 did not overshadow the premiere of *The Brilliant and The Dark* as the AGM's decisions had done in 1950.[79] Unlike *Folk Songs*, *The Brilliant and The Dark* received a good number of reviews in the national newspapers, aided by Millard's publicity photographs (which

---

75 MFS-C (20 September 1968), n.p. and (28 February 1969), n.p. Two further performances of *The Brilliant and The Dark* took place on 11 July 1969 at the Royal Albert Hall.

76 A letter from Brian Trowell to Joan Battle (dated 19 August 1968). R27/1 182/1 OPERA *The Brilliant and the Dark* (1967–1969) file held at BBC Written Archive Centre.

77 MFS-C (20 September 1968), n.p.

78 MFS-C (20 July 1965), n.p.

79 The resolutions called for married quarters to be provided in homes for the elderly and in geriatric hospitals, a report on the effects of artificial sweeteners, a new campaign to conserve the countryside, and a call for a different method of election to the Executive Committee.

appeared in *The Evening Standard* and *The Guardian*) of the dancers from East Sussex Institutes dressed in their costumes.[80]

Reviews of *The Brilliant and The Dark* in the national press reveal critics' uncertainty about the nature and quality of the work. Auriol Stevens described it in *The Guardian* as 'the ultimate in amateur theatricals', Stanley Sadie in *The Times* as 'a lavish pageant', the critic for the *Evening Standard* as 'operetta' and 'A.E.P' in the *Daily Telegraph* as an 'operatic pageant'. The only critic who quoted the National Federation's press handout, which described it as 'an operatic sequence for women's voices', was Alan Blyth in the *Financial Times*.[81]

Figure 5.1: From the premiere of Malcolm Williamson's *The Brilliant and The Dark*.

---

80 It is likely that approximately twenty seats were allocated for the press for each performance. OFS-C (25 June 1969), n.p.

81 Auriol Stevens, 'The WI Spectacular', *The Guardian* (2 June 1969): n.p; Stanley Sadie, 'Opera; A lavish pageant of women's work', *The Times* (4 June 1969): n.p; 'Focus On the Operetta', *The Evening Standard* (4 June 1969), p. 48; A.E.P., '1,000 women in operatic pageant', *Daily Telegraph* (4 June 1969): n.p; and Alan Blyth, 'Albert Hall; *The Brilliant and The Dark*', *Financial Times* (4 June 1969): n.p.

Recalling comments made in 1950 about *Folk Songs*, critics were united in their admiration for Williamson's ability to create variety in a work for all-female voices. A.E.P. in the *Daily Telegraph* wrote: 'I can think of no one who could have more successfully fulfilled the requirements of such a commission, so inventive was the music in its exploitation of an ostensibly limited medium.'[82] Similarly, Blyth wrote in the *Financial Times*: 'Williamson has gratefully seized the opportunity of writing by and large melodically inclined music for women's voices in all kinds of combination and successfully avoided monotony ...'.[83] Sadie wrote in *The Times*:

> Williamson was the right composer for this project. The style was to be within the scope of small WI choirs; he pours out long, fluent diatonic melodies, with a pastoral air for a whiff of the sea, with imaginatively dancing rhythms, once with an apt touch of the cloister, and with darker hints here and there, sometimes in the melodic lines often supplied by orchestral brass ... and Williamson handles the women's voices, solo and choral, with the greatest skill and variety.[84]

The Brilliant and The Dark was reviewed in only one academic music journal, *The Musical Times*, in which Sadie described Williamson's music as 'fluent, very tuneful, destined for choirs of no great skill ...' and referred to his admiration for Williamson's ability to provide variety through both different combinations of voices and variation in mood.[85] The absence of reviews in other academic journals suggests that, as with *Folk Songs*, reviewers in academia did not take *The Brilliant and The Dark* seriously because it was commissioned for amateur musicians.

As in reviews of *Folk Songs*, critics referred to the limitations of composing for female voices, but otherwise their tone had changed. In particular, reviewers of *The Brilliant and The Dark* expressed surprise at the quality of the singing. Sadie wrote in *The Musical Times*: 'There was some excellent solo singing (how many Janet Bakers are there who prefer to stay at home and remain amateurs?)' and in *The Times*: 'There were some outstandingly good solo singers and very capable choral work under Marcus Dods.'[86] A reviewer signed as 'A.E.P.' wrote in the *Daily Telegraph* that the standard of performance of both the soloists and choir was 'outstanding', and Blyth described the contralto solo by Elizabeth Lamb as 'richly sung'.[87]

The Brilliant and The Dark was first broadcast on 30 September 1969 on Radio 3. Whereas the premiere had captured critics' attention, the BBC's Audience Research Report reveals that the first broadcast attracted only a fraction of the listeners that had been anticipated, even though 100,000 listeners was considered 'a fairly unusual

---

82 A.E.P., '1,000 Women in Operatic Pageant', *Daily Telegraph*.
83 Alan Blyth, 'Albert Hall; *The Brilliant and The Dark*', *Financial Times*.
84 Stanley Sadie, 'Opera: A Lavish Pageant of Women's Work', *The Times*.
85 Stanley Sadie, 'Review of *The Brilliant and The Dark*', *The Musical Times* vol. 110 (1969): p. 755.
86 Stanley Sadie, 'Opera: A Lavish Pageant of women's Work', *The Times*.
87 A.E.P., '1,000 Women in Operatic Pageant', *Daily Telegraph*, and Alan Blyth, 'Albert Hall; *The Brilliant and The Dark*', *Financial Times*.

feat for a modern work'.[88] The disappointing number of listeners was attributed to the BBC's failure to notify the National Federation of the broadcast in enough time for the information to be distributed amongst Women's Institute members. In a letter to Trowell, Battle explained:

> We immediately sent particulars to all County Secretaries, County Festival Secretaries and County Press Officers, but it was a bad time of year, with many County Secretaries still on holiday, and many individual Music and Press Personnel also away. I know that many of these did make every effort to get the news around, but it was physically impossible to get complete circulation.[89]

Trowell offered to repeat the broadcast of *The Brilliant and The Dark* and requested that Battle find out when would be a good time for Institutes to tune in.[90] Battle replied that she had gauged opinion from Institute members whilst teaching a course on *The Brilliant and The Dark* at Denman College and guaranteed that a broadcast at a different time of day would secure a larger audience, but did not specifically state a time. She wrote to Trowell:

> Some of my audience had already seen [the live performance] and heard it [on the radio], but were still as interested, and those who had not done either were also eager to hear about it, and when I told them of the possibility of another broadcast there was great jubilation all around! As I said in my previous letter, I am sure that if the proposed broadcast could be at a time when members and their families could listen there would be a very large audience indeed.[91]

The timing of the repeat broadcast was also discussed with Julian Budden (then Producer of Radio 3). A memo written to the controller on 20 April 1970 reveals that Budden had objections to another broadcast of the work on Radio 3's Music programme. He wrote:

> Although described as an operatic sequence, *The Brilliant and The Dark* is not an opera at all and should never have landed in our court in the first place. It contains no sequence of events nor any real impersonation, since the various Edith Swannecks and Florence Nightingales are no more operatic principals than the crowning figures in carnival floats are *dramatis personae*. Fifty years ago, Williamson would have been only too happy to have called it a cantata, a masque or what you will. It is not a bad piece. The restricted compass curbs Williamson's tendency to that self-indulgence which mars most of his operas while

---

88 Memo from Brian Trowell to the controller of Radio 1 and 2 (dated 2 December 1969) from R27/1 234/1 OPERA FILE.

89 A letter to Miss S.R. Butcher (secretary to Brian Trowell) from Joan Battle (dated 5 November 1969) from R27/1 234/1 OPERA FILE.

90 A letter from Brian Trowell to Joan Battle (dated 11 November 1969) from R27/1 234/1 OPERA FILE.

91 A letter from Joan Battle to Brian Trowell (dated 17 November 1969) from R27/1 234/1 OPERA FILE.

at the same time allowing full play to his gift for simple but unpredictable melody. I suggest a repeat therefore, <u>but not in one of our hard-contested operatic spaces</u>![92]

Budden rejected a repeat performance for essentially two reasons: firstly he did not consider *The Brilliant and The Dark* to be a serious operatic work, and second he appears to have been critical of Williamson's operas *per se*. In Budden's view, if *The Brilliant and The Dark* had to be repeated, it should not be played during 'peak' listening time on Radio 3.

Budden's comments must have been well heeded, as the second broadcast of *The Brilliant and The Dark* was not given on Radio 3, but followed 'Woman's Hour' on Radio 4 on 30 June 1970 (between 10.15 and 11.30 am). Despite changing the timing and context of the broadcast, the Audience Research Survey indicates that the second broadcast of *The Brilliant and The Dark* attracted even fewer listeners than the first. Trowell wrote to the Head of Audience Research, Mr B.P. Emmett:

> I am a little surprised that this work should only have achieved audiences of 0.2% for the first broadcast and 0.1% for the second. There are, I believe, 750,000 Women's Institute members who were informed of the TXS through the National Federation of Women's Institutes; and there was much talk about the original performances in *The Archers*. Is it possible that specialist groups of this kind are somehow avoiding the BBC's Audience Research Investigations?[93]

Within the context of the average 'reaction index' for Radio 3, which was 68 for an oratorio or choral music and 61 for opera, *The Brilliant and The Dark*'s 58 scored well. It was also the highest among Williamson's recent dramatic works: *Lucky Peter's Journey* reached 56, and *Julius Caesar* and *The Happy Prince* both obtained 50.[94] In comparison with broadcasts of his other operatic works, the listener figures for the broadcasts of *The Brilliant and The Dark* appear therefore to have been good.

The Brilliant and The Dark: After the Premiere

The Music Festival Ad Hoc Committee celebrated the success of the four performances at its final meeting on 19 September 1969. In addition to thanking the professionals who had taken part in the festival, the minutes described Dods's arrangement of the National Anthem as 'an outstanding success', the actors and dancers as 'extremely good and well co-ordinated' and mentioned the 'excellent work' that had been put into the making of the costumes. There appears to have been only one criticism of the festival, which stemmed from some members' dissatisfaction at the cheaper seats being offered only when the more expensive ones had been sold.[95]

---

92 Original underlining. A letter from Julian Budden to the Controller of Radio 3 (dated 20 April 1970) from R27/1 234/1 OPERA FILE.
93 Memo from Brian Trowell to Head of Audience Research (dated 21 August 1970) from R27/1 234/1 OPERA FILE.
94 '*The Brilliant and The Dark* Audience Report' from R27/1 234/1 OPERA FILE.
95 MFS-C (19 September 1969), n.p.

Williamson hoped that smaller dramatic performances of *The Brilliant and The Dark* would take place in the Institutes after its London premiere, and approached Vooght to write a book about the possibilities of different dramatic presentations of the work in the villages.[96] It is likely that this was not pursued following the Music Festival Ad Hoc Committee's decision to allow producers the opportunity to develop and experiment with their own ideas.[97] The number of applications requesting the use of the costumes (from Hertfordshire, East Sussex and Cornwall Federations, among others) indicates that counties were indeed interested in performing the work after its official premiere.[98] In addition, the 'News in the Institutes' section of *Home and Country* recorded that excerpts of *The Brilliant and The Dark* were sung at the Selwood Group Meeting in Somerset,[99] and that performances took place in Cornwall,[100] Staffordshire[101] and Nottinghamshire Federations[102] during 1969 and 1970, which indicates that performances in the Institutes took place on various scales well into 1970.

The Brilliant and The Dark dominated the agendas of music and drama (and later handicrafts) during its three years of preparation in the Institutes and provided a much-needed sense of direction in music policy during the mid to late 1960s. Although it is difficult to assess the recruitment levels in the immediate aftermath of the Festival, the National Federation's Annual Reports indicate that *The Brilliant and The Dark* did not significantly boost membership within the organization: the total for December 1969 was recorded as being 437,283, and by the end of 1970 had increased by only 918 members. The first increase since 1967 was recorded at the end of 1971, when the number of members reached 439,984.[103] However, it seems that some women did join the organization in order to take part in *The Brilliant and The Dark*: Elizabeth Lamb, the contralto soloist at the premiere, joined after hearing about the second Music Festival, but left soon afterwards (to pursue a career as a professional soloist).[104] The lack of a significant number of newcomers may have been because the recruitment campaign was solely based on offering an opportunity to take part in the premiere of *The Brilliant and The Dark*. No other incentives appear to have been offered. For example, the National Federation did not offer discounted tickets to the premiere in return for membership, or encourage members to bring friends to Institute events.

---

96 MFS-C (28 February 1967), n.p.

97 MFS-C (2 April 1968), n.p.

98 MFS-C (26 November 1968), n.p.

99 Mrs K.L. Young, 'News from the Institutes – Somerset Federation', South-Western counties supplement, *Home and Country* vol. 50 no. 7 (July 1969): p. 294.

100 Mrs M. Sharman, 'News from the Institutes – Cornwall Federation', South-Western counties supplement, *Home and Country* vol. 50 no. 8 (August 1969): p. 329.

101 Meredith Brown, 'News from the Institutes – Staffordshire Federation', North-Western counties supplement, *Home and Country* vol. 50 no. 12 (December 1969): p. 506.

102 Mrs M.J. Taylor, 'News from the Institutes – Nottinghamshire Federation', North-Western counties supplement, *Home and Country* vol. 51 no. 8 (August 1970): p. 334.

103 As recorded in the December of each year listed in the NFWI Annual Reports.

104 Recorded in a telephone interview with Elizabeth Lamb on 12 October 2001.

Like *Folk Songs*, *The Brilliant and The Dark* appears not to have made a significant impact outside of the organization. Critics' reviews of *The Brilliant and The Dark* reveal a similar concern with the limitations of composing for all-female voices, but also express surprise at the musical abilities of Institute members. Beyond newspaper reviews it is difficult to gauge the extent to which the Music Festival engaged attention outside the organization, despite two BBC radio broadcasts of the commission. Examination of the Audience Research Reports reveals that Williamson's commission achieved a good audience for a contemporary opera, but raises the question as to whether those who heard the broadcasts of *The Brilliant and The Dark* were usual Radio 3 listeners or Institute members.

Within the organization, *The Brilliant and The Dark* represents the departure in music policy from the promotion of folk song in favour of 'modern' high culture. It also can be seen to affirm the organization's commitment to 'moderate feminism', which encouraged women to empower themselves within traditional feminine roles at a time when the second 'wave' of feminism was starting to gain momentum. In addition, the 1969 Music Festival boosted confidence in members' musical abilities to the extent that the possibility of Institute members becoming professional musicians was considered. As a direct result of the premiere the National Society Choir was formed in 1970 (discussed in the next chapter). It was these professional singers who maintained the legacy of *The Brilliant and The Dark*; a commercial recording was made for mass production to commemorate the organization's Silver Jubilee in 1977.

Chapter 6

Afterburn: The National Society Choir, 1969–1975

Whereas the premiere of *Folk Songs* had left a void in music activities (until the mid-1960s), the aftermath of *The Brilliant and The Dark* saw an active music policy that resulted in the formation of the National Society Choir. By the end of 1969, there appears to have been an air of confidence within the National Federation, not only in members' musical abilities, but also about the future of music within the organization.[1]

The Formation of the National Society Choir

The idea of a National Society Choir came from a Music Sub-Committee member, Janet Cannetty-Clarke.[2] The possibility of a small national choir being formed to sing work of high standard and perform at county events was discussed at a meeting of the Music and Drama Sub-Committee held on 15 September 1969.[3] By the next Sub-Committee meeting (which was held in December), the budget for the proposed choir and the venue for the first concert (the Fairfield Halls in Croydon) had been decided, and the nature of the choir had changed: it was now hoped that an area choir could be formed in the south which would be followed by one in the northern counties.[4] Possible conductors were also considered. The minutes reported 'that a nationally known conductor be invited to work with the choir; it would ensure both members' co-operation and the success of the concert'. Names suggested included Antony Hopkins, Dods, and David Willcocks, all of whom were well-known figures in the world of music at the time.[5] Dods's engagements included conducting the BBC Concert Orchestra and BBC Chorus, and the London Concert Orchestra (which appears to have been based at the Fairfield Halls in Croydon),[6] Willcocks was involved with conducting the Cambridge University Musical Society (since 1958)

---

   1   Due to the incomplete nature of the archival material, the final section focuses on the South East Section (which later changed its name to the Avalon Singers) rather than the Wales and North-West Section for which there is little detailed information.
   2   A document titled 'Proposed National or Area WI choir' (undated).
   3   Executive Minutes vol. 32, MDS-C (15 September 1969), p. 211.
   4   Executive Minutes vol. 32, MDS-C (10 December 1969), p. 371.
   5   Ibid., p. 371.
   6   References to Dods conducting the BBC Concert Orchestra and BBC Chorus can be found in *The Musical Times* vol. 110 no. 1514 (April 1969): p. 400, and to the London Concert Orchestra in vol. 116 no. 1585 (March 1975): p. 266.

and the Bach Choir in London (since 1960),[7] and Hopkins would have been best known as a broadcaster and lecturer on music.[8]

It is unclear whether Dods or Willcocks were ever approached; but, of the three, the choice of Hopkins as conductor of the National Society Choir, is perhaps the most surprising. Hopkins's fame primarily stemmed from his weekly radio programme, 'Talking About Music' (it ran for a total of 36 years), which discussed the history, content and structure of a major work. By 1970, he had published *Talking About Symphonies* (1961), *Talking About Concertos* (1964) and *Music All Around Me* (1967), and had composed numerous stage works: *Lady Rohesia* (1946), *The Man from Tuscany* (1951), *Scena* (1953), *Three's Company* (1953), *Ten O'Clock Call* (1956), *Hands Across the Sky* (1959), *A Time for Growing* (1967), *Rich Man, Poor Man, Beggar Man, Saint* (1968) and *Dr Musickus* (1969). Hopkins had written only one piece for female voices by this time: *Magnificat and Nunc Dimittis* (1961) which he dedicated to Enid Wood and the girls of Michlefield School. The *Magnificat* is a two part vocal setting with piano or organ accompaniment, and *Nunc Dimittis* is written for an unaccompanied 'echo choir'. The frequent changes in key and tempo in the *Magnificat* and the unaccompanied nature of the second section (which divides into four parts at the end) indicates either that Michlefield School had an advanced choir or that Hopkins had high expectations of amateurs.

Reviews of Hopkins's works often referred to the educational value of his music. Frank Dawes described Hopkins's *Sonatine* (for piano) as 'eminently practicable' and 'eminently useful to children'. The reviewer J.A. Caldwell wrote in *Music & Letters* that his stage work *Doctor Musikus* had a score of educational value.[9] Indeed, it was his stage works for children that attracted the National Federation to Hopkins. A letter asking for him to become involved with the choir drew parallels between *A Time for Growing* (which is about the story of the evolution of the world and the growth of mankind) and *The Brilliant and The Dark*.[10] Mrs Curry, then the administrative secretary for the Music Sub-Committee, wrote:

> The performance of your *Time for Growing* in the Royal Albert Hall last April was greatly enjoyed by many Women's Institute Members. Possibly you saw or heard of the most successful performances given by our members from all parts of England and Wales of Malcolm Williamson's Operatic Sequence *The Brilliant and The Dark* in June and July, also in the Royal Albert Hall. We feel that there is a real link between these two works in that they both brought together amateur choirs with the use of the Arena for dramatic presentation.[11]

---

7 Arthur Jacobs and Ian Carson, 'Sir David Willcocks', *The New Grove Dictionary of Music* vol. 27. 2nd ed. London: Macmillan, 2001, p. 402.

8 Richard Cooke, 'Antony Hopkins', *The New Grove Dictionary of Music* vol. 11. 2nd ed. London: Macmillan, 2001, pp. 697–8.

9 Frank Dawes, 'Modern Piano', *The Musical Times* vol. 113 (July 1972): p. 700, and 'J.E. C[aldwell]', 'Antony Hopkins – *Doctor Musickus*', *Music & Letters* vol. 54 (April 1973): p. 115.

10 Hopkins recalls his work with the Women's Institute choir in his autobiography entitled *Beating Time*. London: Futura Macdonald and Co.1982, pp. 166–8.

11 A letter from Mrs I.L. Curry to Antony Hopkins (dated 29 January 1970).

It seems most likely that it was because of Hopkins's involvement with amateur musicians through his compositions that he was chosen over Dods and Willcocks as conductor of the National Society Choir.

In view of the organization's involvement in training conductors (since the 1930s) and the Choir Leaders' Training Scheme that had recently been launched during the preparations for the 1969 Music Festival, the decision to invite a male conductor may seem somewhat surprising. After all, conducting a female choir adhered to the 'feminine' sphere of conducting. Even if there was not a suitable member from within the organization, Iris Lemare (who had been involved in the adjudication of the area festivals for *Folk Songs* and the regional festivals for *The Brilliant and The Dark*) or a female member of the Music Panel could have been approached.[12] The decision not to consider a female conductor suggests that the National Federation wanted to ensure that the reception of the Society Choir was not hindered by critics' concern with female conductors' abilities, but that it was treated on a par with other choirs on the concert scene.

The music for the first concert was chosen at a meeting of the Music Sub-Committee on 5 May 1970. The programme was essentially a celebration of the organization's past musical achievements. It consisted of extracts from the two music commissions composed for the National Federation, Britten's arrangement of *The Oxen* and songs by Shena Fraser, Imogen Holst, Elizabeth Poston and John Joubert. Only Joubert's works would have been unfamiliar in the National Federation's repertoire.[13] In view of the repertoire chosen, the decision not to include English folk songs (but to include 'new' songs) in the programme suggests that the Music Sub-Committee did not want the choir (or its future activities) to be associated with the same genre that had dominated 'early' music making within the organization.

As with the national music events held in 1950 and 1969, a Sub-Committee was set up to deal specifically with matters relating to the National Society Choir. The first meeting of the Music Society Ad Hoc Committee appears to have taken place on 6 April 1970, with Hopkins and three members of the Music and Drama Sub-Committee (Cherry Vooght, Miss Bower and Janet Cannetty-Clarke) present. The minutes reveal that the Committee was committed to involving young amateur musicians from outside the organization (rather than hiring professional musicians) in the inaugural concert, which enabled the National Federation to avoid any charges of overt professionalism (a criticism that had been levied by newspaper reporters during the preparations of *Folk Songs*). Indeed, the decision to use youth orchestras rather than musicians from the RMSA suggests either that the National Federation wished to branch out in its promotion of amateur music-making beyond organizations that shared similar ideologies, or that the youth orchestras were of a higher quality.

Discussions appear to have taken place with Mr Pinkett, the Leicestershire Local Education Authority Adviser, for a collaboration with the Leicestershire Youth

---

12 Dorothy Erhart (who had led the conducting courses at Denman College) died in 1971.

13 The NFWI Song List published in 1938 included arrangements by Imogen Holst (*Pretty Caroline*, *The Seeds of Love*, *It's a Rosebud in June*, *Hares on the Mountain*, *Sweet Kitty* and *The Virgin Unspotted*), while the 1958 song list also includes songs by Poston and Fraser. A draft programme is included in the minutes. MSCh (5 May 1970), n.p.

Orchestra. However, this was not pursued because the date of the choir's first concert fell in the middle of 'O' and 'A' Level examinations.[14] It was later decided to approach the Young Musicians' Symphony Orchestra (YMSO) of which Hopkins was President, conducted by James Judd, even though there was a request for a WI Orchestra to be set up in time to perform at the concert. The latter suggestion was rejected on the grounds that it would be too difficult to arrange for the immediate concert, but a National Orchestra might be considered the following year. The topic however, does not appear to have been discussed at a Committee meeting again.[15]

Auditions for the National Society Choir took place between 28 September and 6 October 1970 in a flat in Bayswater belonging to Mrs Curry. The adjudicator, Christopher Slater (who had been chosen by Hopkins),[16] devised a method of selection based on a ten-minute individual audition which included singing scales on different vowel sounds, a three-minute solo from *Messiah* (which was assessed for quality in tone and expression), a part from *Cuckoo Dear* arranged by Poston (which tested diction) and a piece of easy sight-reading accompanied on the piano.[17] From over 70 members who applied from 19 counties, Slater selected a choir of 48. The majority were from the Home Counties (six members from Hertfordshire, six from East Kent, eight from Middlesex and six from Surrey) which is unsurprising in view of the location of the auditions and the fact that rehearsals were also scheduled to take place in London. Although it is difficult to gauge the standard of the choir, a 'Sight Reading Day' held in February 1971 suggests that this was the area that most needed improvement.[18]

Early responses indicate that not all Institute members welcomed the idea of a National Society Choir. The minutes of a meeting of the Music and Drama Sub-Committee refer to instances when County Federation Executive Committees stepped in and objected to members taking part.[19] Correspondence was also received from Institutes in Somerset, Hampshire, Cumberland, Guernsey, the Isle of Anglesey, Montgomery, Cheshire, Merioneth and Lancashire, objecting to the expense incurred by choir members selected to sing at the concert.[20] The Ad Hoc Sub-Committee considered asking choir members to pay a subscription (as is common practice in other national choirs) as a means to finance the choir's activities, but the suggestion appears to have been declined on the grounds that members already paid an annual subscription to join the organization and that asking for another fee would open the choir to charges of elitism. Examination of members' comments reveals that their main objection was to the term 'National Choir' and the concept of a selected group specially chosen for high level performance. Many, it seems, recognized that the nature of the National Society Choir contravened the National Federation's principle of giving each member a chance to develop her abilities.

---

14 MS-C (1 July 1970), n.p.

15 MSCh (2 December 1970), n.p.

16 The minutes state that Hopkins did not want to audition the members as he found it 'extremely embarrassing when dealing with amateurs', MSCh (16 January 1970), n.p.

17 MSCh (5 May 1970), n.p.

18 The idea of holding a sight-reading day is recorded in the Executive Minutes vol. 32, MS-C (7 October 1970), p. 850.

19 Executive Minutes vol. 32, MDS-C (8 April 1970), p. 556.

20 MS-C (1 July 1970), n.p.

The National Society Choir's Inaugural Concert

The National Society Choir's first public appearance was on 9 June 1971 at the Fairfield Halls, Croydon. The event was open to the public as well as members of the Women's Institutes, as it was hoped that the concert would attract a wide audience.[21] The publicity that surrounded the event (which was arranged by a member of the Publicity Sub-Committee, Mrs Jenkins) highlights the extent to which the National Federation hoped to attract the media's attention. The concert was also advertised in local papers and 12 tickets were allocated to members of the press (although it is difficult to gauge whether this included reporters from the major nationals).[22] Other complimentary tickets issued were to members of the National Federation Executive and Music and Drama Sub-Committees, and 'special guests' (who included Dods, Ursula Vaughan Williams and Williamson).[23]

Figure 6.1: Antony Hopkins and Janet Cannetty-Clarke with the Avalon Singers.

---

21 'Chronological outline of the origins and history of the NFWI Music Society – up to July 1971' (dated 1 September 1971).
22 MSCh (3 February 1971), n.p.
23 MSCh (2 December 1970), n.p.

As happened with the premiere of *Folk Songs*, the events of the previous day's AGM overshadowed the debut of the National Society Choir. In particular, the overturning of the non-political and non-sectarian ruling of the Constitution captured newspaper critics' attention. The resolution was reported in the major national press: *The Times*, *The Daily Telegraph* and *The Daily Mail* all covered it, as did some local newspapers (such as *The Croydon Advertiser and Croydon Times*).[24] The *Coulsdon and Purley Advertiser* appears to have been one of the few newspapers that included a review of the concert, a decision likely to have been influenced by the fact that the reviewer's wife was a Women's Institute member.[25] In view of a general absence of detail about this event, David Squibb's review is worth citing at length. He wrote:

> Conducted by Antony Hopkins, the forty eight singers picked by audition from all over the country gave a kind of shop-window display of the range of music WIs can tackle. Apparently the tonal quality of the individual singers had largely determined their selection for this top-team, for their blend of voices, beautifully controlled, was the hallmark of their achievement. Intonation was of a high order too, but their diction lacked absolute precision owing to the unclear ends of words. Though I had been placed right at the side of the hall (an uncustomary position for me) I found the vocal balance firmly judged, with the contraltos providing some particularly steady contributions. Of the group of ten songs during the first half of the programme, Britten's 'May' and 'The Oxen' were the best projected, with Elizabeth Poston's 'Cuckoo Dear' sensitively phrased and Imogen Holst's 'In Heaven it is Always Autumn' having musicianly poise. The most substantial singing and in all ways the most absorbing, came from the four choral hymns from 'Rigg [sic] Veda' by Gustav Holst. This third group is full of rich scoring for women's voices, and the choir showed some really poetic feeling in their shading and chording.[26]

The remainder of Squibb's review is concerned with the Young Musicians' Symphony Orchestra who provided the music for the second half of the concert with Berlioz's *Carnival Romain* overture and Hindemith's *Symphonic Metamorphoses on Themes by Weber*. The choir and orchestra combined for the final item of excerpts from *The Brilliant and The Dark*, which Squibb reported as sounding 'rather vacuous after the preceding works, though it received an attractive performance'. Despite criticism of the choir's diction lacking absolute precision, the use of terms 'sensitively phrased', 'musicianly poise' and 'poetic feeling' indicate that Squibb was impressed by the choir's performance, unlike the YMSO whom he criticized for not performing as well as other youth orchestras that had appeared at the same venue.[27]

Four months after the choir's debut, a conference was held in London on 26 October 1971 to discuss the future of music within the organization, and in particular, the future of the National Society Choir. However, the minutes for a meeting of the

---

24 Penny Hunter, 'Women Vote for Free Speech at Institutes', *The Times* (9 June 1971): p. 2, Gerda Paul, 'Women's Institutes: Politics Replaces Jam', *The Daily Telegraph* (9 June 1971): p. 6, unsigned articles 'Now the W.I. Can Talk About Sex', *The Daily Mail* (9 June 1971): p. 3 and 'WI Welcome Politics', *The Croydon Advertiser and Croydon Times* (18 June 1971): p. 9.

25 He refers to her being a 'member of a small west country WI'.

26 David Squibb, 'WI Fully Choral', *Coulsdon and Purley Advertiser* (11 June 1971): p. 21.

27 Ibid., p. 21.

Music Sub-Committee on 1 September 1971 reveal that decisions had already been made as to the choir's future, namely that the next event would be held in the spring of 1972 (in Leicester, Manchester or Chester) and that the programme and performers would be the same as that for the launch concert, conducted by Dods (Hopkins was unavailable).[28] Representatives from each county (who had been chosen by the County Federation Committees) were invited to attend the conference. The agenda included discussions led by members of the Music Sub-Committee: Miss Bower gave a session on the Choir Leaders' Training Scheme, Janet Cannetty-Clarke on 'Music in the Institutes', Mrs Gordon on 'Music in the Counties', Mrs Lock on 'Denman College courses' and Lady Burnham on 'The Future of the NFWI Music Society'. Hopkins is also reported as speaking about the choir.[29] An 'appendix' reveals that suggestions from county representatives included the idea of the choir visiting the Home Counties to give concerts for special events, and the recommendation that because of the expense of travelling, regional choirs be formed to meet the demand for large concerts on special occasions. It also appears that delegates asked questions about the nature of the choir and its membership.[30] The main result of the conference was that preparations for the choir's second concert began to take shape.

The 'Leicestershire' Concert

The choir's second performance took place on 11 April 1972 at the Queen's Hall in Leicestershire. Complimentary tickets were sent to the Mayor and Mayoress of Leicester, the County Music Adviser and Assistant Adviser, members of the University's Music Department, the County Chairman of Leicestershire and Rutland Music Committee and Hopkins, with special invitations to Sir Arthur Bliss, the Vice-Chancellor of Leicester University and Williamson and his wife.[31] As with the Fairfield Halls concert, the National Federation invested in publicity for the event, with Mrs Jenkins notifying newspapers and radio stations,[32] as well as television stations. In addition, the Music Sub-Committee specifically requested that music critics of the national newspapers (including the Sunday press) be notified, which indicates that the National Federation hoped the concert would achieve serious critical attention.[33] A reference to press cuttings being passed around at a Music Sub-Committee meeting suggests that the media reception was greater than that for

---

28 MS-C (1 September 1971), n.p.

29 Ibid., n.p.

30 A document entitled 'NFWI Music Society – Appx' (undated).

31 MS-C (8 March 1972), n.p. The Chairman of Leicestershire and Rutland (Mrs Gibson), Bliss, Williamson, and the Lord and Lady Mayoress of Leicester and Vice-Chairman of the University were all unable to attend.

32 The only information I have been able to find is a reference to the National Society Choir, in a programme on Radio Leicester called 'Coffee Break' on 12 April 1972 between 10.31 and 11am. The radio station's interest in the concert and the nature of the programme is unclear.

33 MS-C (9 February 1972), n.p.

the launching concert, but preliminary research indicates that reviews were mainly confined to local newspapers.[34]

The idea was that the National Society Choir would give its second performance, after which auditions for a second choir would be held in the Midlands area, with members from the first choir joining it if they wanted to. The Midlands Choir would then give a concert in 1973, and another concert in a different area where a third choir would be formed. A document listing the objectives of the choir (dated 8 March 1972) states: 'This "snowballing" should then be continued to cover the north and the west of the country, with the possibility of the first three or four choirs combining at a certain stage to give a truly national concert.'[35] The National Federation was to take financial responsibility for each choir so long as it carried the title 'NFWI Music Society', paying for expenses such as auditions, rehearsals for concerts, and the hiring of professional musicians (such as the conductor and soloists). All other costs were to be paid for by the individual choirs.[36] The scheme encouraged Music Society Choirs to collaborate with local county youth orchestras and male voice choirs, and to include Institute musicians (other than singers) at their public concerts in the hope that instrumentalists within the organization could be 'discovered'. Indeed, this was an area that had the potential for development within music policy as only a few courses on instrumental music had been held at Denman College, namely courses for recorder players and accompanists, and 'For those who play stringed instruments'.[37] A mixed course for wind and string players was introduced in 1960, but appears to have been discontinued after 1963 (see Appendix 5).

However, there was resistance to the National Federation's policy on the National Society Choir. Lady Burnham, a member of the Music Sub-Committee, made an announcement during the interval at the Leicestershire concert that the original choir was to disband immediately. The National Federation had replaced the 'snow-balling' concept with a pair of demonstration concerts followed by a deliberate break-up of the talent to enrich music in the regions.

The correspondence received by the National Federation reflects choir members' uproar at this decision. The main objection was not towards the financial responsibility that Institutes would have to bear or the attention that was being given to music within the organization, but about what would happen to the 'original' National Society Choir (which had become known as the South Eastern Section because most of the members came from this region). One choir member, Joan Mathews, wrote: 'We have been told that the choir is a beautiful instrument, and I cannot believe that the National Federation of Women's Institutes would allow such an instrument, with all the foregoing hard work and expense, not to mention talent, to go to waste.'[38]

---

34 MS-C (10 May 1973), n.p.

35 'Paper on the objectives formulating a clear policy, including financial policy, for the future of the NFWI Music Society' (dated 8 March 1972), n.p.

36 Ibid., n.p.

37 Executive Minutes vol. 33, MS-C (10 May 1972), p. 344.

38 Extract from Joan H. Mathews's letter recorded in a document titled 'Extracts from letters sent in my members of the first NFWI Music Society Choir concerning the future of this section of the choir' (dated 10 May 1972), n.p.

Rosemary Stephens and Audrey Drake also wrote to the National Federation conveying their dismay at the prospect of the choir disbanding and offered their skills (the former as a secretary and the latter as an accompanist) if that might enable the choir to continue. Other suggestions included those of M.E. Crawshaw and Betty Hall, who recommended that members pay a monthly or yearly subscription as a means of continuing the original choir.[39]

The National Federation sought to rectify the situation by arranging a conference for the 44 original choir members on 5 October 1972 to discuss the future of the South Eastern Section. The report indicates that the first half of the conference was concerned with outlining the Music Sub-Committee's general future policy for the choir, which included when and where future concerts would be held (the Midlands in 1973, Wales in 1974, and then the South West, the North, and East Anglia), the name of the choirs (for example 'NFWI Music Society Choir Midlands Section'), how they would be financed and the choice of professional musicians. The second half was concerned with venues for performances, future broadcasts, membership, possible long-term conductors and the establishment of a committee of five choir members to administer the choir and help decide its future. The decision was also made to allow the original choir to have its own sub-committee (on which a member of the National Federation Music Sub-Committee served), which had the responsibility of organizing its finances, planning future engagements and their publicity, arranging auditions and supplementing membership when necessary, continuing the employment of Hopkins as conductor for as long as feasible and seeking possible sources of income. It seems that whereas the National Federation was keen to maintain control of the new Society Choirs by laying down rules that enabled them to vet the professional musicians employed, the South Eastern Section was granted a greater degree of autonomy from its early days.[40]

The 'Midlands' Concert

Only two members of the South Eastern Section, Mrs Eyre and Mrs Scorer, joined the Midlands Section of the Society Choir. Auditions for the remaining members were held on 7–9 October 1972, adjudicated by Robin Gritton.[41] The standard of entries appears to have been lower than that for the original choir, as members had written to the National Federation informing the Music Sub-Committee that alternative arrangements were needed because many were unable to sight-read. The minutes also refer to a local member, Mrs Smith, who had mentioned that many Leicestershire and Rutland members had considered the standard required to be too high.[42] Only 18 singers (with ten reserves) were selected over the first two days

---

39 Ibid., n.p.

40 'Report on the conference held to discuss the future of the NFWI Music Society Choir, South East Area Section on 5 October 1972', Executive Minutes vol. 33 (MS-C), p. 652.

41 Mrs Payne, who had played at the final performance of *The Brilliant and The Dark*, provided the piano accompaniment at these auditions.

42 MS-C (6 December 1973), n.p.

of auditions.[43] The Music Sub-Committee decided to hold further auditions in Derbyshire in January 1973 in order to find enough singers to make up a choir which was envisaged would comprise about 40 singers.[44] Gritton's opinion of the auditions held in Nottinghamshire and Derbyshire was summarized in the minutes:

> Mr Gritton said that he had been impressed in all cases by the enthusiasm of the members who had attended for audition, although he had not found the level of musicianship to be very high. He had therefore only been able to select a total of 24 singers who would be able to reach the required high standard in the time given and had named 16 people as reserves. He added that the pattern was generally that half of those who entered for audition were suitable for selection and also that he felt it to be most important that the proposals for a concert should go ahead, perhaps in a modified form.[45]

In view of the lack of suitable members to start a Midlands Section of the choir, the Music Sub-Committee made the decision not to hold a musical event on 9 June 1973, but to hold a music-making day (entitled 'Spring Entertainment') earlier in the year in the hope of stimulating further interest in the project. The option of opening the Music Society Choirs to non-Institute members does not appear to have been considered until 1975, following an enquiry by Hertfordshire Federation as to the ruling on the percentage of 'outsiders' allowed in a choir.[46]

The 'Spring Entertainment' was held on 17 April 1973 at the University of Nottingham, conducted by Dods.[47] The programme was based on songs considered suitable for use by county choirs which were interspersed with readings by members of the County Drama Sub-Committee: Dyson's 'Pleasure It Is', three madrigals by Morley, two songs by Williamson (one of which was from *The Brilliant and The Dark*) and a relatively new work by Michael Hurd called *Charms and Ceremonies*.[48] The event was advertised in local newspapers (which included *The Lincoln, Rutland and Stamford Mercury* and Nottingham's *Evening Post*). However, little is known about the concert as reviews in *The Derby Evening Telegraph* and Nottingham's *Evening Post* provide little information apart from the venue and the programme.[49]

---

43 MS-C (11 October 1972), n.p.

44 MS-C (10 November 1972), n.p.

45 MS-C (7 February 1973), n.p.

46 The Music Sub-Committee stated that 20% of the choir could be non-WI members, MS-C (14 March 1975), n.p.

47 Letters in the 'NFWI Music Society' file reveal that David Willcocks declined the offer to conduct the Midlands Section on 20 August 1972 due to work commitments, after which Dods was approached on 5 September 1972.

48 Michael Hurd's *Charms and Ceremonies* was commissioned for Downs School, Malvern, and premiered on 12 July 1969.

49 Advertisements include 'WI Music', *Lincoln, Rutland and Stamford Mercury* (stamped 16 April 1973): n.p., and 'New Midlands Choir', [Nottingham] *Evening Post* (stamped 12 April 1973): n.p. Reviews include 'First Concert of WI Choir', *Derby Evening Telegraph* (stamped 24 April 1973): n.p, and 'WI Choir's First Concert', [Nottingham] *Evening Post* (stamped 18 April 1973): n.p. The only other reference appears in the minute books, which refers to the choir's performance as being of a 'very fine quality'. MS-C (9 May 1973), n.p.

The National Federation's music conference held in Leicester on 9 November 1973 was another attempt by the Music Sub-Committee to rally new members to come forward and audition for the Midlands Section. Mrs Eyre spoke of her enthusiasm at belonging to the South Eastern Section and the importance of the scheme within the organization. The report noted: 'She felt that the reason for having a National Music Society was, as with all other WI activities, that there should be a chance to excel.'[50] However, during the discussion delegates criticized various aspects of the scheme ranging from the procedure for selection, the fact that certain members had not been successful in audition, the choice of songs for audition, the venue, the level of achievement expected, the use of reserves, and the time of day for auditions, rehearsals and the concert.[51] It seems that many were aware that excelling in music was somewhat at odds with the organization's promotion of communality. Attempts to encourage singers to audition for the choir (which included advertising in *Home and Country* and local newspapers such as the *Norwich Mercury*) failed; only seven interested members later came forward from Warwickshire Federation.[52] As a result, the Midlands Section never materialized.

The Welsh and North-West Section

Plans for the Welsh and North-West Section of the Society Choir took shape in 1974 after the Midlands Section failed to come to fruition. The choir was open to all the Institutes in Wales, as well as members of Cheshire, Hereford, Lancashire and Shropshire Federations, although Welsh members tended to dominate the Section. It was hoped that a choir of between 45 and 50 members would be formed.[53] If too few members were found, then 'Music for Pleasure' days were planned to take place in eight regions in the north, with smaller 'days' in the Island Federations, as a means to encourage an interest in musical activities within the organization (such as the Choir Leaders' Training Scheme), and gauge what assistance was needed in these areas.[54] Early reports from Institutes in Wales indicate that the scheme was positively received. The minutes refer to a Sub-Committee member, Mrs Hughes, making initial contacts with Caernarvonshire, Flintshire, Montgomery, Merioneth and Anglesey Federations, and finding 26 members who were interested in auditioning.[55]

The auditions for the Welsh and North-West Section were again adjudicated by Gritton and, like those held in 1970 and 1972, included excerpts from *Messiah*. However, members were allowed to choose their own part song and the sight-reading test was dropped (as this was seen to be the main cause for some members not

---

50 'Report of the NFWI Music Society Conference held on 9 November 1973', n.p.
51 Ibid., n.p.
52 Daphne Harmer's article 'Norfolk WI Notes: The Allure of Music' in the *Norwich Mercury* (stamped 15 September 1973): n.p. MS-C (5 December 1973), n.p.
53 MSCh (10 January 1974), n.p.
54 MS-C (13 March 1974) lists the eight regions as the West Country, North Wales, South Wales, the North East, the North West, East Anglia, the Midlands and the Island Federations.
55 MSCh (13 February 1974), n.p.

auditioning).[56] The decision to allow a less regimented approach to the audition was successful, as from a total of 61 members who attended, 39 members were chosen. Gritton reported: 'Of the 39 – 12 are soloists, a further 8 have very good voices, 12 are excellent readers (1 perfect pitch). The remainder have melodic voices and reading ability, 4 cannot read at all! But have been accepted for vocal reasons.'[57] His recommendations for improving the choir included developing breathing techniques and increasing members' knowledge of musical notation. He wrote that this might be achieved by individual lessons and group work being integrated into choir rehearsals.[58] His comments suggest that standards of musicianship had not greatly altered within the organization since 1950 and that the aims choir were somewhat ambitious.

The conductor of the Welsh and North-West Section was William Llewellyn, who at the time was also Director of Music at Charterhouse boys' school (a position he had held since 1965). In view of Hopkins being chosen for the Fairfield Halls concert and Dods for the Midlands Section, the decision to employ a less high-profile figure might suggest that this Section was not intended to attract significant media attention. Indeed, the guest list for the choir's debut did not include any particularly well-known figures active in the British musical scene at the time.[59]

The minutes do not reveal why Llewellyn was chosen, and the decision seems curious in view of his being based some distance away (in Godalming, Surrey). However, he had been involved with the Women's Institutes as an adjudicator at the county festivals of *The Brilliant and The Dark*.[60] In addition, he had extensive experience of choral conducting. A review of the Section's first concert in the *Wrexham Leader* reveals that he had been the conductor of the Linden Singers – a group that by 1974 had had numerous performances broadcast on the radio and television.[61] He also had experience of working with amateurs as President of the

---

56 MSCh (10 January 1974), n.p. The decision to drop the sight-reading element is recorded in MSCh (13 February 1974), n.p.

57 A hand-written document titled 'Wales and NW Choir Auditions' signed Robin Gritton and (dated 8 April 1974), n.p.

58 Ibid., n.p.

59 MS-C (8 May 1974), n.p. These include O. Jones (Secretary of the North Wales Association for the Arts), Mr and Mrs Robin Gritton, William Llewellyn's family, Mrs Robert Williams, Roland Morris (Chief Music Adviser for Clwyd), the Principal of the William Aston Technical College, Howard Davies (Director of Education for Clwyd), the National Federation Chairman, Maria Lyon (Chairman of Clywd Council and Governor of Cardiff), Chairman of 'America in Wales' Year scheme and music advisers of the counties involved. Other special guests who were later invited were Mrs Roland Morris (wife of the Chief Music Adviser, Clywd), Mr and Mrs Bruce Brown (Chairman of Denbighshire Federation and her husband), Antony Hopkins, Mrs Margetts (Chairman of the South Eastern Choir), Janet Cannetty-Clarke (Adviser NFWI Music Sub-Committee), Mrs Howard Davies (wife of the Principal of Denbighshire Technical College) and Mervyn Jones (Chairman of the Welsh Tourist Board).

60 The only reference I have been able to find to his conducting is in a review by Michael Kennedy, 'Charterhouse', *The Musical Times* vol. 114 no. 1559 (January 1973): p. 61 which states that he conducted four performances of *The Pilgrim's Progress* at Charterhouse School (held from 25–28 October 1972).

61 [Unsigned], 'WI Choir Concert.' The *Wrexham Leader* (8 November 1974): n.p.

Godalming Operatic Society, Musical Director of 'Music for Youth' (which gave Saturday morning concerts for young people in the area), President of the Music Masters' Association and Warden of the Incorporated Society of Musicians School Music Section. A biographical entry included in a programme also reveals that Llewellyn had Welsh roots, having been brought up in Colwyn.[62]

The debut of the Welsh and North-West Section took place on 2 November 1974 at the William Aston Hall, Wrexham. The first half of the programme was accompanied by a local orchestra, the Clwyd Concert Band and included Purcell's *Sound the Trumpet*, Giovanni Croce's *Basciami Vita Mia*, Peter Warlock's *The First Mercy*, Britten's *The Oxen*, *Three Hungarian Folk Songs* arranged by Matyás Seiber, and eight nursery rhymes arranged by Walford Davies. The second half included an arrangement by Llewellyn of Welsh folk songs for women's voices and orchestra (which he composed especially for the Section's debut), and choral hymns from Holst's *Rig Veda* which were accompanied by Denbighshire County Youth Orchestra (conducted by the Deputy Music Adviser for Clwyd, Robert Williams). Of the repertoire performed, the *Three Hungarian Folk Songs* and songs from *Rig Veda* (which have difficult intervallic leaps) were perhaps the most complex of all the choral pieces performed by a Music Society Choir.[63]

Press releases had been sent to television companies such as the BBC, ITV, HTV, BBC Bangor and BBC Cardiff, as well as newspapers which included *The Farmers' Guardian*, *The Liverpool Daily Post*, the *Wrexham Leader*, the *Denbigh Free Press* and the *North Wales Chronicle*, and Radio Blackburn and Radio Merseyside. However, there does not appear to have been much media interest in the event. It can only be assumed from the fact that the choir was later booked for future engagements, which included performing as part of the Clwyd Federation's Diamond Jubilee celebrations on 16 September 1976, and at concerts in Hereford, Cheltenham and Shropshire, that it had been favourably received, at least locally.[64]

On 7 June 1975, the Welsh and North-West Section became known as 'The Llewellyn Singers'.[65] The change of name had been on the agenda since October 1974 as the Music Sub-Committee considered 'Wales and North-West Section Choir' to be too long.[66] The change of name symbolized a degree of independence from the National Federation. This final section examines the development of the South Eastern Section and reveals the extent to which the National Federation was willing to loosen its control over music-making activities within the organization.

---

62 Programme for a concert by The Llewellyn Singers at the Shire Hall, Hereford, on 26 June 1976.

63 The programme is listed MSCh (7 September 1974), n.p.

64 WN-WSC (7 June 1975), n.p.

65 An untitled document states that the name was partly in recognition of their conductor, but also their origin in North Wales, as Llewellyn was a Welsh prince. The choir disbanded in February 1981.

66 MS-C (9 October 1974), n.p.

The South Eastern Section

The South Eastern Section was much in demand within the organization, and Institutes invited the choir to give concerts. Its first official concert (as the 'South Eastern Section') was held at The Lees Cliffe Hall, Dorking Halls, Folkestone, on 21 February 1973 and was reported in the minutes as being 'a tremendous success'.[67] Further concerts took place at The Grange School in Aylesbury on 10 November 1973, The Mercury Theatre in Colchester on 20 May 1974, The Dome in Brighton on 29 May 1974, Central Hall in Chatham on 4 November 1974, The Mary Ward Festival in London on 9 June 1975, The Dorking Halls in Folkestone on 13 June 1975 and The Pavilion in Hemel Hempstead on 23 October 1975.

The South Eastern Section soon carved out its own repertoire. The programme for the Folkestone concert was largely based on that performed at the Fairfield Halls concert, but with harp music (performed by Skaila Kanga) instead of an orchestra providing interludes to the choir's pieces. However, the concert in Aylesbury in November 1973 had a very different programme. It did not include excerpts from either of the National Federation's two music commissions. The concert began with the choir singing Gustav Holst's *Ave Maria*, which was followed by two items performed by Buckinghamshire Youth Orchestra (conducted by Kenneth Collingham): Mendlessohn's overture *Fingal's Cave* and Beethoven's Symphony no. 5. The second half consisted of songs by Jacob Handl, Kodàly, Britten, Gustav Holst, Ralph Nicholson and two arrangements by Norman Fulton and Copland performed by the choir (accompanied on piano by Janet Cannetty-Clarke).

The choir performed the same repertoire at its concerts in 1974, with the addition of Hopkins's *Riding to Canobie* at The Dome concert in Brighton on 29 May 1974.[68] The inclusion of religious songs such as Kodàly's *The Angels and the Shepherds* and Handel's *Pueri Concinite* reflects an increased freedom in the choice of repertoire that followed the end of the Constitutional non-sectarian ruling in 1971. Bryn Williams' arrangement of three Welsh Songs, Vaughan Williams's *Dirge for Fidele*, Bliss's *Prayer of St Francis of Assisi* and Joyce Barthelson's arrangement of a Negro spiritual *Rock-a y Soul* were added to the programme for the concerts in Chatham, Hemel Hempstead, Dorking and The Mary Ward Festival, and extended further the choir's repertoire.

One of the most notable features of the South Eastern Section is the sheer number of compositions written for it. Ralph Nicholson wrote *Herrick's Carol*, which he dedicated to Hopkins and the South Eastern Choir, after hearing the choir at Folkestone and the Fairfield Halls (it was also premiered at the Brighton concert).[69] Hopkins, who remained its conductor (with Janet Cannetty-Clarke as its official accompanist), wrote *Riding to Canobie*, a work for women's voices, especially for the choir. The

---

67 MS-C (14 March 1973), n.p.

68 *Riding to Canobie* was recorded on side B of The Readers' Digest recording of *The Brilliant and The Dark* in 1977 to commemorate the Queen's Silver Jubilee, sung by The Avalon and The Llewellyn Singers (accompanied by the English Chamber Orchestra), conducted by Antony Hopkins and accompanied by Janet Cannetty-Clarke (a copy of which is in the National Sound Archive).

69 MS-C (9 May 1973), n.p.

work is based on Cara Lockhart Smith's set of 26 poems. Each poem is linked to a fictitious personality, their names arranged alphabetically, for example Annabel Avalon, Bertram Bloggs, Caterina Carter.[70] Hopkins also commissioned a song (at his own expense) from one of his former pupils at the Royal College of Music, Joan Littlejohn, called *The Bonny Earl of Murray*, which was premiered at the choir's first London performance.[71] Yet despite publicity for each of the premieres, which for *Herrick's Carol* and *Riding to Canobie* included a broadcast on 'Women's Hour' on 8 November 1973 and a live broadcast on Radio Brighton, as well as advertisements in the local press, they did not attract significant attention from the critics.[72] In fact, none of the major national newspapers or music journals included reviews of any of the South Eastern Section's concerts.

The Avalon Singers

The South Eastern Section changed its name to the Avalon Singers in July 1975.[73] Discussion surrounding renaming the South Eastern Section had taken place in November 1974 as the choir's Sub-Committee considered its current name as problematic for publicity reasons.[74] The suggestion 'WI Singers S.E.' was put forward at a Music Sub-Committee meeting on 14 March 1975, and it was hoped that any decision could be postponed for a year.[75] The programme for the concert at The Mary Ward Centre in June 1975 refers to it as the 'Top Note Choir' although there is no evidence to suggest that the National Federation officially sanctioned this name.

Examination of the 'Constitution of the Avalon Singers' reveals that the choir's change in name brought with it a change in role. Originally formed to develop musical talent within the organization and to perform at national events (as discussed earlier), the objective of the choir was now to 'educate the public in the arts and sciences, and in particular the art and science of music, by the presentation of concerts and other activities'.[76] Other differences include the new category of Associate Members (who were elected as members by the Committee but who were unable to take part in performances), the introduction of subscriptions for choir members and the issuing of invitations to possible patrons (who would be chosen by the choir's committee).

---

70 Janet Cannetty-Clarke was the official accompanist for the South Eastern Section who deputized at rehearsals if Hopkins was unable to attend. The National Federation had hoped to publish *Riding to Canobie*, but plans failed to materialize because of financial concerns (as *Folk Songs* and *The Brilliant and The Dark* had not been financially lucrative for their publishers).

71 MS-C (9 October 1974), n.p. It should be mentioned that Dods wrote a new arrangement of the second verse of the National Anthem which the Music Sub-Committee decided would be performed at the Midlands Section Choir.

72 The *Midhurst and Petworth Observer* and the *Bognor Regis Observer* both included advertisements on 17 May 1974 for the Brighton concert.

73 TAS (7 July 1975), n.p. Various names appear to have been considered, and 'The Avalon Singers' was Hopkins's choice.

74 SESS-C (11 November 1974), n.p.

75 SESS-C (7 October 1974), n.p.

76 A document entitled 'Constitution of The Avalon Singers' (undated).

However, perhaps the most significant difference was that the choir had its own bank account and was therefore financially independent of the National Federation. Whereas the National Federation had previously stepped in even when important decisions had to be made, for example in deciding whether a recording of the South Eastern Section should take place (which was declined), the Avalon Singers now had complete control over the direction of the choir, although the choir maintained some link in its marketing by referring to itself as a choir of Institute members.[77] The National Federation appears to have given it back its former importance.

The Purcell Room Concert

The Avalon Singers made their London debut at the Purcell Room on 19 November 1975. It was the first time that the National Federation had not been at the heart of such a public music event involving WI members. Indeed, it is difficult to gauge the extent to which the National Federation assisted the Avalon Singers in their preparation for the concert. It appears that Hopkins and the choir's committee shouldered the bulk of the responsibility for its organization. That said, a note published in the programme by the National Federation's Chairman at the time, Pat Jacob, wishing the choir 'every success', indicates that the National Federation supported the choir, at least publicly.[78]

The publicity material issued provides a valuable insight into the aspirations behind the concert. It states:

> Until now the Choir have been performing under WI Hostess auspices. That is, a local Federation within the S.E. Section were promoters and carried out all [of] the organisation and booking that was necessary. Now it has become evident that they have outgrown this system of WI umbrella protection and need to leave the nest and spread their wings to become nationally known. Thus the opportunity came up for a performance at the Purcell Room, and they will be singing to a sophisticated London audience in the presence of national music critics.[79]

The aim of the concert was not to elevate WI music-making to the professional sphere but to introduce the choir to a London audience. The minutes reveal that it was Hopkins's suggestion that the choir perform at the venue to commemorate the National Federation's Diamond Jubilee and premiere two works: Littlejohn's *The Bonny Earl of Murray* and Poston's *The English Day Book* (the latter coincided with the composer's seventieth birthday).[80] Other items in the programme included Hopkins's arrangement of three folk songs (which seems ironic in view of the organization's attempt to distance itself from the genre) and items that the choir had performed at concerts in the federations (such as *Riding to Canobie*, and songs by Handl, Durufle, Nicholson, Britten, Gustav Holst and Kodály).

---

77 SESS-C (10 October 1973), n.p.

78 Programme for 'The Avalon Singers' on 19 November 1975 at the Purcell Rooms, London.

79 A document entitled 'The Avalon Singers' (undated).

80 A document entitled 'From: Music Sub-Committee report 10 July 1974'. I have been unable to find copies of either of these works.

It was not the first time that the organization had been faced with media attention, as music critics from the national press had been present at the premieres of both *Folk Songs* and *The Brilliant and The Dark*.[81] A brief review published in the *Woking News and Mail* refers to the choir winning 'acclaim from audience and critics alike' although the paucity of reviews in the national newspapers and major music journals suggests this was not entirely the case.[82] The Avalon Singers' London debut actually received less media attention than the premieres of the National Federation's music commissions; the concert was referred to in only two of the national newspapers. A.E.P., the music critic of *The Daily Telegraph*, wrote:

> The Avalon Singers who appeared at the Purcell Room last night under the conductor Antony Hopkins consisted of members of the National Federation of Women's Institute's National Choir, and were all chosen by audition. The results of this rigorous approach to amateur music-making were immediately evident in the quality of the sound produced. In Kodály's *The Angels and Shepherds*, for example, one of the works that made imaginative use of ladies' voices, a ringing affirmative climax was reached.[83]

The article in *The Evening Standard* did not review the concert but instead reported the story of Hopkins forgetting to bring his evening dress trousers. The unsigned critic wrote:

> His [Hopkins's] dilemma might normally have been solved by borrowing from a less exposed performer, but alas last night he was conducting the Women's Institute Avalon choir. Happily, 42 ladies rallied round, and on the second attempt a pair of black ladies slacks were found of the right waist measurement. Two minutes before he was due on the rostrum, Hopkins was standing like a Colossus in his dressing room with two WI members busy tacking up the legs of his make-shift apparel. 'I don't think anyone in the audience noticed; but the embarrassing thing was that being ladies trousers, the zip was on the outside. I managed to diplomatically conceal it with both hands when I turned round to take my bows,' said an amused Hopkins this morning.[84]

The absence of reviews demonstrates once again the lack of critics' interest in concerts performed by amateurs, despite this one being held at such a prestigious venue and conducted by a well-known figure in the world of music. Although the concert may not have attracted significant attention outside the organization, it was regarded as being highly beneficial for the choir itself. The minutes reported: 'The experience of making an appearance on a completely non-WI platform, in London, is felt to have been of immense benefit as a whole, and the choir is hopeful of receiving

---

81 *Folk Songs* was reviewed in *The News Chronicle* and *The Times* as well as in *The Musical Times*, and *Music & Letters*, among others, and *The Brilliant and The Dark* was reviewed in *The Times*, *The Daily Telegraph*, *Financial Times*, *The Evening Standard* and *The Musical Times* (among others).

82 [Unsigned], 'Avalon Singers' London debut', *Woking News and Mail* (undated): n.p.

83 A.E.P., 'Quality of Sound From Women's Choir', *The Daily Telegraph* (20 November 1975): n.p.

84 [Unsigned], 'WI Save The Man Who Forgot His Trousers', *The Evening Standard* (20 November 1975): p. 14.

further engagements of the same kind.'[85] Other performances of the Avalon Singers took place at The Town Hall in Reading on 27 September 1975, Snape Maltings on 6 and 7 November 1976, Castle Hall in Hertford on 26 January 1977, and The Thames Hall in Slough on 18 May 1977.

The Avalon Singers lasted only three years. They disbanded following their Annual General Meeting on 7 December 1978. It seems that further auditions did not take place after 1975 and, as a result, membership dwindled (due to health, age, husbands' retirements, and issues of finance). Hopkins backed the decision, adding that other problems included difficulties in finding the time and space for the choir to rehearse and the burden on Janet Cannetty-Clarke to take rehearsals in his absence.[86]

After the choir disbanded in 1978, the National Federation continued its public-faced promotion of music with WI choirs, and was involved in two concerts held at the Royal Albert Hall: on 9 March 1978, WI choirs joined in massed singing with male voice choirs (which included local police choirs) in a performance of Handel's *Messiah*, and on 15 March 1979 performed with other amateur choirs in a performance of Mendelssohn's *Elijah* (which was organized by the British National Committee for the Prevention of Blindness). In 1979, a new work entitled *Early One Morning* was commissioned from Hopkins, after which the National Federation resumed its role in promoting private music-making within the organization.[87] No national music events have taken place within the National Federation since *The Brilliant and The Dark*.

The South Eastern Section (which became the Avalon Singers) and the Welsh Section (known later as the Llewellyn Singers) were immensely popular within the organization, performing numerous concerts throughout the federations during the early 1970s and should be seen as comprising the best musical talent within the organization. The original aim of the National Society Choir was not to present WI music to the British public, but to demonstrate the high standard of choral music to members as examples within the organization. However, it failed in its original aim (which was to spark the formation of other choirs) because the National Federation stepped in and tried to disband the original choir. The decision appears to have been primarily motivated by the National Federation's wariness of the choir becoming too successful (and thereby contravening the organization's commitment to amateurism) and to quell the discontent being voiced from some Institutes. Members primarily objected to the concept of a select group, specially chosen, which many saw as a contravention of the organization's ideology of communality.

---

85 TAS (3 December 1975), n.p.

86 TAS (7 December 1978), n.p.

87 *Early One Morning* was premiered on 7 November 1981 at the Colston Hall, Bristol. Other performances took place at the Grand Hall in Preston on 14 November 1981, and the Assembly Hall, Tunbridge Wells on 18 February 1982. The libretto (written by Hopkins) is a 64 minute musical story about a woman's life. It is based on a series of episodes that begins with her school days, followed by her teenage romance, being jilted at the altar, finding another man and getting married and ends recalling her duties during wartime.

The renaming of the South East Section as the Avalon Singers brought with it not only independence from the National Federation, but also a change in function – to educate the public in the arts. All of the choirs formed during this period achieved this to an extent by performing relatively unknown (and new) repertoire to audiences throughout England. Since *Folk Songs*, musical standards within the organization had increased dramatically, progressing from simple homophonic settings of folk songs, to complex works such as *Riding to Canobie* which has awkward intervals and difficult diction. However, auditions for the Sections reveals that musical standards were by no means uniform within the organization.

Examination of the National Federation's policy for the National Music Society Choir demonstrates the organization's commitment to promoting amateur rather than professional music-making. This can be seen in the decision not to employ professional musicians in the concerts and to use local youth orchestras at concerts of the South Eastern and Welsh Sections. Although collaborations with male voice choirs were also encouraged, there is no evidence that this took place while the choirs were in existence. It is within this context that the concert at the Purcell Rooms should considered – not as an attempt to infiltrate the sphere of professional music-making, but as an opportunity for members to commemorate the organization's Diamond Jubilee and its achievements in choral singing.

However, the choirs failed to make a significant impact outside the organization. The lack of reviews, even for concerts when works such as Nicholson's *Herrick's Carol* and Hopkins's *Riding to Canobie* were premiered, reveals that the choirs failed to attract the attention of critics. The Avalon Singers' London debut was referred to in only two national newspapers despite its being held at such a prestigious venue, including premieres of two works, and being conducted by a well-known figure in the world of music. Critics' lack of interest in the Music Society's concerts may have been because the choirs did not seek to challenge the acceptable 'female' boundaries of music-making. The Sections not only adhered to the 'feminine' sphere of choral music, but also chose a male conductor (rather than taking it as an opportunity to display female 'empowerment') and repertoire by both male and female composers (rather than promoting just women composers). That said, like its provision of conducting, singing in a Society Choir may have provided some members with a sense of empowerment by allowing them to attain the highest standards possible.

Conclusion

The National Federation's archival documents provide a valuable insight into women's involvement in musical activities in Britain's rural communities during the twentieth century. This book has shown that music in the Women's Institute went far beyond the singing of *Jerusalem* at monthly meetings and that the organization made a significant contribution to British musical culture during this period.

The National Federation commissioned two musical works for its national events in 1950 and 1969, the premieres of which involved a large number of women: over 3000 members took part in the premiere of *Folk Songs of the Four Seasons*, and over 1300 for the premiere of *The Brilliant and The Dark*. However, these numbers represent only a small proportion of the women who took part in some form or another in these national music events. The selection of choirs (and soloists for *The Brilliant and The Dark*) by process of competition meant that, for many members, their involvement in the festivals did not go beyond local or area events. However, this is not to say that the national music events should be dismissed as being only enjoyed by a minority of members, but rather that the organization's contribution to British musical culture should not be confined to these musical works.

Once we look beyond the National Federation's two music commissions it becomes clear that the organization has had a wider role through its music activities within Britain's village communities. The 'News from the Institutes' section of *Home and Country*, for example, reveals that for many Institutes, music extended beyond the monthly meeting and included participating at local music events such as county music festivals.

The extent of Institutes' involvement outside the organization through their music activities can be seen from the relationship with other bodies that similarly promoted amateur music-making. Although the National Federation's associations with organizations such as the EFDSS, the RMSA, the NUTG and the BFMCF, have been shown not to have indicated a neat match of aims, the links that it fostered extended the range of amateur music-making taking place within Britain's rural communities. Indeed, although it has been beyond the scope of this book to examine the ways in which these organizations interacted on a local level, future research in this area would yield useful information about the highly networked nature of amateur music-making within Britain.

The National Federation also had involvement with other leading institutions, namely the Arts Council, CUKT and the BBC, and with key figures involved in Britain's music scene: these included composers (Vaughan Williams, Williamson, Britten, Elizabeth Poston and Imogen Holst, as well as lesser-known figures such as Ralph Nicholson and Joan Littlejohn), conductors (Dods, Boult and Hopkins), soloists (Dame Clara Butt, Nancy Evans and April Cantelo), academics (W.H. Hadow), and others prominent in the amateur music scene (for example W.H. Leslie and Geoffrey Shaw), to name only a few. This richness of contacts helps refute the popular image of the Women's Institute as an insular organization and shows the extent to which the organization was involved in British musical culture.

Jerusalem, too, is more than it seems. The ritualistic singing of the hymn has provided a vital source of strength within the organization by binding the Institutes through communal music-making; and it has remained the Women's Institute's unofficial 'anthem' because it has enabled a range of interpretations to exist simultaneously. However, unlike the structure of the organization (which has not changed since its origins), music policy did not remain static; and the study of *Jerusalem* provides a useful means to assess policy changes over this period.

However, *Jerusalem* has not been the only means of uniting the organization through music-making. Examination of the Social Half Hour reveals that choral music has remained at the heart of the National Federation's policy since the 1920s, and thus reinforced the organization's ideological concern of promoting communality and community spirit by allowing all members to take part, irrespective of ability or resources. In addition to practical music-making, the Social Half Hour provided an opportunity for members to educate themselves by means of attending lectures and demonstrations from visiting speakers on an array of topics (which included those on music), and can be seen to have been part of the organization's broader educational policy.

The promotion of conducting, examined within the context of the National Federation's educational policy, reveals that it has served more than one function within the organization. Although conducting was first introduced into the Institutes in the 1930s to curb the shortage of village conductors, the fact that it became a regular part of the organization's musical activities suggests that its function changed. Whilst for some it provided musical training (which could be used for the benefit of Institute and community music-making), for others it provided an opportunity for Institute members to experience empowerment, by exploring 'unfeminine' qualities of leadership and assertion (that are associated with feminism) within the 'protected' confines of the organization.

Music has also been central to the organization's identity. Folk songs and part songs not only provided a plentiful supply of easy repertoire for amateur music-making, but also acted as a means within which to assert the Women's Institute as a British organization for countrywomen; it also aided interaction with other (amateur music-making) organizations on a local level. The move away from folk songs after the National Federation's first music commission can be seen to reflect wider changes in policy and the quest for a new identity.

Whereas music policy has changed within the organization, the National Federation's support of amateur music-making has remained steadfast. The organization's commitment to promoting amateur music-making can be seen in its relationship with organizations, both on local and national levels, that shared similar ideologies such as the EFDSS, and the use of youth orchestras to accompany the National Society Choir. The use of professional orchestras for the premieres of the two music commissions should not be seen as a breach of the National Federation's commitment to amateurism, but the result of composers' requests.

The extent of the organization's commitment to amateur music-making can be seen in its unwillingness to be associated in any way with any accusations of 'professionalism'. Although 'amateur' and 'professional' are not terms widely used in the National Federation's archival documents, it appears that the National Federation was keen to maintain a distinction in its music activities. During the preparations of *Folk Songs*, for example, it was reported in the minutes that the National Federation had had a report from a newspaper journalist criticizing the festival for its 'professionalism'. Although no immediate reaction is apparent, the National Federation made the format and scope of the Women's Institute's undertaking clearer in later press releases.

It may seem surprising, therefore, that the National Federation even sanctioned the concept of the National Society Choir – a select group specially chosen for high level performance. Indeed, its very nature can be seen to contravene the National Federation's principle of giving each member a chance to develop her abilities. Examination of the National Federation's policy on the National Society Choir reveals that it was willing to allow a certain amount of status to be given to music activities within the organization. Concomitantly, the decision to disband the choir after its second performance (in Leicestershire) can be seen as an attempt to maintain control of music activities and prevent it from gaining too much success. When it became clear that the South Eastern Section was to take on a life of its own (with the possibility of its entering the professional music sphere), the National Federation loosened its tie (and responsibility) and granted the Choir independence, thereby reaffirming its commitment to amateur music-making. The National Federation had no direct involvement in the Avalon Singers' London debut at the Purcell Rooms.

Although examination of music in the Women's Institute fills a gap in knowledge about women and amateur music-making in twentieth century Britain, it raises questions about whether such activity has a place within musicology. What do we do with music written for and performed by amateurs? Does it have any valid contribution to make to musicological discussions or should it simply be disregarded as 'bad' music?

In order for the Women's Institute's contribution to be recognized within musicology, the nature of enquiry requires a refocus. As noted in the Introduction, recent musicological writings have focused on composition, and with regard to the twentieth century, have been dominated by music discussions of modernism. However, by definition, modernism focuses on the exceptional and excludes the representative. As a result, music composed outside this area such as Vaughan Williams's *Folk Songs* and Williamson's *The Brilliant and The Dark*, which might be classed as 'conservative' music, has been excluded. Musicology needs to embrace the pluralism of twentieth-century music in order to look beyond modernist composition.

In addition, the role of music history within the discipline needs to be readdressed. 'Traditional' music history is inadequate for dealing with subject matter such as the Women's Institute. Its focus on composition and on individuals (namely the composers) leave it ill-equipped to deal with a group for whom the source material available is largely performance-based and generated by the institution to which these women belong.

Social music history provides a valuable means within which to give representation to women such as members of the Women's Institute, who would otherwise be excluded from history, by providing the means to examine the reasons behind collective music-making and its role within social organizations. It also allows study of the contexts within which music is produced, which, in the case of the Women's Institute, provides a valuable insight into women's roles as patrons and consumers of music within British musical culture.

Bibliography

Monographs

Andrews, Maggie, *The Acceptable Face of Feminism: The Women's Institute as a Social Movement* (London: Lawrence and Wishart, 1997).

Bailey, Peter (ed.), *Music Hall: The Business of Pleasure* (Milton Keynes: Open University Press, 1986).

Banfield, Stephen (ed.), *The Twentieth Century*, The Blackwell History of Music in Britain no. 6 (Oxford: Blackwell, 1995).

Barr, Cyrilla and Ralph Locke (eds), *Cultivating Music in America: Women Patrons and Activists since 1860* (Berkeley: University of Berkeley Press, 1997).

Bashford, Christina and Leanne Langley (eds) *Music and British Culture, 1785–1914: Essays in Honour of Cyril Ehrlich* (Oxford: Oxford University Press, 2001).

Blackstone, Bernard, *English Blake* (Cambridge: Cambridge University Press, 1949).

Blake, Andrew, *The Land Without Music: Music, Culture and Society in Twentieth Century Britain* (Manchester: Manchester University Press, 1997).

Bottrall, Margaret, *The Divine Image: A Study of Blake's Interpretation of Christianity* (Oxford: Oxford University Press, 1948).

Boult, Adrian C., *My Own Trumpet* (London: Hamish Hamilton, 1973).

Bowers, Jane and Judith Tick (eds) *Women Making Music: The Western Art Tradition, 1150–1980* (Chicago: University of Illinois Press, 1987).

Bowles, Michael, *The Art of Conducting* (New York: Doubleday and Co., 1959).

Boyes, Georgina, *The Imagined Village: Culture, Identity and the English Folk Revival* (Manchester: Manchester University Press, 1993).

Bracey, H.E., *English Rural Life – Village Activities, Organizations and Institutions* (London: The Humanities Press, 1959).

Citron, Marcia J., *Gender and the Musical Canon* (Cambridge: Cambridge University Press, 1993).

Clarke, Alfred C., *Leith Hill Musical Festival 1905–1955: A Record of Fifty Years of Music Making in Surrey* (Surrey: Pullinger Ltd., 1955).

Coleman, Henry, *Choral Conducting for Women's Institutes* (London: Oxford University Press, 1932).

Colles, H.C. and John Cruft, *The Royal College of Music: A Centenary Record, 1883–1983* (London: Royal College of Music, 1982).

Cook, Nicholas and Mark Everist (eds) *Rethinking Music* (Oxford: Oxford University Press, 1999).

Corder, Frederick, *A History of the Royal Academy of Music, 1822–1932* (London: F. Corder, 1922).

Courtney, Janet, *Countrywomen in Council: The English and Scottish WIs* (London: Oxford University Press, 1933).

Courtney, Janet, *The Adventurous Thirties: A Chapter in the Women's Movement* (London: Oxford University Press, 1933).

Cox, Gordon, *A History of Music Education in England, 1872–1928* (Aldershot: Scolar, 1993).

Darke, Jane, Sue Ledwith and Roberta Woods, *Women and The City: Visibility and Voice in Urban Space* (Basingstoke: Palgrave, 2000).

Davies, Constance, *A Grain of Mustard Seed* (Bangor: Jarvis and Foster, 1954).

Delafield, E.M., *The Diary of a Provincial Lady* (London: Macmillan and Co Ltd., 1930).

Deneke, Helena, *Grace Hadow* (London: Oxford University Press, 1946).

Dibble, Jeremy C., *Hubert H. Parry: His Life and Music* (Oxford: Clarendon Press, 1992).

Dolmetsch, Rudolph, *The Art of Orchestral Conducting* (London: Bosworth and Co., 1942).

Doughan, David and Peter Gordon, *British Women's Organizations, 1825–1960* (London: Woburn Press, 2001).

Doughan, David and Peter Gordon, *Women, Clubs, and Associations in Britain* (London: Routledge, 2006).

Drage, Dorothy, *The Growth of Women's Institutes in Wales* (Caernarvon: Caernarvonshire Women's Institute, 1956).

Dudgeon, Piers, *Village Voices* (London: Pilot Productions Ltd., 1989).

Ehrlich, Cyril, *The Music Profession in Britain since the Eighteenth-Century: A Social History* (Oxford: Clarendon Press, 1985).

Everitt, Sybil, *Please Stand for Jerusalem: The Story in Words and Pictures of Gloucester WI* (Gloucester: Gloucestershire Federation of Women's Institutes, 1989).

Fairburn, Miles, *Social History: Problems, Strategies, and Methods* (London: Macmillan Press Ltd., 1999).

Freedman, Jane, *Feminism: An Introduction* (Buckingham: Open University Press, 2001).

Frogley, Alain (ed.), *Vaughan Williams Studies* (Cambridge: Cambridge University Press, 1996).

Fuller, Sophie, *The Pandora Guide to Female Composers: Britain and the United States, 1629–Present* (London: Pandora, 1994).

Gillett, Paula, *'Encroaching on all man's privileges': Musical Women in England, 1870–1914* (London: Macmillan, 2000).

Goodenough, Simon, *Jam and Jerusalem* (London: Collins, 1977).

Graves, Charles L., *Hubert Parry: His Life and Works* vol. 2. (London: Macmillan and Co. Ltd., 1926).

Green, Lucy, *Music, Gender, Education* (Cambridge: Cambridge University Press, 1997).

Grout, Donald J. and Claude V. Palisca, *A History of Western Music* (4th ed., London: Norton, 1988).

Harker, Dave, *Fakesong: The Manufacture of British 'Folksong' 1700 to the Present Day* (Milton Keynes: Open University Press, 1985).

Harrison, Brian, *Prudent Revolutionaries: Portraits of British Feminists Between the Wars* (Oxford: Clarendon Press, 1987).

Heffer, Simon, *Vaughan Williams* (London: Weidenfeld and Nicolson, 2000).

Holst, Imogen, *Thematic Catalogue of Gustav Holst's Music* (London: Faber Music Ltd., 1973).

Hopkins, Antony, *Beating Time* (London: Futura Macdonald and Co., 1982).

Hopkins, Antony, *Talking About Symphonies: An analytical study of a number of well-known symphonies from Haydn to the present day* (London: Heinemann 1961).

Hopkins, Antony, *Talking About Concertos; An analytical study of a number of well-known concertos from Mozart to the present day* (London: Heinemann Educational 1964).

Hopkins, Antony, *Music All Around Me: A personal choice from the literature of music* (London: Frewin, 1967).

Horn, Pamela, *Rural Life in England in the First World War* (London: St Martins Press, 1984).

Horn, Pamela, *Women in the 1920s* (Gloucester: Alan Sutton, 1995).

Howes, Frank, *The Music of Ralph Vaughan Williams* (London: Oxford University Press, 1954).

Hughes, Meirion and Robert Stradling, *The English Musical Renaissance, 1840–1940: Constructing A National Music* (2nd ed., Manchester: Manchester University Press, 1993).

Huxley, Gervas, *Lady Denman G.B.E., 1884–1954* (London: Chatto and Windus, 1961).

Hyde, Derek, *New-Found Voices: Women in Nineteenth-Century English music* (3rd ed., Aldershot: Ashgate, 1998).

Ibberson, Mary, *For the Joy That We Are: Rural Music Schools, 1929–1950* (London: N.C.S.S., 1977).

Jenkins, Ignez, *A History of the Women's Institute Movement of England and Wales* (Oxford: Oxford University Press, 1953).

Jones, Helen, *Women in British Public Life, 1914–1950: Gender, Power and Social Policy* (London: Pearson Education Ltd., 2000).

Karpeles, Maud, *An Introduction to English Folk Song* (London: Oxford University Press, 1973).

Kaye, Barbara, *Live and Learn* (London: NFWI, 1970).

Kelly, Thomas, *A History of Adult Education from the Middle Ages to the Twentieth Century* (Liverpool: Liverpool University Press, 1970).

Kennedy, Michael, *A Catalogue of the Works of Ralph Vaughan Williams* (London: Oxford University Press, 1964; 2nd ed. 1982).

Kitchen, Penny, *For Home and Country: War Peace and Rural Life As Seen Through the Pages of the WI Magazine, 1919–1959* (London: NFWI, 1996).

Kitchen, Penny, *The Works of R.V.W.* (London: Oxford University Press, 1964, repr. 1966).

Langhamer, Claire, *Women's Leisure in England, 1920–1960* (Manchester: Manchester University Press, 2000).

Legge, Derek, *The Education of Adults in Britain* (Milton Keynes: Open University Press, 1982).

Livingstone, Richard, *The Future in Education* (Cambridge: Cambridge University Press, 1941).

Livingstone, Richard, *Education in a World Adrift* (Cambridge: Cambridge University Press, 1943).

Lowe, John, *Adult Education in England and Wales: A Critical Survey* (London: Michael Joseph, 1970).

Mackinnon, Niall, *The British Folk Scene: Musical Performance and Social Identity* (Buckingham: Open University Press, 1994).

Marshall, Kimberley (ed.), *Rediscovering The Muses: Women's Musical Traditions* (Boston: Northeastern University Press, 1993).

McCall, Cicely, *Women's Institutes* (London: Collins, 1943).

McClary, Susan, *Feminine Endings: Music, Gender and Sexuality* (Minneapolis: University of Minnesota Press, 1991).

McRobbie, Angela, *In the Culture Society: Art, Fashion, and Popular Music* (Oxford: Routledge, 1999).

Merz, Caroline, *After the Vote: The Story of the National Union of Townswomen's Guilds in the Year of its Diamond Jubilee* (Norwich: NUTG, 1988).

Nettel, Reginald, *Seven Centuries of Popular Song: A Social History of Urban Ditties* (London: Phoenix House, 1956).

Newby, Howard, *Green and Pleasant Land: Social Change in Rural England* (London: Hutchinson and Co. Ltd., 1979).

Offen, Karen, *European Feminisms, 1700–1950: A Political History* (Stanford, California: Stanford University Press, 2000).

Pendle, Karin (ed.), *Women in Music: A History* (Bloomington: Indiana University Press, 1991).

Pike, Lionel, *Vaughan Williams; The Symphony* (London: Toccata Press, 2003).

Pirie, Peter, *Furtwängler and The Art of Conducting* (London: Duckworth, 1980).

Potter, Keith, *Four Musical Minimalists: La Monte Young, Terry Riley, Steve Reich, Philip Glass* (Music in the Twentieth Century Series. Cambridge: Cambridge University Press, 2002).

Pratt, Edwin A., *The Organisation of Agriculture* (London: John Murray, 1904).

Pugh, Martin, *Women and The Women's Movement in Britain, 1914–1959* (London: Macmillan, 1972).

Purvis, June and Sandra Stanley Holton (eds.), *Votes for Women* (London: Routledge, 2000).

Russell, Dave, *Popular Music in England, 1840–1914: A Social History* (Music and Society Series. 2nd ed., Manchester: Manchester University, 1997).

Sadie, Stanley (ed.), *The New Grove Dictionary of Opera* vols. 1–4 (London: Macmillan, 1992).

Sadie, Stanley, (ed.) with Alison Latham, *The Cambridge Music Guide* (Cambridge: Cambridge University Press, 1993).

Scholes, Percy, *The Mirror of Music 1884–1944* vol. 2 (London: Novello, 1947).

Scott, Derek, *The Singing Bourgeois: Songs of the Victorian Drawing Room and Parlour* (2nd ed., Aldershot: Ashgate, 2001).
Sharp, Cecil, *English Folk-Song: Some Conclusions* (London: Novello and Co., 1907).
Sharp, Cecil, *Folk Singing in Schools* (London: EFDSS, 1912).
Sheail, John, *Rural Conservation in Inter-War Britain* (Oxford: Clarendon Press, 1981).
Stamper, Anne, *Rooms Off the Corridor: Education in the WI and 50 years of Denman College, 1948–98* (London: NFWI, 1988).
St John, Christopher, *Ethel Smyth: A Biography* (London: Longman Green and Co., 1989).
Stott, Mary, *Organization Women: The Story of The National Union of Townswomen's Guilds* (London: Heinemann, 1978).
Talbot, Kathleen, *Village Music* (London: Oxford University Press, 1934).
Tong, Rosemarie, *Feminist Thought: A Comprehensive Introduction* (London: Routledge, 1997).
Vaughan Williams, Ralph, *National Music* (London: Oxford University Press, 1934).
Vaughan Williams, Ralph, *The Making of Music: Four Lectures Given at Cornell University, Autumn 1954* (New York: Cornell University Press, 1955).
Vaughan Williams, Ursula, *R.V.W.: A Biography* (London: Oxford University Press, 1964).
Warrack, Guy, *The Royal College of Music: The First 85 Years, 1883–1968 and Beyond* part 5 (London: Royal College of Music, 1977).
Watt, Sholto (ed.), *What In The Country: What Women Of The World Are Doing* (London: Chapham Hall Ltd., 1932).
Weiner, M.J., *English Culture and the Decline of the Industrial Spirit, 1850–1980* (Cambridge: Cambridge University Press, 1981).
Whalley, David, *Teenage Nervous Breakdown: Music and Politics in the Post-Elvis age* (London: Insight Books, 1998).
Whatmore, Sarah, *Farming Women: Gender, Work and the Family Enterprise* (Basingstoke: Macmillan, 1991).
White, Eric W., *The Arts Council of Great Britain* (London: Davis-Poynter, 1975).
Whittall, Arnold, *Musical Composition in the Twentieth-Century* (Oxford: Oxford University Press, 1999).
Wood, Henry, *My Life of Music* (London: Victor Gollancz Ltd., 1938).
Zweiniger-Bargielowska, Ina, *Women in Twentieth Century Britain* (Harlow: Longman, 2001).

Articles

Andrews, Paul, 'Herbert Howells', *The New Grove Dictionary of Music* vol. 11, ed. Stanley Sadie (2nd ed., London: Macmillan, 2001): pp. 770–74.
Austin, Christopher, 'To Be a Pilgrim – Malcolm Williamson at 70', *British Music* vol. 23 (2001): pp. 5–9.

Bearman, C.J., 'Cecil Sharp in Somerset: Some Reflections on the Work of David Harker', *Folklore* vol. 113 (2002): pp. 11–34.

Beaumont, Caitriona, 'Citizens not Feminists: the boundary negotiated between citizenship and feminism by mainstream women's organisations in England, 1928–1939', *Women's History Review* vol. 9 no. 2 (2000): pp. 411–29.

Broadwood, Lucy E., 'On the Collecting of English Folk-Song', *Proceedings of the Royal Musicological Association 1904–5* (14 March 1905): p. 101.

Brooks, Jeanice, 'Nadia Boulanger and the Salon of the Princesse de Polignac', *Journal of the American Musicological Society* vol. 46 no. 3 (1993): pp. 415–68.

Caldwell, J.E., 'Hopkins, Antony, *Doctor Musickus*', *Music & Letters* vol. 54 (April 1973): p. 115.

Cockrell, Dale, 'Beatles', *The New Grove Dictionary of Music* vol. 2, ed. Stanley Sadie (London: Macmillan, 1980): p. 321.

Cooke, Richard, 'Antony Hopkins', *The New Grove Dictionary of Music and Musicians* vol. 11, ed. Stanley Sadie (2nd ed., London: Macmillan, 2001): pp. 697–8.

Cooke, Richard, 'Arthur (William) Oldham', *The New Grove Dictionary of Music and Musicians* vol. 18, ed. Stanley Sadie (2nd ed., London: Macmillan, 2001): p. 379.

Crichton, Ronald, 'Adrian Boult', *The New Grove Dictionary of Music* vol. 1, ed. Stanley Sadie (2nd ed., London: Macmillan Press, 2001): p. 108.

Davidoff, Leonore, Jean L'Esperance and Howard Newby, 'Landscape with Figures: Home and Community in English Society', in *The Rights and Wrongs of Women* ed. and introduced by Juliet Mitchell and Ann Oakley (Harmondsworth: Penguin, 1976, repr. 1979): pp. 139–76.

Dawes, Frank, 'Modern Piano', *The Musical Times* vol. 113 (July 1972): p. 700.

De Val, Dorothy, 'The Transformed Village: Lucy Broadwood and Folksong' in Christina Bashford and Leanne Langley (eds.), *Music and British Culture, 1785–1914: Essays in Honour of Cyril Ehrlich* (Oxford: Oxford University Press, 2001): pp. 341–67.

Ellis, Katharine, 'The Fair Sax: Women, Brass-Playing and the Instrument Trade in 1860s Paris', *Journal of the Royal Musical Association* vol. 124 part 2 (1999): pp. 221–55.

Gillett, Paula, 'Entrepreneurial Women in Britain', William Weber (ed.), *The Musician as Entrepreneur, 1700–1914: Managers, Charlatans, and Idealists* (Bloomington: Indiana University Press, 2004): pp. 198–220.

Howes, Frank, 'Review of *Folk Songs of the Four Seasons* by Ralph Vaughan Williams', *Journal of the English Folk Dance and Song Society* vol. 6 no. 1 (December 1949): p. 56.

Howkins, Alun, 'The Discovery of Rural England', *Englishness: Politics and Culture* R. Colls and P. Dodds (eds) (London: Croom Helm, 1986): pp. 89–98.

Howkins, Alun, 'Greensleeves and the Idea of National Music', *Patriotism – The Making and Unmaking of British National Identity* vol. 3, ed. Raphael Samuel (London: Routledge, 1987): pp. 89–99.

Jacobs, Arthur and Ian Carson, 'Sir David Willcocks', *The New Grove Dictionary of Music* vol. 27, ed. Stanley Sadie (2nd ed., London: Macmillan, 2001): p. 402.

Kennedy, Michael, 'The Unknown Vaughan Williams', *Proceedings of the Royal Musical Association* vol. 99 (1972–3): p. 34.

Layton, Mary, 'Women as Organists and Choir Trainers', *The Music Student* vol. 10 no. 9 (May 1918): p. 336.

Lawson, Ray, 'Women Conductors: Credibility in a Male-Dominated Profession', *The Musical Woman: An International Perspective* vol. 3, ed. Judith Lang Zaimont (London: Greenwood, 1991): pp. 197–219.

Lester, A., 'Review of Dave Harker: Fakesong', *Lore and Language* vol. 9 no. 1 (1985): p. 104.

MacGregor, Lynda, 'Ernest Read', *The New Grove Dictionary of Music* vol. 20, ed. Stanley Sadie (2nd ed., London: Macmillan Press, 2001): p. 894.

Marshall Jones, K., 'The Use of Folk Song in Village Choir Training', *English Dance and Song Journal* vol. 3 no. 2 (November and December 1938): p. 19.

Mason, Colin, 'The Music of Malcolm Williamson', *The Musical Times* vol. 103 (1967): pp. 757–9.

Matthews, Jill Julius, 'They had such a lot of fun: the Women's League of Health and Beauty Between the Wars', *History Workshop* vol. 50 (Autumn 1990): pp. 22–51.

McKay, Martin J., 'Vaughan Williams and the Amateur Tradition', *Making Music* no. 21 (Spring 1953): pp. 6–8.

Morgan, Maggie, 'Jam and Jerusalem', *Oral History* (Spring 1995): pp. 85–8.

Morgan, Maggie, 'Jam Making, Cuthbert Rabbit and Cakes: Redefining Domestic Labour in the Women's Institute, 1915–60', *Rural History* vol. 7 no. 2 (1996): pp. 207–219.

Oakley, Ann, 'Telling the Truth about Jerusalem', *New Society* (25 October 1984): pp. 136–8.

Payne, Elsie, 'Vaughan Williams and Folk Song: The Relation Between Folk Song and Other Elements in his Comprehensive Style', *The Music Review* vol. 15 (1954): pp. 103–126.

Pugh, Martin, 'Domesticity and the Decline of Feminism, 1930–50', *British Feminisms in the Twentieth Century*, ed. Harold C. Smith (Aldershot: Elgar, 1990): pp. 144–63.

Reich, Nancy, 'Women and the Music Conservatory', *Aflame with Music: 100 years of Music at the University of Melbourne*, ed. Brenton Broadstick et al. (University of Melbourne: Centre for Studies in Australian Music, 1996): pp. 427–37.

Rosenthal, Harold, 'Nancy Evans', *The New Grove Dictionary of Music* vol. 6, ed. Stanley Sadie (London: Macmillan, 1980): p. 319.

Russell, Dave, 'Amateur musicians and their repertoire', *The Twentieth Century*, ed. Stephen Banfield, The Blackwell History of Music in Britain no. 6 (Oxford: Blackwell, 1995): pp. 145–76.

Sadie, Stanley, 'Review of *The Brilliant and The Dark*', *Musical Times* vol. 110 (1969): p. 755.

Shaw, Geoffrey, 'Response to G.H. Clustam, "Classicism and False Values"', *Proceedings of the Musical Association* vol. 44 (1917–1918): p. 141.

Smyth, Ethel, 'England, Music, and – Women', *The English Review* vol. 22 (1916): p. 198.

Stebbing, S., 'Women's Roles and Rural Society', *Locality and Rurality*, ed. T. Bradley and P. Lowe (Norwich: Geo Books, 1984): pp. 200–207.

Sykes, Richard, 'The Evolution of Englishness in the English Folksong Revival, 1890–1914', *Folk Music Journal* vol. 6 no. 4 (1993): pp. 447–89.

Thompson, Lynne, 'The Promotion of Agricultural Education for Adults: The Lancashire Federation of Women's Institutes', *Rural History* vol. 10 no. 2 (1999): pp. 217–34.

Vaughan Williams, Ralph, 'English Folk Song', *The Musical Times* vol. 52 no. 816 (February 1911): pp. 101–104.

Vaughan Williams, Ralph, 'Traditional Arts in the Twentieth Century', *English Dance and Song Society Journal* vol. 2 no. 6 (June–July 1938): pp. 98–9.

Vaughan Williams, Ralph, 'The Composer in Wartime, 1940', *Heirs and Rebels: Letters Written to Each Other and Occasional Writings on Music by Ralph Vaughan Williams and Gustav Holst*, Ursula Vaughan Williams and Imogen Holst (eds) (London: Oxford University Press, 1959): pp. 91–3.

Vaughan Williams, Ralph, 'The Justification of Folk Song', *English Dance and Song Society Journal* vol. 5 no. 6 (July–August 1941): pp. 66–7.

Vaughan Williams, Ralph, 'Let Us Remember', *English Dance and Song Society Journal* vol. 6 no. 3 (February 1942): pp. 27–8.

Vaughan Williams, Ursula, 'Vaughan Williams and Amateur Music', *Journal of the Rural Music Schools Association* vol. 78 (Spring 1972): pp. 7–8.

Walsh, Stephen, 'Malcolm Williamson', *The New Grove Dictionary of Music and Musicians* vol. 20, ed. Stanley Sadie (London: Macmillan, 1980): p. 437.

Walsh, Stephen, 'Williamson the Many-Sided', *Music and Musicians* (July 1965): p. 26.

Wiley, Christopher, 'A Relic of an Age Still Capable of a Romantic Outlook: Musical Biography and The Master Musicians Series, 1899–1906', *Comparative Criticism* vol. 25 (November 2003): pp. 161–202.

Unpublished theses

Beaumont, Caitriona, 'Women and Citizenship: A Study of Non-Feminist Women's Societies and the Women's Movement in England, 1928–50', PhD thesis, University of Warwick, 1996.

Drews, Walter, 'The British Short-Term Residential College for Adult Education, 1941–1995', PhD thesis, University of Ulster, 1995.

Fuller, Sophie, 'Women Composers During the British Musical Renaissance, 1880–1918', PhD thesis, University of London, 1998.

Laverick, Alyson, 'The Women's Institute: Just Jam and Jerusalem?', MA. Dissertation in Women's Studies, University of Wales, 1990.

McCarthy, Elizabeth, 'Attitudes to Women and Domesticity in England, c.1939–1945', DPhil thesis, University of Oxford, 1994.

McHale, Maria, 'A Singing People: English Vocal Music and Nationalist Debate, 1880–1920', PhD thesis, University of London, 2004.

North, David L., 'Middle-class Suburban Lifestyles and Culture in England, 1919–1939', DPhil thesis, University of Oxford, 1989.

Payne, Elsie, 'The Folk-Song Element in the Music of Ralph Vaughan Williams', PhD thesis, University of Liverpool, 1953.

Unpublished papers

Thompson, Lynne, '"Conservative" Women and Feminist History: The Case of The Women's Institute Movement in England and Wales 1915–1945', unpublished paper given at the 'Conservative Women' Conference at University College Northampton in November 2001.

Articles from *Home and Country*

Bavin, J.T., 'The Care of the Piano,' *Home and Country* vol. 10 no. 1 (January 1928): pp. 32–3.

Barker, George, 'On Record', *Home and Country* vol. 46 no. 2 (February 1964): p. 49.

Barker, George, 'Shakespeare and Music', *Home and Country* vol. 46 no. 4 (April 1964): pp. 125–6.

Barker, George, 'The Lure of Opera', *Home and Country* vol. 46 no. 9 (September 1964): pp. 301–302.

Barker, George, 'On Listening to Modern Music', *Home and Country* vol. 46 no. 6 (June 1965): p. 95.

Barker, George, 'The Beggar's Opera', *Home and Country* vol. 47 no. 2 (February 1965): p. 51.

Battle, Joan, 'Taking Shape', *Home and Country* vol. 49 no. 9 (September 1968): p. 311.

Belletti, Lilian, 'Women's Institute Choirs', *Home and Country* vol. 4 no. 6 (November 1922): p. 8.

Belletti, Lilian, 'Madrigals', *Home and Country* vol. 5 no. 11 (November 1923): p. 304.

Bernard, Joan, 'The Queen's Musick', *Home and Country* vol. 35 no. 6 (June 1953): p. 191.

Berwick, Teresa, 'A Short History of Music I', *Home and Country* vol. 13 no. 11 (November 1931): p. 567.

[Brocklebank, Joan], 'A Home of Music in Germany', *Home and Country* vol. 19 no. 4 (April 1937): p. 187.

Brocklebank, Joan, 'Choosing Music for Women's Institutes', *Home and Country* vol. 21 no. 3 (March 1939): p. 92.

Brown, Meredith, 'News from the Institutes – Staffordshire Federation', North-Western counties supplement, *Home and Country* vol. 50 no. 12 (December 1969): p. 506.

Comber, W.M., 'News in the Institutes – Cheshire Federation', *Home and Country* vol. 32 no. 6 (June 1950): p. 154.

Darling, Diana, 'Music in the English Family', *Home and Country* vol. 34 no. 8 (August 1952): p. 235.
Drew, Sylvia H., 'Correspondence', *Home and Country* vol. 1 no. 7 (September 1919): p. 2.
Evans, Edwin, 'Master of the King's Musick', *Home and Country* vol. 24 no. 3 (March 1942): p. 41.
Evans, Edwin, 'Sir Henry Wood', *Home and Country* vol. 26 no. 10 (October 1944): p. 147.
Foss, Hubert, 'Our English Folk Song: A Great Possession', *Home and Country* vol. 32 no. 2 (February 1950): pp. 32–3.
Foss, Hubert, 'The Singer in Our Music – 1', *Home and Country* vol. 32 no. 4 (April 1950): p. 88.
Foss, Hubert, 'The Singer in Our Music – 2', *Home and Country* vol. 32 no. 4 (May 1950): p. 119.
Foss, Hubert, 'The Singer in Our Music – 3', *Home and Country* vol. 32 no. 5 (June 1950): p. 153.
Foss, Hubert, 'The Singer in Our Music – 4', *Home and Country* vol. 32 no. 8 (July 1950): p. 179.
Gaskell, C.J., 'The Folk Dance Society and the Institutes', vol. 14 no. 7 (July 1932): p. 328.
Grant, Peter, 'Felix Mendelssohn Bartholdy, 1809–1847', *Home and Country* vol. 29 no. 11 (November 1947): p. 192.
Grant, Peter, 'Frederic François Chopin, 1810–1849', *Home and Country* vol. 31 no. 10 (October 1949): pp. 216–7.
Grant, Peter, 'Johann Sebastian Bach', *Home and Country* vol. 32 no. 7 (July 1950): p. 176.
Grant, Peter, 'A Mercurial Genius', *Home and Country* vol. 38 no. 1 (January 1956): p. 7.
Green, Paul, 'Music for Folk Dancing', *Home and Country* vol. 42 no. 2 (February 1960): p. 43–5.
Hadow, W.H., 'Music for Country People', *Home and Country* vol. 6 no. 5 (July 1924): pp. 614–16.
Harrison, Atherton, 'Our Rock 'n' Rolling Teenagers', *Home and Country* vol. 40 no. 7 (July 1958): p. 157.
Hobbs, M.E., 'Singing', *Home and Country* vol. 3 no. 3 (July 1921): p. 6.
Hobbs, M.E., 'Dancing and Music II', *Home and Country* vol. 7 no. 7 (June 1925): p. 232.
Hughes, Mrs, 'News in the Institutes – Hertfordshire Federation', *Home and Country* vol. 32 no. 8 (August 1950): p. 210.
Kennedy, D.N., 'Singing and Dancing in the Village', *Home and Country* vol. 15 no. 8 (August 1933): p. 390.
Lampson, Gertrude, 'The Gramophone', *Home and Country* vol. 12 no. 1 (January 1930): p. 19.
Lemare, Iris, 'For Those Who Play Stringed Instruments', *Home and Country* vol. 36 no. 12 (December 1954): p. 439.

Neville-Smith, Esther, 'Singing Across the Centuries', *Home and Country* vol. 35 no. 8 (August 1953): p. 255–6.

Nugent Harris, J., 'A Village in Somerset', *Home and Country* vol. 2 no. 4 (June 1920): p. 5.

Olive, Phyllis, 'Towards Opera', *Home and Country* vol. 44 no. 2 (February 1962): p. 42.

Radford, M., 'On Hearing Music', *Home and Country* vol. 3 no. 2 (June 1921): p. 17.

Rigg, Elise, 'Music in Wartime', *Home and Country* vol. 22 no. 7 (July 1940): p. 159.

Rigg, Elise, 'New Music for WI Choirs', *Home and Country* vol. 27 no. 12 (December 1945): p. 187.

Robertson Scott, J.W., 'The Cottage Housewife's Earphones', *Home and Country* vol. 9 no. 1 (October 1932): p. 422.

Sharman, M., 'News from the Institutes – Cornwall Federation', South-Western counties supplement, *Home and Country* vol. 50 no. 8 (August 1969): p. 329.

Tatham, M. and Mrs Tylor, 'Ralph Vaughan Williams', *Home and Country* vol. 31 no. 2 (February 1949): p. 23.

Taylor, M.J., 'News from the Institute – Nottinghamshire Federation', North-Western counties supplement, *Home and Country* vol. 51 no. 8 (August 1970): p. 334.

Tennant, Nancy, 'The Uses of Leisure in the Country', *Home and Country* vol. 16 no. 5 (May 1934): pp. 240–42.

Wyatt, Honor, 'Ursula Vaughan Williams', *Home and Country* vol. 48 no. 5 (May 1966): p. 179.

Wyatt, Honor, 'Malcolm Williamson', *Home and Country* vol. 48 no. 7 (July 1966): p. 267.

Wyatt, Honor, '*The Brilliant and The Dark*', *Home and Country* vol. 48 no. 9 (September 1966): p. 315.

Young, K.L., 'News from the Institutes – Somerset Federation', South-Western counties supplement, *Home and Country* vol. 50 no. 7 (July 1969): p. 294.

Unknown authors

'Association of Musical Competition Festivals', *The Musical Times* vol. 46 (1 August 1905): p. 541.

'Centenary: Arthur Seymour Sullivan', *Home and Country* vol. 24 (April 1942): p. 75.

'Conductor's School held in London, November 31st', *Home and Country* (January 1932): p. 32.

'Correspondence', *Home and Country* vol. 11 no. 6 (September 1919): pp. 2–3.

'Drama and Music in Country Villages', *Home and Country* vol. 2 no. 7 (September 1920): pp. 6–7.

E.L., 'Review of *A Ceremony of Carols*', *Music & Letters* vol. 25 no. 2 (April 1944): p. 119.

I.K., 'Reviews of Music – Choral Music', *Music & Letters* vol. 31 no. 4 (October 1950): pp. 373–4.

'Introduction to Jazz', *Home and Country* vol. 47 no. 2 (February 1965): p. 55.

Leith Hill Musical Festival, *And Choirs Singing: An Account of The Leith Hill Musical Festival, 1905–1985* (Dorking: The Festival, 1985).
'Letters to the Editor', *Home and Country* vol. 5 no. 6 (December 1923): p. 355–6.
'Letters to the Editor', *Home and Country* vol. 6 no.11 (November 1934): p. 608.
'Letters to the Editor', *Home and Country* vol. 9 no. 5 (June 1937): p. 323.
'Letters to the Editor', *Home and Country* vol. 9 no. 8 (August 1937): p. 437.
'Letters to the Editor', *Home and Country* vol. 9 no. 5 (June 1937): p. 383.
'Letters to the Editor', *Home and Country* vol. 9 no. 7 (July 1937): p. 383.
'Letters to the Editor', *Home and Country* vol. 9 no. 10 (September 1937): p. 485.
'Letters to the Editor', *Home and Country* vol. 19 no. 10 (October 1937): pp. 539–40.
'Letters to the Editor', *Home and Country* vol. 19 no. 11 (November 1937): p. 599.
'Letters to the Editor', *Home and Country* vol. 25 no. 11 (November 1943): p. 179.
'Letters to the Editor', *Home and Country* vol. 26 no. 1 (January 1944): p. 15.
'News in the Institutes', *Home and Country* vol. 26 no. 6 (June 1944): p. 93.
'News in the Institutes', *Home and Country* vol. 32 no. 8 (December 1950): p. 326.
'Notes from the Music Sub-Committee', *Home and Country* vol. 7 no. 7 (July 1925): p. 254.
'Notes from Headquarters', *Home and Country* vol. 8 no. 2 (February 1936): p. 76.
[Unsigned], 'Review of The Women's Symphony Orchestra – A Charity Performance', *The Times* (27 June 1924): p. 12.
[Unsigned], 'Should Mothers Visit Their Children in Hospital?', *News Chronicle* (15 June 1950): p. 3.
[Unsigned], 'Music Review', *The Times* (16 June 1950): p. 719.
[Unsigned], 'WI Save The Man Who Forgot His Trousers', *The Evening Standard* (20 November 1975): p. 4.
[Unsigned], 'Obituary for Ruth Gipps', *The Daily Telegraph* (30 March 1999): p. 15.
'Woman in a Man's World', *Home and Country* vol. 50 no. 1 (January 1969): p. 11.
'Woman in a Man's World', *Home and Country* vol. 50 no. 2 (February 1969): p. 54.
'Woman in a Man's World', *Home and Country* vol. 50 no. 5 (May 1969): p. 189.

Websites

[Unsigned], 'Dame Clara (Ellen) Butt', *The New Grove Dictionary of Music Online* ed. L. Macy (Accessed 4 May 2004), <http.www.grovemusic.com>.
Colles, H.C. and E.D. Mackerness, 'Leslie, Henry (David)', *The New Grove Dictionary of Music Online* (Accessed 30 January 2001) <http: www.grovemusic.com>.
Fortune, Nigel, 'W.H. Hadow', *The New Grove Dictionary Online* ed. L. Macy (Accessed 4 May 2004), <http.www.grovemusic.com>.
National Federation of Women's Institute website (Accessed 12 February 2005), <http.www.womensinstitute.org.uk>.
Ottaway, Hugh and Lewis Foreman, 'Sir (Henry) Walford Davies', *The New Grove Dictionary of Music Online* (Accessed 4 May 2004), <http.www.grovemusic.com>.

Material consulted at the British Newspaper Library

Canning, Hugh, 'Lightning conductor', *The Sunday Times Magazine* (12 January 2003): p. 10.
Chesterton, Joyce, 'Cruel to Keep Us Away Plead 438, 000 women', *Daily Mirror* (15 June 1950): p. 7.
Fraser, Cicely, 'Mothers Place is in the Home', *Daily Herald* (Thursday 15 June 1950): p. 3.
Graham, Clive, 'Let These Mothers See Them', *Reynolds News and Sunday Citizen* (11 June 1950): p. 6.
S.G., 'WI Choirs in New Cantata', *News Chronicle* (16 June 1950): p. 3.
Squibb, David, 'WI Fully Choral', *Coulsdon and Purley Advertiser* (11 June 1971): p. 21.

Material consulted at the NFWI Archives at Denman College

National Federation's minute books 1923–75: Music Sub-Committee minutes, Executive minutes Office and Finance Minute Books.
WI Handbook (NFWI, 1951)
NFWI publications on music: *Music in the Institutes* (London: NFWI, 1925, 1946), *The Women's Institute Song Book* (NFWI, c. 1925), *The Women's Institute Second Song Book* (NFWI, 1926), *Women's Institute Song List* (c. 1938), *Welsh Women's Institute Song List* (National Council of Music, c. 1939), *Suggested Items Suitable for Variety Programme* (c. 1943), *Supplement* (1948), *Music Handbook* (London: NFWI, 1954), *NFWI Song List* (c. 1958), *NFWI Song List* (1965), Imogen Holst, *Singing for Pleasure: A Collection of Songs* (London: Oxford University Press, 1957), *Time to be Social* (London: NFWI, 1957), *Keeping Ourselves Informed* (London: NFWI, 1964), *Book of Carols* (London: NFWI, 1968), *Accent on Music* (London: NFWI, 1971).
A review of 'Folk Songs of the Four Seasons', *Music in Education* (July–August 1950), n.p.
Newspaper reviews of *The Brilliant and The Dark* which include Auriol Stevens, 'The WI Spectacular', *The Guardian* (2 June 1969), Stanley Sadie, 'Opera; A Lavish Pageant of Women's Work', *The Times* (4 June 1969), [Unsigned] 'Focus On the Operetta', *The Evening Standard* (4 June 1969), p. 48, A.E.P. '1,000 Women in Operatic Pageant', *Daily Telegraph* (4 June 1969) and Alan Blyth, 'Albert Hall; The Brilliant and The Dark', *Financial Times* (4 June 1969).
Newspaper reviews of the National Society Choir which include [Unsigned] 'WI choir's First Concert' [Nottingham] *Evening Post* (stamped 18 April 1973), [Unsigned] 'First Concert of WI Choir', *Derby Evening Telegraph* (stamped 24 April 1973), [Unsigned] 'Norfolk WI Notes: The Allure of Music', *Norwich Mercury* (stamped 15 September 1973), [Unsigned] 'WI Choir Concert', *Wrexham Leader* (8 November 1974), [Unsigned] 'Avalon Singers' London Debut', *Woking News and Mail* (n.d.), A.E.P., 'Quality of Sound From Women's Choir', *The Daily Telegraph* (20 November 1975).

Programmes for concerts, which include *Folk Songs of the Four Seasons* (Royal Albert Hall, 15 June 1950), *The Brilliant and The Dark* (Royal Albert Hall, 3 June 1969), 'The Avalon Singers' (Purcell Rooms, 19 November 1975) and performances of the South East Section on the following dates: The Lees Cliff Halls in Dorking, 21 February 1973 and 13 June 1975; The Grange School in Aylesbury, 10 November 1973; The Mercury Theatre in Colchester, 20 May 1974; The Dome in Brighton, 29 May 1974; Central Hall in Chatham, 4 November 1974; The Mary Ward Festival in London, 9 June 1975; and The Pavilion in Hemel Hempstead, 23 October 1975). A performance of The Llewellyn Singers at Shire Hall Hereford, on 26 June 1976.

Denman College Archives

'The Story of Denman College' (n.d.)
'Denman College: Past, Present and Future' (n.d.)
'Denman College: its First Thirty Years' (1973)

Material consulted at the NFWI Head Office (London)

Executive minute books 1919–1975.
Music Sub-Committee minutes 1923–1975.
NFWI Annual Reports 1918–1973.

Material consulted at the BBC Script Archives

Transcript of 'Woman's Hour' on 15 June 1950 (transmission 14.00–15.00, 15.00–15.30).
'Contributors, Williams Ralph Vaughan. Composer file 3, 1947-51 COM 3'.
'Contributors, Williams Ralph Vaughan. Composer file 4, 1952-62 COM 4'.
LIV T297 Talk Scripts.
Woman's Hour, M101/102.
Files R27/1 182/1 OPERA and R27/1 234/1 OPERA.

Material consulted at the EFDSS Archives, Cecil Sharp House

EFDS Executive minutes 1920–1932.
Davies, H.W., *The Fellowship Songbook* (London: J. Curwen and Sons, 1916).
The Motherland Song Book: Songs for Unison and Mixed Voices (London, n.d.).
The Pocket Sing-Song Book for Schools, Homes and Community Singing (London: Novello and Co., 1927?).
News Chronicle Song Book (Words edition. London: News Chronicle Publications Department, 1931?).

Material consulted at the RCM Archives

Conducting registers for Gordon Jacobs, Constant Lambert, Reginald Jacques and Richard Austin.
The Society of Women Musician archives – Boxes 1 and 2.

Royal Academy of Music Archives

Royal Academy prospectuses from 1921–1970.
The minutes for the Committee of Management from 1923–1935.

Material consulted at the Britten-Pears Foundation Library

Files labelled 'Pike 1 of 2', 'Pike, 2 of 2', 'East Coke WI 53' and 'National Federation of Women's Institutes'.

Song books (consulted at the British Library)

Brocklebank, Joan (ed.), *Songs for All Seasons* (Oxford: Oxford University Press, 1937).
Brocklebank, Joan and Biddie Kindersley (eds), *A Dorset Book of Folk Songs* (London: EFDSS, 1948).
Songs of Faith, Nature and Comradeship (Stockport: Co-Operative Holidays Association, 1902).

Material consulted at the V&A Archives

'File EL1 Council for the Encouragement of Music and the Arts: Minutes and Papers, 1939–1945.'
'File EL2 Council for the Encouragement of Music and the Arts: Minutes and Papers, 1939–1960.'
'File EL3 Council for the Encouragement of Music and the Arts: Correspondence, 1942–1956.'
'File EL4 Council for the Encouragement of Music and the Arts: Minutes and Papers, 1942–1945.'
'File EL5 Council for the Encouragement of Music and the Arts: Secretariat and Correspondence, 1945–1961.'
'File EL4 Council for the Encouragement of Music and the Arts Council of Great Britain: Minutes and Papers.'
'File EL6 Council for the Encouragement of Music and the Arts: Festival of Britain. Records.'

Material loaned by kind permission of Prof. Lionel Pike (Royal Holloway)

Letter from Ursula Vaughan Williams to Mr [Lionel Pike] dated 30 September 1989.
Letter from Ursula Vaughan Williams to Mr [Lionel] Pike dated 7 October 1989.

Other

Goddard, Scott, 'Concerto Grosso for All Comers', Souvenir Programme of the Rural Music Schools Association 21st Birthday Festival on 18 November 1950.

Carnegie United Kingdom Trust, 'Music and Drama in the Villages – Report for 1928–31 of the Joint Committee Administering a Fund provided by the CUKT' (1931).

Interviews with Ursula Vaughan Williams (on 25 May 2001) and Antony Hopkins (on 21 July 2003).

Programme for The Avalon Singers at The Thames Hall, Fulcrum Centre, Slough (on 18 May 1977).

Telephone interviews with Mrs Elizabeth Lamb (on 12 October 2001), Mrs Cannetty Clarke (on 2 November 2001) and Mr Stuart Neame (on 13 February 2002).

The Musical Directory, Annual and Almanack (London: Rudall, Carte and Co.) 1899–1930.

Personalia

This appendix lists the names of Institute members, and those involved in music making activities within the organization, mentioned in the book. In certain cases, background information is provided about individuals for whom more details are known. Inevitably, information has been more accessible for some individuals than for others, in particular those involved in the National Federation's committees. Finding information about members has been problematic for a number of reasons. Firstly, sources often provide little detailed information apart from members' names and the Institute to which they are affiliated. Second, it is often difficult to differentiate between members that share the same name.

The information provided is largely compiled from the National Federation's minute books which listed those members present at committee meetings and provides an insight into the length of individuals' service. In addition, I have made preliminary investigation into the membership of the National Federation's Executive Committee in order to examine its relationship with the Music Sub-Committee. It appears that many members held joint membership of other Sub-Committees which is an area yet to be fully researched and would provide a valuable insight into the internal workings of the National Federation. Other sources which have been consulted in compiling the appendix of personalia include *Home and Country* which had occasionally included articles and obituaries about members and concert programmes.

For information about 'outsiders' I have consulted *The New Grove Dictionary of Music Online*. In addition, the appendix of Michael Kennedy's *A Catalogue of the Works of Ralph Vaughan Williams* has been a valuable source that has provided useful information about individuals involved in amateur music-making.[1] However, in majority of cases the information about individuals has been compiled from a variety of sources such as newspaper articles, histories of organizations and archival documents (which include other women's organizations). Although it is by no means a complete list of all those involved in the organization's music activities during this period, the appendix provides an insight into those at the centre of music policy both within and outside the organization.

---

1 Michael Kennedy's, *A Catalogue of the Works of Ralph Vaughan Williams*, London: Oxford University Press, 1964; 2nd ed., 1982.

Name (title if known is given in brackets)	Role or involvement in the WI
Albemarle, Lady	President of Snetterton WI, and member of the Norfolk Federation Executive Committee. NFWI Chairman (1946–1951) and also NFWI representative on the National Council of Social Service Village Halls Sub-Committee.
Aldin, John (Mr)	Chosen by Williamson to adjudicate at the county festivals of *The Brilliant and The Dark*.
Anglesey, Lady	NFWI Chairman (1966–1969). She also served on the Music Festival Ad Hoc Committee (1964–1969).
Arkwright, Marion (Dr)	(d. 1922) President for almost 4 years of Highclere WI, and member of Hampshire Executive Committee. She conducted choral and orchestral societies in her local area and was one of the first women to gain a Mus.Doc from Durham University.
Auerbach, Helen (Mrs)	(d. 1955) NFWI's first Treasurer. She was closely connected with Millicent Fawcett, until 1917, and was also Treasurer of the National Union of Women's Suffrage Societies.
Austin, Richard (Mr)	(b.1903) English conductor. Conductor for the Carl Rosa company (1929–1931), and the Bournemouth Municipal Orchestra (1934–1940). In 1946, joined the staff at the RCM and gave courses on conducting from 1957 to 1959.
Baines, Margaret	WI member. Wrote a letter to the editor of *Home and Country* regarding *Jerusalem* in 1937.
Baker, George (Mr)	Clarinetist and pianist, who for 10 years was programme adviser to the London Philharmonic orchestra. Wrote articles on listening to music which were published in *Home and Country* in 1964.
Ballard, Anne (Mrs)	NFWI General Secretary (1972–1990). Worked in the NFWI archives until 2002.
Bateson, (Mrs)	Member of Buckinghamshire Federation, and the NFWI Music and Drama Sub-Committee (1947–1951).

Personalia

Battle, Joan (Mrs)	Member of the NFWI Music and Drama Sub-Committee (1962–1963), and also served on the Music Festival Ad Hoc Committee (1964–1969).
Batty Shaw, A. (Mrs)	NFWI Chairman (1977–1981).
Barling, (Mrs)	Stood as candidate for the NFWI Executive Committee in 1956, and was a member of the Music Festival Ad Hoc Committee (1964–1969).
Baseley, Geoffrey (Mr)	Producer of the radio programme *The Archers* at the time of the 1969 Music Festival.
Bavin, J.T. (Major)	Adviser on the NFWI's Music Sub-Committee (1926–1929). Wrote 'The Care of the Piano' which was published in *Home and Country* in January 1928.
Beale, Mrs	Served on NFWI Music and Drama Sub-Committee (1946–1950) and was also a member of the Singing Festival Sub-Committee (1948–1950).
Belletti, Lilian M.	Member from Stenwell WI, Middlesex. Wrote to the editor of *Home and Country* in 1919 about music in the WI, and articles entitled 'Women's Institute Choirs' and 'Madrigals' which were published in *Home and Country* in 1922 and 1923 respectively.
Benson, (Mr)	Representative from the publishers Weinbergers who entered into negotiations with the NFWI with regard to a recording of *The Brilliant and The Dark*.
Bernard, Joan	Secretary of the NFWI Music and Dancing Sub-committee (1956–1957). Wrote 'The Queen's Musick' which was published in *Home and Country* in 1953.
Berwick, Teresa	Wrote a series of three essays on the history of music, and 'Musical instruments', which were published in *Home and Country* in 1931 and 1932.
Blackburn, Margery	Member of Knowle WI, Warwickshire. A pianist who played at the premiere of *The Brilliant and The Dark*.

Boscawen, Margaret (Lady)	Served on the NFWI's Music Sub-Committee (1923–1926), at the same time as serving on the Executive Committee (1923–1926), Agriculture and Horticulture Sub-Committee (1923–1925) and Education, Literature and Publicity Sub-Committee (1925–1926).
Boult, Adrian (Mr)	(1889–1983) English conductor. Conducted the premiere of *Folk Songs of the Four Seasons*.
Bower, Mr	Conductor of the Sandhurst WI choir and was granted a bursary in 1936 to attend the Schools for Conductors.
Bower, (Miss)	Member of the NFWI's Music and Drama Sub-Committee (1965–1966), and later served on the Music Festival Ad Hoc Committee (1964–1969), and the Music Society Ad Hoc Committee (1970–1973).
Bowers, (Mrs)	Member of the Music Festival Ad Hoc Committee (1964–1969).
Boweskill, (Mr)	His advice was sought regarding Mrs Vooght's drama script planned for the Golden Jubilee celebrations.
Boyne, Viscountess	Served on the NFWI Music Sub-Committee (1923–1926), at the same time as serving on the Executive Committee (1923–1926), Education, Literature and Publicity Sub-Committee (1923–1926), *Home and Country* Sub-Committee (1925–1926), and Drama Sub-Committee (1925–1926).
Braine, (Mrs)	Member of the Music Festival Ad Hoc Committee (1964–1969).
Brocklebank, Joan (Miss)	Chairman of Leicestershire and Rutland Federation and was elected onto the Council of Shorthorn Society in 1931. Served as Music Adviser of the NFWI (1936–1938). Articles published in *Home and Country* include 'A Home of Music in Germany' (April 1937), 'Music in the Institute' (January 1938), 'Choosing Music for Women's Institutes' (March 1939) and 'Making Music' (August 1951).

Brown, Meredith (Mrs)	Correspondent for 'News from the Institutes' who reported on performances of *The Brilliant and The Dark* in Staffordshire Federation.
Browning, M.C.	WI member. Wrote to the editor of *Home and Country* regarding *Jerusalem* in 1937.
Brooke, M.A. (Mrs)	NFWI Treasurer (1969–1971), and beforehand was a member of the Executive and the Music Festival Ad Hoc Committee (1964–1969).
Brunner, Lady	NFWI Chairman (1951–1956).
Budden, Julian (Mr)	Producer of Radio 3 at the time of the 1969 Music Festival.
Buddug Jones, (Mrs)	Co-opted onto the NFWI Executive in 1956 as Welsh representative, and served on the Music Festival Ad Hoc Committee (1964–1969).
Burnham, (Mrs)	Member of the Music Festival Ad Hoc Committee (1964–1969).
Burnham, (Lady)	NFWI Music Sub-Committee member who gave a talk on 'The Future of the NFWI Music Society' at a conference held in London on 26 October 1971. Made the announcement at the Leicestershire concert that the original National Society Choir was to disband.
Butt, Clara (Dame)	(1872–1936) English contralto. She was invited to sing at the AGM in 1929.
Campbell, Sylvia	Member from Hartford WI, Huntingdon and Peterborough Federation. A vocal soloist at the premiere of *The Brilliant and The Dark*.
Cannetty-Clarke, Janet (Mrs)	Member of Horsted Keynes WI, West Sussex. Served on the NFWI Music Sub-Committee from 1969 and on the Music Society (SE Section) Committee until the Avalon Singers disbanded in 1978 (and was their official accompanist). A pianist who played at the premiere of *The Brilliant and The Dark* and who, according to the minutes, proposed the idea of a National Choir.

Cantelo, April	A distinguished singer, having performed at Glyndebourne, Covent Garden and the Royal Festival Hall and been involved in a production of Britten's *A Midsummer Night's Dream* at Aldeburgh. Sang at the preparatory conference for *The Brilliant and The Dark* in November 1966.
Catheside, Doris	Member of Alnmouth WI, Northumberland. A pianist who played at the premiere of *The Brilliant and The Dark*.
Chaplin, (Lady)	Member of the Music Festival Ad Hoc Committee (1964–1969).
Christmas, Betty	The first warden of Denman College (1948–1955).
Churchill, John (Mr)	Chosen by Williamson to adjudicate at the county festivals of *The Brilliant and The Dark*.
Clarke, Mrs	Member of Somerset Federation, who appears to have written the commentary for the 1934 publication of the leaflet on *Jerusalem*.
Collingham, Kenneth (Mr)	Conducted Buckinghamshire Youth Orchestra at the SE Sections' concert in Aylesbury in 1973.
Comber, W.M. (Miss)	WI member. Reported on activities in Cheshire Federation in *Home and Country* in 1950.
Cox, John (Mr)	Director of the premiere of *The Brilliant and The Dark* at the Royal Albert Hall.
Crawshaw, M.E.	Member of the NFWI Society choir who, in 1972, objected to news it was disbanding.
Crompton, Alice (Miss)	Member from Sutton, Bignor and Barlavington WI, Sussex. Wrote to the editor of *Home and Country* in 1919 about music in the WI.
Curry, (Mrs)	Secretary for the NFWI Music Sub-Committee during the formation of the National Society Choir.

Personalia

Darling, Diana (Mrs)	Chairman of NFWI Music and Dancing Sub-committee (1952–1957) (d.1961). Wrote 'A Mixed Bag of Music' and 'Fun with Music and Dancing' which were published in *Home and Country* in 1954 and 1957 respectively.
Dawkes, Hubert (Mr)	Chosen by Williamson to adjudicate at the county festivals of *The Brilliant and The Dark*. He also played the organ at the NFWI AGMs.
Davies, Walford (Sir)	(1869–1941) Conducted the premiere of *Jerusalem* on 28 March 1914 at the Queen's Hall. He was present at Henry Leslie's summer school in September 1922.
Denman, Gertrude (Lady)	(1884–1954) NFWI Chairman (1917–1946). Served on the Executive Committee of the Women's Liberal Federation and was also Chairman of the Women's Liberal Metropolitan Union. She was the founding Chairman of the Family Planning Association and also Chairman of the Women's Land Army (1939–1945).
Dods, Marcus (Mr)	English conductor. Adjudicator of the regional festivals and conductor of the premiere of *The Brilliant and The Dark*. He was also considered as a possible conductor for the National Choir.
Doman, Kathleen (Miss)	Her advice was sought regarding Mrs Vooght's drama script planned for the Golden Jubilee celebrations.
Drake, Audrey	Member of the NFWI Society choir who, in 1972, objected to news it was disbanding.
Drew, Sylvia (Miss)	Member from Chilworth WI, Surrey. Wrote to the editor of *Home and Country* in 1919 about music in the WI.
Dyer, Lady	NFWI Chairman (1956–1961).
Eaton, Sybil (Miss)	A professional violinist who led the first course at Denman College for instrumental music.
Emmett, B.P. (Mr)	Head of Audience Research at the BBC at the time of the 1969 Music Festival.

Erhart, Dorothy (Miss)	(d. 1971) She served on the NFWI's Advisory Panel during the early 1930s, and was a member of the NFWI's Music Sub-Committee (1938–1940). Taught courses on conducting at Denman College until the 1960s. She wrote 'The Piper and the Tune' which was published in *Home and Country* in December 1935. County Organizer for the RMSA and a member of the Society of Women Musicians.
Evans, Hilda	Member of East Coker WI, Somerset. A pianist who played at the premiere of *The Brilliant and The Dark*.
Evans, Nancy	(b. 1915) She was a renowned mezzo-soprano soloist who made her London stage debut in 1938 in Sullivan's *The Rose of Persia*. During the Second World War she sang with the Entertainments National Services Association and became a member of the English Opera Group in 1946. Sang at the preparatory conference for *The Brilliant and The Dark* in November 1966.
Eyre, (Mrs)	One of only two members who was originally a member of the SE Section who joined the Midlands Choir.
Farquharson, Mr	Secretary of the Joint Committee for Music and Drama in 1934.
Farquharson, Olive (Mrs)	Elected Vice-Chairman of the Executive in 1966, and served on the Music Festival Ad Hoc Committee (1964–1969).
Farrer, Francis (Dame)	(b. 1895) NFWI Organizer in 1926, and became General Secretary (1929–1959). Before she joined the NFWI, she was secretary of the NUSEC. She was also a member of the Colonial Social Welfare Advisory Committee, National Savings Committee, Women's Group on Public Welfare and Women's Committee of Economic Information. Also Hon. Secretary of the Leith Hill Music Festival.
Ferguson, Inez (she later became Mrs Jenkins)	The first paid NFWI General Secretary (1919–1929), and later served on the Executive Committee. Lady Denman's assistant during her Chairmanship of the Women's Land Army and later wrote a history of the organization (published in 1953).

Foss, Hubert (Mr)	(d. 1953) In 1924 he became Director of the newly established Music Department at Oxford University Press. Vaughan Willliams' publisher and friend. Wrote a series of articles published in *Home and Country* entitled 'The Singer and our Music' in 1950.
Gaskell, [C.J] Miss	Served on the NFWI's Executive Committee (1927–1940), and on the NFWI Music Sub-Committee (1933–1934). Also a member of the English Folk Dance Society, and wrote 'The Folk Dance Society and the Institutes' which was published in *Home and Country* in July 1932.
Gee, Anne	Member of Clayton WI, East Sussex. A vocal soloist at the premiere of *The Brilliant and The Dark*.
Gildea, Miss	Reported the events of the Hertfordshire Council Meeting to the Executive in 1922 (at which W.H. Leslie was present). May be the same Miss Gildea who was a member of Dorset Federation until 1926.
Gilles-Wyatt, Monica	Won a conducting competition at the Royal Academy of Music in 1933.
Gipps, Ruth (Dr)	(1921–1999) Conductor and composer. First woman to conduct at the Royal Festival Hall. Founded two orchestras (London Repertoire 1955 and Chanticleen in 1961). Conductor of Co-Operative Orchestra and Listeners' Club choir (1948–1950), Chairman of Composers' Guild of Great Britain (1967). Awarded MBE (1981).
Gittings, Robert (Mr)	(b. 1911) Keats scholar. Wrote *Out Of This Wood* for the National Federation's Drama Festival in 1957.
Glasgow, (Miss)	Secretary of the Arts Council during the early 1940s.
Gordon (Mrs)	NFWI Music Sub-Committee member who gave a talk on 'Music in the Counties' at a conference held in London on 26 October 1971.
Gowring, (Mrs)	Member of the NFWI's Executive Committee (1942–1945).

Grant, Peter (Mr)	Usually wrote for *Home and Country* about films but is also a music devotee. His articles include 'Hot Singing' in 1968.
Gray, Sylvia	NFWI Chairman (1969–1974).
Gritton, Robin (Mr)	Freelance musician, who worked mainly as a conductor but also sang and recorded professionally. Examined for the Associated Board of the Royal School of Music, adjudicated festivals, taught at the University of London and played the cello professionally. Adjudicated the Midlands Section of the Society Choir in 1972.
Hackett Paine, (Mrs)	Member of the Music Festival Ad Hoc Committee (1964–1969).
Hadow, Grace (Miss)	(1875–1940) NFWI's Vice-Chairman (1919–1940). Articles published in *Home and Country* include 'Of Enjoying Ourselves' in February 1929.
Hadow, William Henry (Mr)	(1859–1937) English writer on music, educationist and composer, and the older brother of Grace Hadow. Gave a speech at the AGM in 1924, and was asked for his opinion about the suitability of *The Community Songbook* in 1926.
Hall, Betty	Member of the NFWI Society choir who, in 1972 objected to news it was disbanding.
Harris, Nugent J. (Mr)	Secretary of the Agricultural Organization Society.
Hemingford, Lady	An Executive Committee Officer who also served on the Music Festival Ad Hoc Committee (1964–1969).
Hennar, Anne (Mrs)	Member of Wilbourne WI, Northamptonshire. Featured in a series of articles titled 'Woman in a Man's World' published in *Home and Country* in 1969.
Henslow, Miles (Mr)	Involved in a magazine called 'Music' and approached the NFWI regarding including a section on Institutes' music activities in the counties.

Holst, Imogen (Miss)	(1907–1984) English writer on music, composer and administrator. A reserve composer for the National Federation's first and second music commission. Edited (for female voices) *Singing for Pleasure: A Collection of Songs* (1957) and the *Book of Carols* (1968) which were promoted by the National Federation.
Hoodless, Adelaide (Mrs)	Founder of the Canadian Women's Institutes.
Hopkins, Antony (Mr)	(b. 1921) English composer, broadcaster and writer on music. Conductor of the National Society Choir (later known as the Avalon Singers).
Hudson, (Mrs)	Served on the Music Festival Ad Hoc Committee (1964–1969), and also on the NFWI Music and Drama Sub-Committee (1968–1969).
Hughes, (Mrs)	Reported on Hertfordshire Federation's activities in *Home and Country* in 1950.
Hughes, Audrey	Member of Oxstalls WI, Gloucestershire. A vocal soloist at the premiere of *The Brilliant and The Dark*.
Ibberson, Mary (Miss)	Founded the Rural Music Schools Association in 1929.
Jacob, Gordon (Mr)	(1895–1984). English composer, teacher and writer. On the teaching staff at the Royal College of Music from 1924 to 1966, which included teaching conducting from 1938 to 1941.
Jacobson, Maurice (Mr)	(1896–1976) English composer, pianist, adjudicator and publisher. Composed an arrangement of *Jerusalem* for the NFWI in 1955.
Jacob, Pat (Mrs)	Served on the Music Festival Ad Hoc Committee (1964–1969), and later became Chairman of the NFWI (1974–1977).

Jacques, Reginald (Mr)	(1894–1969). English conductor, adjudicator and teacher. Director of Council for the Encouragement of Music and the Arts, the Bach Choir and founder and conductor of the Reginald Jacques Orchestra. Taught at the Royal College of Music for twenty years, which included aural training, conducting, and teacher training in class singing. From 1936 to 1939 he gave classes on conducting.
Jenney, (Miss)	Studied with Constant Lambert at the Royal College of Music for the whole of her second year.
Jenkins, (Mrs)	Member of the NFWI Publicity Sub-Committee who was in charge of the arrangements for the national Society Choir's debut and the 'Leicestershire' concert.
Jessell, (Mrs)	WI member of Hertfordshire Federation who became a member of the NFWI Music and Dancing Sub-Committee (1950–1954).
Joslin, (Miss)	Member of the Music Festival Ad Hoc Committee (1964–1969).
Judd, James (Mr)	Conductor of the Youth Musicians' Symphony Orchestra that accompanied the National Society Choir at its debut concert.
Justham, Barbara	Member of Rotherfield Greys WI, Oxfordshire. A vocal soloist at the premiere of *The Brilliant and The Dark*.
Kanga, Sheila	Professional harpist who played at the SE Sections' concert at Folkestone Halls in 1975.
Kimpton, Gwynne	(d. 1931) Conductor and distinguished violinist. Founded the Strings Club (1902) and the Gwynne Kimpton Orchestral Concerts for young people before First World War. Conducted the British Women's Orchestra (founded 1923) in a series of concerts.
King, A. (Miss)	NFWI General Secretary (1959–1969), and also served on the Music Festival Ad Hoc Committee (1964–1969).

Kitching, [Frances?] Mrs	(d. 1968) Accompanist for many of the courses on conducting held at Denman College.
Kisch, Miss	Studied conducting in her second and third year at the Royal College of Music, firstly with Jacques (in the Easter term 1936), then with Lambert (from the Midsummer term 1936 to the Christmas term 1937) and finally with Jacob (in the Midsummer term 1938).
Lake, Mary (Miss)	Member of the NFWI's Music and Drama Sub-Committee (1964–1965) and later served on the Music Festival Ad Hoc Committee (1964–1969).
Lamb, Elizabeth (Mrs)	Member of Scotby WI, Cumberland. A vocal soloist at the premiere of *The Brilliant and The Dark* and later became a professional singer.
Lambert, Constant (Mr)	(1905–1951) English composer, conductor and writer on music. Taught at the Royal College of Music, which included conducting from 1934 to 1939.
Lampson, Gertrude (Mrs)	Member of Anstye WI in Sussex, and well-known within the WI music circles. Wrote to the editor of *Home and Country* in 1919 about music in the WI Served on the NFWI Music Sub-Committee (1923–1936).
Le Fleming, Christopher	Reserve composer for the National Federation's first music commission. Involved with the RMSA, and became its Assistant Director.
Lemare, Iris (Miss)	Daughter of Edwin Lemare, the well-known organist and composer. Studied at Geneva and the Royal College of Music and then worked at the Mercury Theatre. During the Second World War she was County Music Organizer in Yorkshire and was on the regional committee for Adult Education in H.M. Forces. Adjudicated the area festivals for the Singing Festival in 1950 and the Music Festival in 1969.
Leslie, Henry [David] (Mr)	(1822–1896) English choral conductor and composer. Father of W.H. Leslie.

Leslie, William Henry (Mr)	Second son of Henry David Leslie. Held a Summer School of Music at his home in September 1922 to which WI members were invited. Co-opted member of the NFWI Music Sub-Committee (1923–1926). Gave a lecture at a VCO Conference in 1922.
Llewellyn, William (Mr)	Director of Music at Charterhouse boys' school (from 1965), and conductor of the Linden Singers. Other positions he held include being President of the Godalming Operatic Society, Musical Director of 'Music for Youth', President of the Music Masters' Association, and Warden of the Incorporated Society of Musicians School Music Section. Chosen by Williamson to adjudicate at the county festivals of *The Brilliant and The Dark*. Conductor of the Llewellyn Singers.
Lloyd Roberts, Enid	Member of Rhoscolyn and District WI, Anglesey. A vocal soloist at the premiere of *The Brilliant and The Dark*.
Listowel, Freda (Lady)	Member of the NFWI Music Sub-Committee (1933–1948), who attended the Founder's Day gathering of Hertfordshire RMS in 1934 and the weekend RMS school in Roehampton in 1947.
Littlejohn, Joan	Composer who was a former pupil of Hopkins' at the Royal College of Music. Composed *The Bonny Earl of Murray*, which was premiered at the Avalon Singer's first London performance in 1975.
Locke, Kathleen (Mrs)	Member of the NFWI Music Sub-Committee member and gave a talk on 'Denman College courses' at a conference held in London on 26 October 1971. Interviewed about her participation in *The Brilliant and The Dark* which featured in Nancy Wise's report broadcast on 'Woman's Hour'.
Lockhart Smith, Cara	Author of the twenty-six poems which Hopkins set to music for the SE Section (*Riding to Canobie*).
Mathews, Joan	Member of the NFWI Society choir who objected to news it was disbanding in 1972.

May (Mrs)	Member of the NFWI's Music and Drama Sub-Committee (1959–1960) and later served on the Music Festival Ad Hoc Committee (1964–1969).
Merritt, [Kathleen?] (Miss)	Applied to be the NFWI's Music Adviser in 1940. May be the same person who was the NUTG's music adviser in 1937.
Moore, Lorna (Miss)	Editor of *Home and Country* (a position from which she resigned in December 1944), and was involved in publicity for *The Brilliant and The Dark*. BBC's Chief Producer of Arts Talks during the preparations for the 1969 Music Festival.
Mounsey, (Mrs)	Representative from the north who served on the Music Festival Ad Hoc Committee (1964–1969).
Mulliner, Michael (Mr)	(1895–1973) English composer, pianist, and copyist. Conductor who led the preparatory conductors' conference in 1949.
Mundy, (Miss)	In charge of press and publicity (which was affiliated to the NFWI Office and Finance Sub-Committee) during the preparations for the Singing Festival.
Musgrave, Thea	Composer and broadcaster. Interviewed Ursula Vaughan Williams and Williamson about the Music Festival on 'The Lively Arts' programme in 1966.
Neame, Shena (maiden name Shena Fraser)	(1910–1977). Scottish composer, adjudicator and performer. Also composed under the pseudonym Sebastian Scott. A member of Ospringe WI, East Kent and Eastling WI, Faversham. She was one of the pianists who played at the premiere of *The Brilliant and The Dark*. She accompanied on the piano at local WI events, adjudicated music festivals, and was involved in the Talbot Lampson School for Conductors.
Neville-Smith, Esther (Mrs)	(d. 1955) Served on the NFWI Executive Committee (1931–1953). Wrote 'Singing Across the Centuries' which was published in *Home and Country* in 1953.

Nicholson, Ralph (Mr)	Composer and county music adviser for Surrey. He dedicated *Herrick's Carol* to Hopkins and the S.E. Section after hearing the choir at Folkestone and the Fairfield Halls.
Nightingale, [Ethel?] Miss	Gave a report on Leslie's summer school in 1922, and may have been Secretary of the Handicrafts Sub-Committee in 1927 and appointed as the new assistant of Kent Rural Community Council in 1928.
Nutley, Lionel (Mr)	Chosen by Williamson to adjudicate at the county festivals of *The Brilliant and The Dark*.
Olive, Phyllis (LRAM, ARCM)	Member of Somerset WI. She wrote 'Towards Opera' which was published in *Home and Country* in 1962.
Payne, (Mrs)	Vice-Chairman of the NFWI's Music and Drama Sub-Committee (1963–1969) and also served on the Music Festival Ad Hoc Committee (1964–1969). Accompanist at the auditions for the Midlands Section of the Society Choir.
Payne, Margaret	Member of Bilton WI, Warwickshire. A pianist who played at the premiere of *The Brilliant and The Dark*.
Pendered, Mary L.	WI member who wrote to the editor of *Home and Country* regarding *Jerusalem* in 1937.
Pike, Gabrielle (Mrs)	NFWI Chairman (1961–1966) and also served on the Music Festival Ad Hoc Committee (1964–1969).
Pinkett, (Mr)	The Leicestershire Local Education Authority Adviser who was approached for the National Society Choir to perform with the Leicestershire Youth Orchestra.
Piper, Myfanwy	(1911–1997). English librettist of Welsh descent. She achieved distinction with her librettos for Britten.
Poston, Elizabeth	(1905–1987). English composer, writer and pianist. Agreed to be musical director for a drama production planned for the Golden Jubilee celebrations in 1964.

Powell, Mrs	Member of the NFWI's Music and Drama Sub-Committee (1963–1964) and later served on the Music Festival Ad Hoc Committee (1964–1969).
Price, Beryl	Won a conducting competition at the Royal Academy of Music in 1936.
Ratliff, Pamela	Her advice was sought regarding Mrs Vooght's drama script planned for the Golden Jubilee celebrations.
Read, Jean (Mrs)	WI member who was interviewed about her participation in *The Brilliant and The Dark* which featured in Nancy Wise's report broadcast on 'Woman's Hour'.
Robertson Scott, J.W. (Mr)	(d. 1962) Author of the first official history of the organization in 1925. Wrote 'The Cottage Housewives Earphones' which was published in *Home and Country* in 1927.
Rice, Peter (Mr)	Designed the settings for the premiere of *The Brilliant and The Dark*.
Rigg, Elsie (Mrs)	Appointed part-time Music Adviser for the NFWI (1940–1948). Articles in *Home and Country* include 'Music in Wartime' in 1940.
Ruggles-Brise, Marjory R.	WI member from a South Eastern Federation who wrote to the editor of *Home and Country* regarding *Jerusalem* in 1937.
Scampton, Ann (Mrs)	WI member from Chew Magna, Somerset. Featured in a series of articles titled 'Woman in a Man's World' published in *Home and Country* in 1969.
Scorer, (Mrs)	One of only two members who was originally a member of the S.E. Section and joined the Midlands Choir.
Sharman, M. (Mrs)	Correspondent for 'News from the Institutes' who reported on performances of *The Brilliant and The Dark* in Cornwall Federation.
Sharpe, Rita	Won a conducting competition at the Royal Academy of Music in 1945 and 1947.
Shaw, Geoffrey (Mr)	Served as H.M. Inspector of Education.

Shillabeer, A.	WI member from Cornwall who wrote to the editor of *Home and Country* regarding *Jerusalem* in 1937.
Sidmouth, Lady	WI member from Devon Federation who, at the Devonshire Federation AGM in 1956, announced that the use of prayer at WI meetings was a breach of the Constitution.
Slater, Christopher (Mr)	Freelance conductor who had taught opera at Trinity College, conducted the London Philharmonic and the Royal Philharmonic, and had been on the staff of a German Opera House. Adjudicator of the National Society Choir auditions in 1970.
Smith, Mrs	Member of Leicestershire Federation who mentioned that many members considered the standard required to join the National Society Choir was too high.
Smith, R.A. (Mr)	Chosen by Williamson to adjudicate at the county festivals of *The Brilliant and The Dark*.
Smithwick, Cecily	WI member of East Coker, Somerset to whom Britten dedicated his song *The Oxen* (which was published in the NFWI's *Book of Carols*).
Somerset, (Mrs)	WI member who was interviewed about her participation in *The Brilliant and The Dark* which featured in Nancy Wise's report broadcast on 'Woman's Hour'.
Stephens, Rosemary	Member of the NFWI Society choir who, in 1972, objected to news it was disbanding.
Stobart, H.G. (Mrs)	Served on the NFWI Executive (1919–1925), the Education, Literature and Publicity Sub-Committee (1923–1925), as well as the *Home and Country* Sub-Committee (1923–1925) and was a member of the Music Sub-Committee (1923–1926).
Stockley, Susan (Mrs)	Chairman of the National Federation (1991–1994). She worked in the NFWI archives until 2002.
Surplice, Ronald (Mr)	Chosen by Williamson to adjudicate at the county festivals of *The Brilliant and The Dark*.

Talbot, Kathleen (Miss)	(d. 1958) Chairman of the Mid and West Hertfordshire Music Festivals and was Hon. Organizer of the County Garden Produce Central Committee. Served on the NFWI Music Sub-Committee (1931–1936).
Tatham, Mona (Miss)	The Arts Councils' representative on the NFWI Music Sub-Committee (1946–1954). Served on the Singing Festival Ad Hoc Committee (1948–1950). Wrote 'Art, Music and Drama for the Countryside: the Arts Council Plans Ahead', and 'Ralph Vaughan Williams', which were published in *Home and Country*.
Taylor, M.J. (Mrs)	Correspondent for 'News from the Institutes' who reported on performances of *The Brilliant and The Dark* in Nottinghamshire Federation.
Tennant, Nancy (Miss)	Served on the NFWI Executive Committee (1934–1936) and (1940–1951) and was Music Adviser until 1937. Chairman of the Music Sub-Committee (1939–1942?) and later served on the Singing Festival Ad Hoc Committee (1948–1950). A member of International Sub-Committee. Wrote articles for *Home and Country* which include 'The Social Half Hour', 'Singing Festival', 'Spinet to Skiffle' and 'Dr. Ralph Vaughan Williams'.
Thompson, Isabel	Member of Graft Green WI, West Kent. A pianist who played at the premiere of *The Brilliant and The Dark*.
Thorfold, Phyllis (Mrs)	Accompanist at the preparatory conductors' conference in 1949.
Tovey, E.M.	WI member who wrote to the editor of *Home and Country* regarding *Jerusalem* in 1937.
Travers, Mrs	Vice-Chairman of the NFWI Music and Dancing Sub-Committee as well as Chairman of the Music Festival Committee (1964–1969).
Trowell, Brian (then Dr)	Chief Assistant of Opera at the BBC at the time of the 1969 Music Festival.

Tylor, (Mrs)	Served on NFWI Music and Drama Sub-Committee (1947–1950) and was also a member of the Singing Festival Sub-Committee (1948–1950).
Unwin, (Miss)	Served on the Music Festival Ad Hoc Committee (1964–1969) and was involved in the National Federation's publicity.
Vann, Stanley (Mr)	Chosen by Williamson to adjudicate at the county festivals of *The Brilliant and The Dark*.
Vaughan Williams, Ursula	(b. 1911) English novelist, poet and librettist. Second wife of the late Ralph Vaughan Williams. Wrote the libretto for *The Brilliant and The Dark*.
Viles, Patricia	Member of Baddow Hall WI, Essex. A vocal soloist at the premiere of *The Brilliant and The Dark*.
Vincent, (Mrs)	Member of the Music Festival Ad Hoc Committee (1964–1969).
Vooght, Cherry (Mrs)	Member of the NFWI Music and Drama Sub-Committee (1960–1961) and then co-opted onto the Executive. Served on the Music Festival Ad Hoc Committee (1964–1969), and the National Society Choir Ad Hoc Committee (1970–1972). Wrote a drama which was to be accompanied by music composed by Poston for the Golden Jubilee celebrations, but which the Executive later rejected.
Walker, Mr	Music Advisor for Warwickshire during the 1920s.
Walker, M.S.	WI member who wrote to the editor of *Home and Country* regarding *Jerusalem* in 1937.
Watt, Madge (Mrs)	Brought the organization to Britain and was involved in founding the first WI in Llanfair.
Watt, Janet	Composed an arrangement of *Jerusalem* for the NFWI in 1977.
Wells, (Mrs)	Member of the Music Festival Ad Hoc Committee (1964–1969).

White, Felicity	Member of Bilton WI, Warwickshire. A pianist who played at the premiere of *The Brilliant and The Dark*.
Willcocks, David (now Sir)	(b. 1919) English conductor, organist and teacher. One of the conductors considered for the National Society Choir.
Williams, Robert (Mr)	Deputy Music Adviser for Clwyd, and conducted the Denbighshire County Youth Orchestra at the debut of the Welsh and North West Section in 1974.
Wilson, Steuart (Mr)	(1889–1966) English tenor, scholar, administrator, and adjudicator. Director of the BBC (1948–1949) during preparations for the National Singing Festival.
Wise, Nancy	Report on *The Brilliant and The Dark* featured in 'Woman's Hour' in 1969.
Withall (Miss)	NFWI General Secretary (1969–1972), and also served on the Music Festival Ad Hoc Committee (1964–1969).
Would, Margery	Member of Bookham Afternoon WI, Surrey. A vocal soloist at the premiere of *The Brilliant and The Dark*.
Wright, Doreen (Mrs)	WI member from Chenies and Latimer, Buckinghamshire. Featured in a series of articles titled 'Woman in a Man's World' published in *Home and Country* in 1969.
Wyatt, Honor	Her interviews with Ursula Vaughan Williams and Williamson were published in *Home and Country* in 1966.
Young, K.L. (Mrs)	Correspondent for 'News from the Institutes' who reported on performances of *The Brilliant and The Dark* in Somerset Federation.

Appendices

APPENDIX 1

'Jerusalem' – Words by William Blake (1757–1827)

    And did those feet in ancient time
    Walk upon England's mountains green?
    And was the Holy Lamb of God
    On England's pleasant pastures seen?
    And did the Countenance Divine
    Shine forth upon our clouded hills?
    And was Jerusalem builded here
    Among those dark Satanic mills?

    Bring me my bow of burning gold!
    Bring me my arrows of desire!
    Bring me my spear! O clouds unfold!
    Bring me my Chariot of Fire!
    I will not cease from mental fight;
    Nor shall my sword sleep in my hand
    Till we have built Jerusalem
    In England's green and pleasant land.

APPENDIX 2

'The story of Jerusalem' (NFWI, 1934)

The poem, Jerusalem, which, with its setting by Sir Hubert Parry, has been adopted by many Women's Institutes as their special song, is of such a mystic character as frequently to demand some sort of interpretation.

William Blake, painter, engraver, poet, was born in London in the reign of George II. His unusual imaginative powers found expression not only in poetry but in illustrations for many books, both in water colours and engraving.

The poem, Jerusalem, is taken from one of his 'Prophetic Books' all of which are highly symbolical and now very obscure.

The title 'Jerusalem', the dwelling place of Peace, embodies his vision of the ideal City of God, where Christ's law of love prevails and where men live in brotherhood with one another.

The first eight lines, which have been puzzling to many, refer to the widely accepted tradition that the living Christ actually visited England, in parts of Cornwall and Somerset. It is a historical fact that a trade in tin and lead existed in the very early times between England and the country of the Phoenecians. There is a persistent tradition that Joseph of Arimathea was engaged in this trade: the idea occurs in a quaint song used by the tin miners. If, as many commentators have surmised John of Arimathica was related to the Mother of Our Land, it is not unlikely that Christ, as a youth, may have accompanied him in some of his journeys, during the period when the Gospels were silent as to his life between the ages of 12 and 30. The tradition survives in Cornwall, at Glastonbury in Somerset and at Priddy on the Mendip Hills, where the trade in lead is known to have existed in the time of Christ.

It was this story that William Blake referred, probably hearing it when on a visit to Priddy, a small village, lying in the very centre of the ancient lead and copper mining area. The entrances to the disused mines still shew, dark and terrible, against the green hillsides. Probably in Blake's time, gaunt machinery rose black against the sky line, causing his reference to 'dark Satanic mills'. Yet beyond them rise the green hills of Somerset, peaceful and unsullied, and the beautiful belief of the country people is that these hills are always green because they were one trodden by holy feet. Possibly also Blake had in mind the great increase of mechanical power all over England, and the cruel use of child labour in the mills.

The vision of England sanctified and claimed for Christ, by Christ himself, leads Blake onto prayer and resolve in the second stanzas. He prays for the bow and arrow of burning enthusiasm, for the spear for closer battle, and above all, for the spiritual forces of heaven, the 'Chariot of Fire', to carry him onwards, till his vision of peace shall find fulfilment in the fertile and smiling English land.

Sir Hubert Parry, for many years the President of the Royal College of Music, composed the music. The accompaniment is difficult, but it is possible to procure a simpler setting, and the marked increase of force and fervour in the second verses, though the air remains the same, should be clearly defined. 'Jerusalem' formed part of the Jubilee celebrations in 1935, when it was included, by special command of King George V, in the programme of the great National Concert in the Albert Hall.

APPENDIX 3

'Jerusalem' (NFWI, 1950)

William Blake, poet and painter, was born in London in 1757. He was a visionary, mystic and reformer. Considered a madman by many of his contemporaries, even now, when he is recognised as one of the world's greatest artists, much of his poetry remains obscure. Like all prophetic writers he used the language of allegory and metaphor and any literal translation of his poems is impossible.

The stanzas which form the song 'Jerusalem' were written in 1804 and form part of the preface of a long poem called 'Milton'. Jerusalem, as Blake thought of it, was not a heavenly city, but rather a state of mind which was attained by practising the virtue of love and the 'healing power of constructive imagination'. He believed if men would achieve this state of mind, this Jerusalem, they would live in harmony with each other, practising 'mutual toleration' and working for each other's good.

The first verse has as its theme the legend that Christ came to Britain as a child, but it really throws out a challenge. Blake is asking us what we think about our country, what does it mean to use with all its beauty and traditions? Do the right spiritual and physical conditions prevail in it for its people to develop what is best in themselves? In the second verse he answers the challenge and as we sing it we answer it too, for it is a challenge to the individual. 'Bring me my bow of burning gold,' 'I will not cease from mental fight.'

We shall all interpret this challenge according to our lives; the bow, the chariot and the spear will mean something different for each of us; but the belief that it is only by men using their knowledge and their imagination and by their working together in love, that a solution of the world's problems can be found.

APPENDIX 4

'An Institute Song' from 'Letters to the Editor' in Home and Country

Vol. 5 no. 6 (December 1923): p. 355–6.

Dear Editor,

I have recently been at Exhibitions or Council Meetings at which the whole assembly has joined in singing Sir Hubert Parry's setting of Blake's 'Jerusalem'.

Many WI members have said how much they would like to sing at our Annual Meeting in London, and I write to urge the WIs or County Federations which approve this suggestion might write to Headquarters and ask if this could be arranged.

It should be clearly understood that when a WI makes this request it pledges itself to learn [the] words and tune by heart. The attempt cannot be a success unless every delegate is ready to sing whether she thinks she can sing or whether she thinks she can't. Both words and music are simple and dignified and are easy to learn. Incidentally, the learning would give pleasure to any WI and would afford an excellent opportunity for a short talk either on Blake's poetry, or on poems about England.

We have long looked in vain for a national 'Institute song'. Here is one made to our hand and one which some counties have already adopted.

Yours truly,
Grace E. Hadow

Dear Editor,

In England we are feeling our way to a song peculiarly fitted to Institutes, as witness the production of East Kent in our August number. Canada, too, feels the need, and last year produced a song with music, entitled 'Home and Country', by two WI members. Mrs Denton, the composer of the music, is anxious that it shall be of use to Institutes. In selling the song she wishes only to cover the cost of production. Mrs Alfred Watt has introduced the song into several English Institutes. Copies with music, 10d. each, can be obtained from Benita, Lady Lees, Thorngrove, Gillingham, Dorset. This song is of a more generally patriotic nature than the production of our East Kent friends. Personally, I do not think that even yet the ideal WI song has been written, but either of the two now available will form a fitting close to our meetings.

Yours, etc.
E.P.S.

Vol. 19 no. 6 (June 1937): p. 323.

Dear Editor,

I suggest that it would be a good thing is we could have a new song to sing at our meetings instead of *Jerusalem*.

In the Albert Hall, sung by thousands of voices, it is perhaps beautiful and inspiring; but dragged out, as often it is, in a country village, at a snail's pace, by the few members who happen to be present and know it, it is not beautiful.

The words are not particularly applicable to the Women's Institute Movement, and the music is not easy for everyone to learn, having no striking melody in it.

Many of us remember the Suffrage Movement and how heartily everyone joined in singing the inspiring words they had set to the familiar tune of the 'Marseillaise'. Surely it would be better if we had suitable words adapted to a well-known tune such as 'Onward Christian Soldiers' or 'Land of Hope and Glory'?

Yours faithfully,
M.C. Browning

Vol. 19 no. 6 (July 1937): p. 383.

Dear Editor,

I have felt ever since I became a member of the Women's Institute that though the music of *Jerusalem* is inspiring, if played by a good accompanist, the words convey nothing understandable to the ordinary Institute member and especially so in the Southern and Eastern Counties. We have not got 'dark Satanic mills' and have never seen them. We may interpret to ourselves the last verse, as meaning that we should each do our bit to build up a better land on our beloved country, but why not say so in plain language?

Yours faithfully,
Marjorie M. Ruggles-Brise (A Women's Institute President for seven years, and ten years a member. Finchingfield, Braintree.)

Vol. 19 no. 6 (July 1937): p. 383–4.

Dear Editor,

May I be permitted to support Mrs Browning's suggestion that another song or hymn be found to take the place of *Jerusalem* at monthly meetings?

Far be it from me to decry the merits of such a noble work, but I am sure that all will agree that certain technical difficulties such as range and time render *Jerusalem* unsuitable for general use, unless the singers are content to give a performance which approximates only in a small degree to Sir Hubert Parry's wishes.

One possible alternative occurs to me – those beautiful and simple words of Sir Cecil Spring-Rice, 'I vow to thee, my country', to that glorious tune by Gustav Holst, to be found in 'Songs of Praise', no. 319.

I realise that as an 'outsider' I have little right to criticise the actions of such a splendid organization as the Women's Institute, but as a village organist, and choirmaster of a small Women's Institute Choir, I feel this particular point is really worth serious consideration.

Yours faithfully,
William J. Pain, Organist-Choirmaster Lowick Church

Vol. 19 no. 6 (July 1937): p. 384.

Dear Editor,

I agree that more appropriate words and a *simpler tune* would be far better. For an unmusical Institute to sing *Jerusalem* every month results in a most painful rendering of what is a very beautiful tune. Headquarters do not seem to realise that many Institutes have no member with outstanding musical talent, or they would select easier tunes. A notice reached us early this year asking Institutes to learn 'England', among other songs. For any body of women to give a tolerable rendering of this song, requires a greater amount of musical ability than is to be found in an average Women's Institute.

Yours truly,
A.M.B. Swanton, President [of] Wellington Heath [WI]

Vol. 19 no. 8 (August 1937): p. 436.

Dear Editor,

No! We do *not* need a new Institute song! If your correspondent cannot see in *Jerusalem* any particular application to the Women's Institute I am sorry for her sense of perception. The fact that it is not easily learned is all the better for it makes it all the more interesting and gives us the more satisfaction when we *have* learned it. We are a tiny Institute in a country village, and I am sure that I speak for all in saying that we would rather miss out a cup of tea than the thrill of *trying* to sing *Jerusalem*.

Yours faithfully,
(Miss) O. Cozens, Secretary [of] St. Mary-in-the-Marsh [WI], Kent

Vol. 19 no. 8 (August 1937): p. 436.

Dear Editor,

The words of 'Jerusalem' seem to me to be singularly applicable to the Women's Institutes, and surely it is not the tune that is at fault, but the people who sing it 'at snail's pace!' *Why* sing it at a snail's pace? It is marked, 'Slow but with animation.' In our Institute we sing it at a good swinging pace – 'with animation' – a pace that carries the fine phrases through as they should be carried. A simple guide to the right pace is that the three beats in each bar should be at the same pace as that of the pendulum of an ordinary 'grandfather's' clock (they mostly have the same swing).

True, the accompaniment is not easy – the accompaniment of a song like this must of necessity be rather broad and spread out; a simplified form, arranged by Gordon Jacob, is published by Curwen's, price 4d.

Yours faithfully,
Emily R. Daymond, Wivelscombe, Somerset[1]

Vol. 19 no. 8 (August 1937): p. 436–7.

Dear Editor,

Yes, indeed, why not alter the song *Jerusalem*, and while we're about it, alter the watchword of the Institute to something less idealistic than for 'Home and Country'?

Every women who tries to understand *Jerusalem* will realise that contained in the lines, 'I will not cease from mental strife, nor shall my sword sleep in my hand till we have built Jerusalem in *every* green and pleasant land', is the answer of all women to the talk of war, strife and bitterness.

But to a large number of Women's Institute members *Jerusalem* means nothing. 'We want something with a catchy tune.' 'For Home and Country' means even less – '*We* have not got the dark, satanic mills', they say (and apparently are not concerned with those who have).

Perhaps 'Boo Hoo' or 'Red sails in the sunset' would be more appropriate for people whose only objective in belonging to the movement is to spend a pleasant week-day afternoon or evening.

I sign myself very bitterly as an ex-President and member.

Yours faithfully,
E.M. Tovey, Bilton, Rugby

---

1   Emily Daymond was Parry's amanuensis (among other activities). She is also mentioned in Appendix 6 as one of the conductors at SWM events.

Vol. 19 no. 8 (August 1937): p. 437.

Dear Editor,

A new song is *not needed* by any human member of the Women's Institute. *Jerusalem* has very inspiring words and a magnificent tune.

Yours truly,
Helen Green, Chobham Surrey

Vol. 19 no. 8 (August 1937): p. 437.

Dear Editor,

I should like to support Mrs Browning's suggestion that another song is needed to replace *Jerusalem*, which is most difficult to sing and has a most dreary and uninspired tune. I doubt if one hundred of our members grasp its symbolism and I have never heard it sung at a village meeting with the least enthusiasm.

Could we not take a vote on this subject from all the Institutes?

Yours truly,
Mary L. Pendered, Kettering

Vol. 19 no. 8 (August 1937): p. 437.

Dear Editor,

Jerusalem is a bit taken out of a long poem. 'Those feet' are Milton's feet. 'The holy lamb of God' is Milton. I feel we are singing one thing and meaning another; and, just as our embroidery advisers tell us that it is bad design to put Jacobean patterns, meant for large curtains, on to small cushions, so it is bad art to take a bit of a long poem and make it mean something else.

And then I hear it sung in the Albert Hall, and feel that it would be revolution to change.

What is one to do?

Yours in a difficulty,
Mariana Hopkinson, Coton, Cambridgeshire

Vol. 19 no. 9 (September 1937): p. 485.

Dear Editor,

Jerusalem is a magnificent song, and the Albert Hall meeting is a magnificent occasion; but we do not attempt to copy the Albert Hall gathering at our monthly meetings, so why try and echo the song? The monthly meeting is a homely, sociable affair, at which we learn things that will help us and our neighbours, and enjoy each other's company in games and talk.

What we want is a homely song to a simple tune that we can all enjoy; something in the style of Kingsley's well known:

Do the work that's nearest,
Though it's dull at whiles;
Helping, when you meet them,
Lame dogs over stiles.

A bow of burning gold is rather a remote idea, but a lame dog appeals to everyone.

Yours sincerely,
Margaret Kendall, Fovant

Vol. 19 no. 9 (September 1937): p. 485.

Dear Editor,

At the Women's Institute to which I belong we always sing the Women's Institute's Ode from Canada, the words of which are as follows:

'A goodly thing it is to meet,
In friendship's circle bright.
Where nothing stains the pleasure sweet,
Nor dims the radiant light;
No unkind word out lips shall pass,
No envy sour our mind,
But each shall seek the common good
The weal of all mankind.'

The tune is 'Auld Lang Sayne'. Every year the words are printed at the head of our programme, so everyone knows it and it makes an excellent end to the meetings.

Yours sincerely,
R.A. MacInnes, Castle Carrock, Scotland

Vol. 19 no. 9 (September 1937): p. 485.

Dear Editor,

To me, *Jerusalem* is a constant offence, with its utterly unchristian sentiments, plus some nonsense, and its pretentious, unsuitable setting – in fact, I try always to make a point of arriving at our monthly meeting *after* the singing of it!

Yours faithfully,
Constance Larymore, St Mawes, Cornwall

Vol. 19 no. 10 (October 1937): p. 539.

Dear Editor,

I cannot believe that Blake, even in his maddest moments, would have applied the title of the 'Lamb of God' – a title inevitably identified with Our Saviour – to a man whom he regarded merely as a poet and, in some degree, a prophet; and I am more inclined to accept the explanation that he was thinking of an old legend to the effect that Our Saviour in his early days sailed as a ship's carpenter on a Phoenician vessel which made a voyage to England. This explanation gives the poem a simple yet profound significance, and one particularly appropriate to Women's Institutes – namely, that the one country (other than the Holy Land itself) which was 'in ancient time' deemed worthy of the supreme honour of Our Saviour's bodily presence, is now being desecrated by the ugly thing which nowadays we speak of as 'urbanization'.

Yours faithfully,
Margaret Baines, Great Rissington, Gloucestershire

Vol. 19 no. 10 (October 1937): p. 539.

Dear Editor,

Like several of your correspondents, I do wish we could replace *Jerusalem*, which I greatly dislike when sung at our meetings. The tune is wobbly, and hard to catch, and the words, with the exception of the beautiful last line, objectionable. In this little Cotswold town, where a considerable part of the population depends, regularly and happily, on employment in two prosperous local textile factories, belonging to a resident and popular land owner, it is rank insincerity to wail about 'dark Satanic mills', nor, I hope, do we women want bows and arrows, spears and swords, however figuratively, to gain our ends.

Yours faithfully,
M.S. Walker, Member [of] Wotton-under-Edge [WI]

Vol. 19 no. 10 (October 1937): p. 539–540.

Dear Editor

Nine years ago our institute voted for 'Mine Own Countrie', words by John Oxenham, air, 'Londonderry', published by Hawkes and Song, Ltd., London, in 'More than Twice 55 Community Songs' and we have sung it ever since. The words are beautiful and the 'old Irish air' familiar.

Yours faithfully,
L.C. Murray, President [of] Longtown [WI], Cumberland

Vol. 19 no. 10 (October 1937): p. 540.

Dear Editor,

I have always thought *Jerusalem* a little above us. I suggest a more suitable song would be 'The Song of the Musicmakers'. It is pleasing tune and goes with a swing, and is quite easy to pick up. We have found it most successfully at our meetings.

Believe me.

Yours very truly,
Miss Mabel Illingworth

Vol. 19 no. 11 (November 1937): p. 599.

Dear Editor,

The National Federation Executive Committee and Music Sub-Committee have watched with interest the correspondence concerning *Jerusalem* in your columns. We realized that some Institutes experience difficulty in singing *Jerusalem* well, but we do not feel that the time has come for a change to be made and for another song to be chosen in its place. The singing of *Jerusalem* is by no means obligatory, and if an Institute wishes to use another song it is at liberty to do so. May I suggest, however, that if it does adopt another song, it should still persevere, and try to sing *Jerusalem* well? Such a rare satisfaction can be found in singing this song, that is well worth while to learn it properly.

Yours sincerely,
Freda Listowel [The Chairman of the Music and Dancing Sub-Committee]

APPENDIX 5

Music courses held at Denman College, 1948–1969

The following list is compiled from information in Denman College brochures and references to courses in the National Federation's Music Sub-Committee minutes.

Date	Title
23–6 September 1948	Residential Music School
12–16 September 1949	Books and Music
5–9 September 1949	Residential Music School
February 1950	Combined Arts Course
28 May–1 June 1950	Folk Music and Folk Dancing
2–7 October 1950	Music
22–26 January 1951	Conductors' School
28 May–1 June 1951	Folk Singing and Dancing
1–5 October 1951	Music for the Institute Meeting
26–30 November 1951	Music
3–7 March 1952	Conductors' School
27–31 October 1952	Music for the Institute Meeting
2–6 February 1953	Conductors' School
26–30 October 1953	Choral Singers and Accompanists
14–18 February 1954	Conductors' School
9–13 May 1954	For Recorder Players and Accompanists
24–28 May 1954	Music for the Institute Meeting
27 September–1 October 1954	For those who play stringed instruments
25–29 October 1954	Eighteenth-Century Music
14–18 February 1955	Conductors' School
9–13 August 1955	For Recorder Players and Accompanists
5–10 September 1955	For those who play stringed instruments
6–10 February 1956	Choir Training
2–6 July 1956	Music and Song
22–26 October 1956	Recorder Playing for Beginners
18–22 February 1957	Conductors' School
17–22 June 1957	For those who play stringed instruments
18–22 November 1957	Music Appreciation (deferred until April 1958)
10–14 February 1958	Choir Training
14–18 April 1958	Music for the WI Meeting

29–31 May 1958	Recorder Course
14–16 November 1958	The Life and Music of Chopin
12–14 December 1958	Music for the WI monthly meeting
25–31 January 1959	Conductors' course
1959	Planning a Combined Arts Programme
17–19 April 1959	Light Music, Songs, and Sketches for the Social Time
4–8 May 1959	Singing for Pleasure
20–24 July 1959	For Choir Conductors
25–31 July 1959	Stringed instruments (men and children invited)
17–19 October 1959	Recorder Playing (Advanced)
22–26 January 1960	Teaching a Choir to Sing
1960	Folk Dance Leaders and Musicians
28 March–1 April 1960	For Wind and String Players
20–25 April 1960	Guitar Players and Folk Singing
28–30 October 1960	Recorder Playing for Beginners
25–27 November 1960	Singing for Pleasure
28 November–2 December 1960	Conductors' course
20–24 February 1961	Accompanying and Choir Training
27 February–3 March 1961	Music – Wind and String Players
8–12 May 1961	The Enjoyment of Music
23–25 June 1961	The County Choir
22–24 September 1961	Singing for Pleasure
21–25 May 1962	Introduction to Opera
27–31 August 1962	Madrigal Singers and Elizabethan Music
19–23 November 1962	Singing for Pleasure
11–5 May 1963	Beginners' Course for Conductors of Choirs
22–26 April 1963	For Wind and String Players
17–19 May 1963	Singing for Pleasure
15–19 June 1963	Singing for Pleasure
29 July–2 August 1963	Choir Training and Conducting
30 September–4 October 1963	Music and Drama Together
6–8 March 1964	Conference for County Music Sub-Committees
11–15 May 1964	Conductors' course
6–8 November 1964	Introduction to Opera
8–12 March 1965	Music in the Institute
1965	Learning to Sing

23–25 July 1965	Introduction to Jazz
23–27 August 1965	Methods of Music Making
17–21 January 1966	Singing for Pleasure
1966	Teachers' course for choir trainers
8–12 May 1966	Conductors' Course
12–16 September 1966	For Conductors of Choirs
30 September–2 October 1966	Music Today
2–6 October 1966	Conductors' course
5–9 December 1966	An Introduction to Opera
13–15 January 1967	An Introduction to Mozart
8–12 May 1967	Conductors' Course
22–26 May 1967	For Conductors of Choirs
7–13 August 1967	Music-making for all ages (Family Week)
27 November–1 December 1967	For Conductors of Choirs
12–14 January 1968	An Introduction to Schubert
1968	'The Brilliant and The Dark'
26 February–1 March 1968	Singing for Pleasure
4–8 March 1968	Conductors' and Accompanists' course
25–29 March 1968	For Village Organists
16–18 August 1968	Introduction to Jazz
30 September–4 October 1968	Conductors' Course
14–18 October 1968	For Conductors of Choirs
10–12 January 1969	An Introduction to Beethoven
13–17 January 1969	For Singers and Choir Leaders
13–17 April 1969	Choir Leaders' Training Scheme
4–10 August 1969	Music-making for all ages (Family Week)
19–21 September 1969	The Beggar's Opera
29 September–3 October 1969	Choir Leaders' Training Scheme
10–14 November 1969	Music of the Twentieth Century

APPENDIX 6

Society of Women Musicians concerts and events conducted by women

The list below is compiled from the archives of the SWM held the library of the Royal College of Music.

Date	Event	Conductor	Programme	Miscellaneous
Summer 1912	Fortnightly meeting of the Society choir	Emily Daymond		
Monday 26 February 1913	SWM 2nd public concert	Emily Daymond	Coleridge Taylor – 'We Strew These Opiate Flowers', Stanford – 'The Shepherd's Serene', Palestrina – 'Hodie Christus Natus Est', Lasso – 'Adoramus Te', Palestrina – 'Pleni Sunt Coeli', Brahms' 'Romances'.	
Autumn term 1913				Emily Daymond resigned as conductor of the SWM Choir (replaced by Dr Harold Darke).
Spring 1923	17 March	First appearance of the SWM String Orchestra conducted by Mesdames Ruby Holland, Elsie Hamilton, Verlliamy, Feltham, and Eiffe.	Other items in the programme are listed as being provided by Miss Murray Lambert, Miss Adelaide Kind, and Mrs Mary Sheldon.	

January 1928	A small choir was formed to practice madrigals and partsongs for female voices	Miss Alice Hare (previously conductor of the Music Society Choir and orchestra at the Welwyn Gardens City.)		A concert was planned to take place at the end of March in 1928 at Grosvenor Street.
Summer 1929	Saturday 15 June 1929	Miss Alice Hare	Programme of music by the SWM Choir	
	Saturday 10 July 1937	Dorothy Erhart	Conducted the String Orchestra	The orchestra comprised of professional and amateur members of the Chamber Music Section.
Spring 1939	Saturday 21 January	Kathleen Riddick	Conducted a concert by the London Women's String Orchestra	
	SWM Otago, New Zealand	Mrs Yetti Bell (conductor of the Society choir.)		Mrs Bell is also listed as conducting part songs (by Philips, Byrd, and Arne) at a concert on 8 August 1949.
18 June 1959	SWM Choir to perform cantatas rather than part songs	Ruth Gipps		The SWM's first appearance at the Christmas party on 18 December 1959 (which included a work by Elizabeth Poston).

Summer 1960	Wednesday 8 June	Ruth Gipps	Concert with Antonia Butler (cello), Norma Greenwood (piano), and the SWM choir. Works by Schubert, Brhams, Beethoven, Bax, and 'The Cloud' by Rutland Boughton.	Accompanied by Mary Mollison (piano).
Autumn 1964	Saturday 12 December	Ruth Gipps	Conducted the London Repertoire Orchestra.	Included Nancy Evans (Mezzo-soprano), Mary Chandler (Accompanist), and 'carols for everybody' conducted by John Wilkinson.
Autumn 1965	Thursday 16 December	Helen Anderson	Christmas carols	Accompanied by Elizabeth Kerry (organ).

APPENDIX 7

Contents of The Women's Institute Song Book *(London: NFWI, 1925)*

- 'Dashing Away With The Smoothing Iron' (Somerset) – collected and arranged by Cecil Sharp
- 'I'm Seventeen Come Sunday' (Somerset) – collected and arranged by Cecil Sharp
- 'The Keeper' (Warwickshire) – collected and arranged by Cecil Sharp
- 'The Lark in the Morn' (Somerset) – collected and arranged by Cecil Sharp
- 'Farmyard Song' – collected by H.E.D. Hammond, arranged by R. Vaughan Williams
- 'The Jolly Plough Boy' – collected and arranged by R. Vaughan Williams
- 'The Tree in the Wood' (Somerset) – collected and arranged by Cecil Sharp
- 'Tis Hum Drum!' – Harrington
- 'Let's Have A Peal' – Anonymous
- 'Farewell, Manchester' – arranged by Alan Gray
- 'Drink To Me Only' – arranged by Alan Gray
- 'Come, Lasses and Lads' – tune 'Away to the Maypole', arranged by Alan Gray
- 'The Blue Bells of Scotland' – tune attributed to Mrs Jordan, arranged by Alan Gray

APPENDIX 8

Contents of The Women's Institute Second Song Book *(London: NFWI, 1926)*

- 'The Faithful Bird' (Y 'Deryn Pur) – Welsh melody arranged by Nicholas Gatty
- 'Shenandoah' – American sea-song arranged by Leslie Woodgate
- 'The Blackbird' (Y Fwyalchen) – Welsh melody arranged by Nicholas Gatty
- 'Round' – Anonymous
- 'The Music-Makers' – words by Arthur O'Shaugnessy, music by Sydney H. Nicholson
- 'Just As The Tide Was Flowing' – arranged by R. Vaughan Williams
- 'The Bonny Blue Handkercher' – noted and arranged by E.T. Sweeting
- 'Fine Knacks for Ladies' – transcribed and edited by Edmund H. Fellowes
- 'Pedlar Jim' – words by Florence Hoare to the tune of 'The Carman's Whistle'
- 'Catch' – Anonymous
- 'Afton Water' – words by Burns, arranged by C. Sanford Terry
- 'A-Hunting We Will Go' – words by Henry Fielding, music attributed to Dr Arne

APPENDIX 9

National Federation National Events, 1928–1980

Date	Event
1928	Suggestion for a National Music Festival (which did not proceed)
1929	Handicraft Exhibition
1933	Drama Festival
1935	Handicraft Exhibition
1938	Handicraft Exhibition
1946	Combined Arts Festival
1948	Home Produce Exhibition
1950	National Singing Festival (*Folk Songs of the Four Seasons*)
1952	Handicrafts Exhibition
1954	County Fare – Ideal Home Exhibition
1957	Drama Festival (*Out of this Wood*)
1960	Handicrafts Exhibition
1961	Market Place – Ideal Home Exhibition
1962	Country Feasts and Festivals Exhibition
1963	Art Exhibition – Painting for Pleasure
1964	Birmingham Exhibition
1965	Golden Jubilee celebrations – The Countrywoman Today Exhibition
1969	National Music Festival (*The Brilliant and The Dark*)
1972	This Green and Pleasant Land rally
1975	Diamond Jubilee celebrations – Tomorrow's Heirlooms Craft Show
1980	Drama Festival – Scene 80

Index

Agricultural Organization Society   9
Albemarle, Lady   73, 82, 83
Aldin, John   101
amateur music-making   1, 2, 4, 5, 12, 14, 16, 17, 32, 33, 34, 41, 57, 58, 60, 64, 75, 78, 81, 85, 87, 95, 100, 103, 105, 106, 107, 108, 114, 115, 124, 129, 130, 131, 133, 134, 135
Andrews, Maggie   7, 8, 43, 44, 48, 137, 142
Anglesey, Lady   vii, 98
Annual General Meeting   8, 12, 13, 17, 25, 35, 76, 83, 91, 106, 118, 130
Area Festivals   21
Arkwright, Marion   59
Arts Council   16, 17, 80, 86, 99, 133
Ashcroft, Peggy   106
Ashton, Frederick   106
Association of Musical Competition Festivals   13
Auerbach, Helen   45

Baines, Margaret   27
Baring-Gould, Sabine   49
Barker, George   67
Barling, Mrs   98
Barlow, David   96
Barns, Ethel   41
Baseley, Godfrey   105
Bateson, Mrs   86
Battle, Joan   97, 98, 102, 104, 105, 106, 109
Bavin, Major J.T.   13, 34
BBC   21, 35, 66, 80, 81, 82, 94, 105, 106, 108, 109, 110, 112, 113, 125, 133
BBC Symphony Orchestra   35, 80, 81
Beaumont, Caitriona   7, 42, 43, 44, 142, 145, 153
Bedford, Herbert   41
Bell, Robert   49
Belletti, Lilian M.   52, 55
Benson, Mr   105

Bernard, Joan   56, 68
Berwick, Teresa   55
Besancon, Carol   94
Blackburn, Marjorie   103
Blake   25, 26, 27, 28
Bliss, Sir Arthur   106, 119
Boosey and Hawkes   19
Boscawen, Lady Margaret   11
Boult, Adrian   34, 35, 41, 50, 71, 76, 77, 85, 133
Bourne, Mrs   38
Bower, Miss   98, 115, 119
Bower, Mr   34
Bowers, Mrs   98
Boweskill, Mr   91
Boyne, Viscountess   11
Braine, Mrs   99
British Drama League   17
British Federation of Music Competition Festivals   xi, 13, 26, 34, 79, 133
Britten, Benjamin   5, 12, 37, 67, 68, 69, 85, 90, 91, 92, 93, 94, 95, 115, 118, 125, 126, 128, 133
Broadwood, John   49
Broadwood, Lucy   49, 50
Brocklebank, Joan   20, 21, 58, 62
Brooke, Mrs M.A.   98
Browning, M.C.   27
Brunner, Lady   35, 91
Buckinghamshire Youth Orchestra   126
Budden, Julian   109, 110
Buddug-Jones, Miss   98
Burnham, Lady   119, 120
Burnham, Mrs   99
Butt, Dame Clara   12, 133

Camilleri, Charles   96
Campbell, Sylvia   103
Canada   8, 9, 178, 183
Cannetty-Clarke, Janet   11, 103, 113, 115, 117, 119, 126, 130, 157
Cantelo, April   100, 103, 133

Carnegie UK Trust   16, 17, 18, 33, 133
Casson, Hugh   106
Catheside, Doris   103
Chaplin, Lady   99
Chappell, William   49
Chater, Mary   93
Chesterman, Linda   94
Christmas, Betty   36
Churchill, John   101
Clwyd Concert Band   125
Collingham, Kenneth   126
Comber, Miss W.M.   87
composition   1, 2, 42, 53, 61, 71, 131, 135
conducting   4, 13, 17, 18, 21, 31, 32, 33, 34, 35, 37, 38, 39, 40, 41, 42, 44, 47, 48, 59, 67, 77, 82, 100, 101, 102, 103, 113, 115, 120, 121, 124, 129, 131, 133, 134
Constitution   14, 21, 22, 23, 28, 29, 31, 37, 46, 52, 61, 65, 74, 77, 118, 127
Consultative Council   17, 73
County Federation Committee   19, 20, 21, 119
County Federation Music Committees   11, 29, 34, 78
County Music Organisers   19, 33
Cox, John   105
Crawshaw, M.E.   121
Crompton, Alice   52
Curry, Mrs   114, 116
Curwen   19

Darling, Diana   64
Davies, Walford   17, 25, 50, 52, 125
Dawkes, Hubert   101
Dawn, Muriel   94
Daymond, Emily   41
Denbighshire County Youth Orchestra   125
Denman College   4, 20, 31, 35, 36, 37, 38, 41, 42, 43, 44, 54, 67, 69, 93, 109, 115, 119, 120
Denman, Lady   45, 46, 61
descant singing   18, 55
Dods, Marcus   41, 89, 100, 101, 102, 106, 108, 110, 113, 114, 115, 117, 119, 122, 124, 133
Doman, Kathleen   91
Donska, Miss   39
Drake, Audrey   120
Drew, Sylvia H.   51
Driver, Ann   94

Dudgeon, Piers   8
Duks, Miss Jessie   38

Eaton, Gertrude   41
Eaton, Sybil   67
education   7, 9, 10, 26, 31, 32, 35, 36, 54, 63, 66, 82, 114, 134
Eggar, Katharine   41
Elgar   2, 26, 67, 83
Empire Musical Fellowship   16
empowerment   4, 22, 27, 31, 42, 44, 47, 48, 98, 112, 131, 134
English Chamber Orchestra   89
English Folk Dance and Song Society   xi, 16, 19, 56, 57, 69, 82, 85, 86, 133, 134
English Folk Dance Society   50
Erhart, Dorothy   19, 38
Evans, Edith   106
Evans, Hilda   103
Evans, Nancy   100, 103, 133
Eyre, Mrs   121, 123

Family Planning Association   46
Farquharson, Mr   18
Farquharson, Olive   98
Farrer, Dame Frances   45, 73, 76, 80
Fawcett, Millicent   23, 45
feminism   1, 4, 5, 7, 28, 31, 37, 42, 43, 44, 46, 47, 48, 97, 112, 134
Ferguson, Ignez   72
Fight for the Right   25
Fiske, Roger   93, 94
folk dancing   10, 50, 53, 56, 67, 86
folk song   2, 5, 10, 19, 26, 49, 50, 51, 52, 53, 54, 55, 56, 57, 58, 59, 60, 61, 62, 63, 64, 67, 69, 74, 75, 80, 85, 87, 92, 112, 115, 125, 128, 131, 134
Folk Songs of the Four Seasons   5, 11, 12, 27, 50, 58, 63, 64, 65, 67, 69, 71, 72, 77, 78, 79, 80, 81, 82, 83, 84, 85, 86, 87, 88, 89, 92, 95, 96, 106, 108, 112, 113, 115, 118, 125, 129, 131, 133, 135
Fonteyn, Margot   106
Forvargue Eva   94
Foss, Hubert   50, 63, 64
Fox-Male, Miss   39
Fraser, Shena   1, 94, 115
Fuller-Maitland, J.A.   49

Index

Gaskell, Miss [C.J.]   13, 56 n.36
Gee, Anne   103
Gibbs, Mr Armstrong   15 n.39, 34, 69
Gillies-Myatt, Monica   39
Gipps, Ruth   41, 42
Gittings, Robert   89, 90
Glasgow, Miss   17
Gordon, Mrs   119
Gowring, Mrs   16
Grant, Peter   65, 66
Gray, Sylvia   98
Gritton, Robin   121, 122, 123, 124
Grove, George   50

Hackett Paine, Mrs   99
Hadow, Grace   13, 25, 36, 45
Hadow, William Henry   13, 50, 133
Hall, Betty   121
Hambourg, Miss   39
Harrison, Marjory   94
Hemingford, Lady   98
Hennar, Anne   98
Henslow, Miles   19
Hobbs, M.E.   53
Holst, Gustav   2, 28, 57, 77, 118, 125, 126, 128
Holst, Imogen   5, 16, 17, 58, 60, 73, 91, 94, 115, 118, 133
Home and Country   5, 10, 18, 19, 20, 21, 22, 25, 27, 32, 33, 34, 35, 51, 53, 54, 55, 56, 61, 62, 63, 64, 65, 66, 67, 68, 69, 74, 75, 87, 93, 95, 98, 102, 104, 105, 111, 123, 133
Hoodless, Mrs of Hamilton   8
Hopkins, Antony   5, 41, 113, 114, 115, 116, 118, 119, 121, 124, 126, 127, 128, 129, 130, 131, 133
Howells, Herbert   93, 94
Hudson, Mrs   98
Hughes, Audrey   103
Hughes, Mrs   87, 123

Ibberson, Mary   14
instrumental music   11, 14, 15, 41, 67, 69, 74, 87, 103, 116, 120, 125, 126, 131

Jacob, Gordon   39, 93, 94
Jacob, Pat   98, 128
Jacques, Reginald   39
jazz   54
Jenkins, Ignez   8
Jenkins, Mrs   117, 119
Jenny, Miss   39
Jerusalem   4, 7, 8, 18, 21, 22, 23, 24, 25, 26, 27, 28, 29, 83, 85, 87, 133, 134
Jessel, Mrs   86
Johnstone, Lucie   41
Joslin, Mrs   99
Joubert, John   115
Judd, James   116
Justham, Barbara   103

Kanga, Skaila   126
Karpeles, Maud   50
Kent, Duchess of   106
Kewish, Miss   39
Kimpton, Gwynne   40
King, Miss   98
Kisch, Miss   39
Kitching, Mrs   38

Lake, Mary   98
Lamb, Elizabeth   3, 103, 105, 108, 111
Lambert, Constant   39
Lampson, Gertrude   11, 13, 19, 20, 34, 52, 66, 72
Laverick, Alyson   7, 43, 44, 48
Lax, F. Gertrude   86
Layton, Mary   38, 39
Le Fleming, Christopher   73, 83
Lehmann, Liza   41
Leicestershire Youth Orchestra   116
Lemare, Iris   20, 67, 78, 79, 80, 84, 101, 115
Leslie, William Henry   13, 17, 19, 32, 33, 55, 59, 133
Linden Singers   124
Listowel, Lady   14, 28
Littlejohn, Joan   5, 127, 128, 133
Llewellyn, William   101, 124, 125
Lloyd Roberts, Enid   103
Local Education Authorities   33, 34, 36, 100
Lock, Mrs   119
Locke, Kathleen   105
Lockhart Smith, Cara   127
London Symphony Orchestra   41, 71, 77, 81
Lutyens, Elizabeth   91

Maconchy, Elizabeth   96
Manson, Mary   94

Mathews, Joan 120
May, Mrs 98
Megary, Ann 94
Menhuin, Yehudi 106
Merritt, Miss 21
Millard, Mrs 105, 106
modernism 1, 5, 135
Moore, Lorna 105
Mothers' Union 9
Mounsey, Mrs 98
Mulliner, Michael 83
Mundy, Miss 82, 87
Musgrave, Thea 105
Music Adviser 19, 21, 79
Music Festival Ad Hoc Sub-Committee 98, 99, 100, 101, 102, 104, 105, 110, 111
musicology 1, 2, 135
Music Panel 11, 21, 38, 79, 115
Music Society Ad Hoc Sub-Committee 115

National Council of Social Services 34
National Federation Agricultural Sub-Committee 90
National Federation Agriculture and Horticulture Sub-Committee 11
National Federation Education, Literature and Publicity Sub-Committee 11
National Federation Executive Committee 11, 12, 13, 15, 16, 17, 19, 20, 22, 23, 32, 36, 45, 65, 72, 76, 82, 83, 89, 90, 91, 98, 99, 100, 103, 104, 117
National Federation *Home and Country* Sub-Committee 11, 105
National Federation Music Adviser 20, 21, 29, 72, 100, 119, 125
National Federation Music and Dancing Sub-Committee 11, 15, 20, 23, 28, 37, 73, 89
National Federation Music and Drama Sub-Committee 11, 27, 72, 76, 90, 92, 94, 98, 113, 115, 116, 117
National Federation Music Sub-Committee 4, 10, 11, 13, 14, 18, 19, 20, 21, 29, 56, 59, 72, 83, 113, 114, 115, 119, 120, 121, 122, 123, 125, 127
National Federation Music, Drama and Dancing Sub-Committee 11, 12
National Federation of Music Societies 17
National Federation Office and Finance Sub-Committee 76, 82

National Federation Organisation Sub-Committee 90
National Federation Royal Show Sub-Committee 90
National Federation Singing Festival Ad Hoc Sub-Committee 75, 76, 79, 85
National Federation song books 5, 13, 18, 19, 21, 52, 53, 54, 58, 59, 60, 74, 91, 95
National Federation song lists 5, 18, 53, 58, 59, 74, 94
National Federation's Music Adviser 20, 58, 76
National Federation's Music Advisory Panel 38
National Music Society Choir 131
National Singing Ad Hoc Sub-Committee 76, 98
National Society Choir 5, 112, 113, 114, 115, 116, 117, 118, 120, 130, 134, 135
National Society Choir Ad Hoc Sub-Committee 116
National Union of Societies for Equal Citizenship xi, 45
National Union of Townswomen's Guilds 14, 15, 60, 133
National Union of Women's Suffrage Societies xi, 14, 45
nationalism 25, 51, 69
Neal, Mary 50
Neame, Shena 1, 103 see also Fraser, Shena
Nettleship, Ursula 34
Neville-Smith, Esther 56, 68
New London Orchestra 81
Nicholson, Ralph 5, 126, 127, 128, 131, 133
Nightingale, Florence 97, 109
Nightingale, Miss 18
Novello 59
Nugent Harris, Mr 9
Nutley, Lionel 101

Oldham, Arthur 93
Olive, Phyllis 68, 69
Olivier, Sir Laurence 106
opera 12, 21, 38, 59, 67, 68, 90, 95, 99, 103, 105, 108, 109, 110, 112
Oxford University Press 58, 81, 83

Parke, Dorothy 94
Parry 23, 24, 25, 83
part song 51, 52, 55, 57, 58, 59, 60, 69, 77, 134
patriotism 25, 26, 54
patronage 1, 2, 56, 136
Payne, Margaret 103
Payne, Mrs 98
pedagogy 1
Pendered, Mary L. 27
performance 1, 10, 12, 21, 23, 38, 39, 67, 68, 79, 84, 85, 86, 87, 89, 92, 99, 100, 105, 106, 108, 109, 110, 114, 116, 118, 119, 120, 127, 128, 130, 135
Perrin, Susan 94
Philharmonia Orchestra 81
piano 8, 38, 64, 67, 73, 100, 114, 116, 126
Pike, Gabrielle 90, 92, 93, 98
Pinkett, Mr 115
Piper, Myfanwy 95
pop music 2, 53, 54
Poston, Elizabeth 5, 91, 93, 94, 115, 116, 118, 128, 133
Powell, Mrs 98
Price, Beryl 39
professional 11, 16, 33, 39, 42, 80, 81, 85, 92, 103, 111, 112, 115, 120, 121, 128, 131, 134, 135

Queen Mother 83

Ratliff, Pamela 91
Read, Ernest 34, 35
Read, Jean 105
Riding to Canobie 5, 126
Rigg, Elsie 20, 21, 61, 62, 76, 118
Robertson Scott, J.W. 66
Robson, Flora 106
rock 'n' roll 54
Rowlands, Miss Olwen 39
Royal Academy of Music 11, 35, 39, 103
Royal College of Music 12, 39, 73, 94, 103, 127
Ruggles-Brise, Marjory R. 28
Rural Music Schools Association 14, 16, 19, 38, 60, 62, 77, 78, 82, 83, 85, 115, 133

Saumarez Smith, Mabel 41
Scampton, Ann 98

Schools for Conductors 4, 12, 15, 18, 21, 34, 35, 38, 42, 44, 76
Scorer, Mrs 121
Scott, Marion 41
Scott, Sebastian *See* Fraser, Shena
Sharp, Cecil 37, 49, 50, 51, 53, 54, 55, 60, 69, 74
Sharp, Evelyn 94
Sharpe, Evelyn 94
Sharpe, Rita 39
Shaw, Geoffrey 34, 55, 133
Shillabeer, A. 28
Sidmouth, Lady 21
Six Point Group 45
Slater, Christopher 116
Smith, Mrs 121
Smith, R.A. 101
Smithwick, Cecily 91
Smyth, Ethel 39, 41
Social Half Hour 10, 15, 62, 63, 134
Society of Women Musicians 4, 38, 41
Somerset, Mrs 105
South Eastern Section 120, 121, 123, 125, 126, 127, 128, 129, 130, 131, 135
Stamper, Anne 8
Stephens, Rosemary 120
Stobart, H.G., Mrs 11
suffrage 4, 23, 25, 26, 28, 29, 44, 45, 46, 48
Suggis, Madame 40
Summer School 17, 18, 32, 34
Surplice, Ronald 101
Swan-Neck, Edith 97, 109

Talbot, Kathleen 19
Tate, Phyllis 91, 94
Tatham, Mona 16, 76, 80
Tennant, Nancy 15, 19, 20, 21, 27, 37, 73, 76
The Beatles 92, 93
The Brilliant and The Dark 5, 11, 27, 33, 50, 68, 69, 89, 95, 96, 97, 98, 100, 101, 103, 104, 105, 106, 107, 108, 109, 110, 111, 112, 113, 114, 115, 118, 122, 124, 129, 130, 133, 135
The Llewellyn Singers 125
Thompson, Isabel 103
Thompson, Lynne 7
Thorfold, Phyllis 83
Thorndike, Sybil 106
Topliff, R. 49

Tovey, E.M.   27
Travers, Mrs   98, 100
Trowell, Brian   105, 106, 109, 110
Turner, Dame Eva   106
Tylor, Mrs   76

Unwin, Miss   99, 104, 105

Vann, Stanley   101
Vaughan Williams, Ralph   2, 5, 12, 26, 27, 37, 50, 51, 58, 61, 63, 64, 71, 73, 74, 75, 76, 77, 78, 79, 80, 83, 84, 85, 86, 87, 89, 95, 96, 126, 133, 135
Vaughan Williams, Ursula   3, 27, 71, 73, 74, 78, 95, 96, 97, 98, 100, 101, 104, 105, 117
Viles, Patricia   103
Vincent, Mrs   99
Voluntary County Organisers   15, 19, 20, 29
Vooght, Cherry   91, 94, 98, 111, 115

Walker, M.S.   28
Walker, Mr   72
Walton, Sir William   106
Watt, Madge   9
Weinbergers   95, 105
Wells, Mrs   99
Whatford, Mrs   38
White, Felicity   103
White, Maude Valérie   41
Willcocks, David   113, 114, 115
Williams, Grace   94
Williams, Robert   125
Williamson, Malcolm   5, 11, 51, 69, 89, 93, 94, 95, 96, 99, 100, 101, 102, 103, 104, 105, 106, 108, 109, 110, 111, 112, 114, 117, 119, 122, 133, 135
Wilson, Sir Steuart   80, 81
Wise, Nancy   105
Withall, Miss   98
Woman's Hour   81, 82, 83, 105, 110, 127
Women's Co-operative Guild   15
Women's Land Army   46, 61
Women's Liberal Federation   45
Women's Liberal Metropolitan Union   45
Women's Social and Political Union   45
Women's Symphony Orchestra   39
Wood, Enid   114
Would, Margery   103
Wright, Doreen   98
Wyatt, Honor   104
Wythes, Mrs   34

Young Musicians Symphony Orchestra   116, 118
Younghusband, General Sir Francis   23